To Je[...]

Thank[...]

own word + ministry

among the Baptists

of Derbyshire.

God bless

Stephen

The Baptists
of
Derbyshire

1650 – 1914

By

Stephen Greasley

British Library Cataloguing in Publication Data.
A catalogue record for this book is available
from the British Library.

ISBN 978 086071 611 2

Commissioned Publication of

MOORLEY'S Print & Publishing
23 Park Rd., Ilkeston, Derbys DE7 5DA
Tel/Fax: (0115) 932 0643

The cover picture is of the old Baptist Meeting House at Barton in
the Beans, found in John Nicholls' 'The History and Antiquities of
the County of Leicester' volume 4 part 2; by kind permission of the
Record Office for Leicestershire, Leicester and Rutland.

DEDICATION

This book is dedicated to the memory of:

Mrs Muriel Bacon: Derbyshire Local Preacher for thirty years

Rev Arthur H. Bonser: Minister of Osmaston Road Baptist Church, Derby 1956 - 1968; East Midland Baptist Association Secretary 1958 - 1968; and General Superintendent 1969 - 1983.

Mr John Butlin: Secretary to the Derbyshire County Union 1988 - 2001

Mrs June Johnson: Secretary to the newly formed Derbyshire Baptists 2001 – 2006

Rev Joan Styles: Minister of Diseworth Baptist Church 1989 – 1999

We give thanks to God for these faithful workers who served the Baptist family in Derbyshire with great diligence, and who stand in a noble line going back to the seventeenth century. We honour their memory.

All profits from the sale of this book will be used to support the Baptist family through Home Mission, and the support of poorer students struggling to access Higher Education, a cause that would have been very dear to our Baptist forebears.

PREFACE

This History has only been made possible through the assistance of a great many people who have given me access to primary and secondary material over the last two years. While I am grateful to all the churches that have allowed me to sit in rooms pouring over aged and dusty books I would like to acknowledge my personal indebtedness to the following people:

To Andrew Eley, whose researches into the history of Willington Baptist Church awakened my own slumbering interest in the wider Baptist story; to Derek Meller at Barton for patiently tolerating my visits to the Church there and giving me access to photocopies of some very useful manuscripts; to Nikki Hening and Roy Chaplin for access to their own studies of Diseworth and Kegworth Baptist churches respectively as well as access to archive material at the Kegworth Church; to Paul Hancock at Long Eaton and June Johnson at Sawley for insights into their church's history; to Tom Robb-Ronald at Castle Donington for his willingness to part with very old minute books as well as his cheery encouragement of the whole project.

Many churches still retain control of their own records, and I am indebted to those who have given me access to these wonderful treasure troves: the late Brian Bamford at Smalley; Alice Dunnicliffe at Melbourne; Jane Webb at Swadlincote; David Howe at Heanor; John Staniland at Swanwick; Melvyn Gilmour at Milford; Alan Flint at Crich; Peter Worrall at Belper; Alan Gordon at Willington; Derek Lander at Birches Lane, South Wingfield; and Tim Paisley at Duffield. I also deeply appreciated the opportunity provided by Trinty Baptist Church, Green Lane, Derby, to explore their archives including those of the Agard Street Particular Baptist Church.

In addition I am most grateful to those who have made available copies of their Chapel Histories: Graham Bunting at Kilburn; Dave Thomas at Overseal; and Paul Clarke at Loscoe. Monty Wood helpfully supplied me with a copy of a 1985 History of Langley Mill Baptist Church. Jenny Few's excellent study of Wirksworth Baptist Church,

'Living Stones,' proved a useful resource. And Blyth Harrison kindly sent me a copy of Chesterfield Baptist Church's 1961 Centenary 'History' which is without doubt the most comprehensive study I have encountered, and is deserving of special mention.

I have been much obliged to Douglas Wooldridge, the East Midland Baptist Association Archivist, for giving me the freedom to explore the Baptist archive material at Market Harborough. Sue Mills, who until recently was the archivist at the Angus Library, Regent's Park College, Oxford, was most helpful in furnishing me with volumes of old Association records, as well as pointing me in the direction of the J.G. Pike material. Her successor, Andrew Hudson, has proved equally helpful over several enquiries. Steve Wing at Didcot obligingly unearthed some old documents pertaining to Loscoe Baptist Church. The staff at the Derbyshire County Record Office and the Local Studies Library in Matlock have been extremely efficient and helpful throughout my various visits, and I would like to thank them for their constant cheerfulness. Likewise, the Record Office for Leicestershire, Leicester and Rutland, has kindly helped me out over a number of enquiries, and also given permission to reproduce some useful items. The Derby Local Studies Library in Irongate has also proved a valuable source for newspapers pertaining to the period of this study. It would also be quite remiss of me if I didn't mention the assistance of Rev Roy Plant who carried out his own detective work into the Riddings and Stonebroom churches for which I am very grateful, and provided a guided tour of the sites of long since disappeared chapels.

There are several people whose own researches into aspects of Baptist history in Derbyshire have been of great help: Sheila Spendlove at Littleover, Ray Thompson at Burton, and Peter Shepherd at Broadway have all made available material, and shared knowledge, which has proved most useful. Enid Measures, also at Littleover, very kindly made available to me research carried out by her late husband. Dr Alasdair Kean, from the University of Derby, has kindly furnished me with material pertaining to the abolition of the Slave Trade and its associations with Derby and the Baptists. While Mrs Margery Tranter helpfully provided a copy of her own M.A dissertation exploring social and geographical aspects of Rural Dissent in Derbyshire. Frank

2

Rinaldi and Margaret Wombwell have also carried out intense investigations into the life of Baptists in the county, and I have been able to draw upon some of their findings in this study.

A number of people have helped through providing photographs. Derek Palmer and Mary Dainty came to the rescue with photographs of Watson Street and Sacheverel Street churches; Keith Malin at Salem, Burton made available some very useful material with respect to his own Church; Des Greenwood and Freda Searson came up trumps with some excellent material on Ripley; while Judith Smith provided the photo of William Shawcroft, one of her distant relatives. Brian Radford and Margaret Wombwell also kindly gave me permission to make use of photographic material accumulated from their own researches.

I have been much obliged to some of our first rate local history societies whose representatives have kindly made available to me some of the fruits of their accumulated wisdom. The Chellaston History Group has compiled some extremely useful sources of photographs, including those of the tiny but persisitent Baptist cause in the village. Hope Historical society put me in touch with Mr Stanley Bradwell who gave me a tour round the old Baptist Meeting House in Bradwell. The Heanor and District Local History Society made some useful corrections in respect of the cause at Loscoe. David Woodruff from the Strict Baptist Historical Society furnished me with plenty of material on the cause at Charlesworth. While Clyde Dissington and his merry band of helpers at The Magic Attic Historical Resource Centre, Swadlincote, were most obliging, and provided several useful snippets of information.

My son, David, deserves particular mention. Not only has he scanned all the photographs into this volume, but he has been constantly on hand when his incompetent and timid father experienced any difficulties with the computer. Without him at the other side of the landing I am not sure I would have made much progress.

Moorleys of Ilkeston have been superb in their assistance and advice in the final format of this book. Peter Newberry in particular has been

3

invaluable in providing technical support in the latter stages of the work.

I am extremely grateful to the Whitley Lectureship for a grant towards the publication of this volume. It really was a tremendous help. Their practical support of this venture is very much appreciated. I am also indebted to those friends who have helped with the costs of publication in memory of their loved ones who have faithfully served the Baptists of Derbyshire in one way or another.

Finally, my particular debt of gratitude is extended to the late Muriel Bacon of Pear Tree Road Baptist Church, Derby. Muriel's own love of all things Baptist (and ecumenical too) came through in her famous Derbyshire Baptist Heritage outings. The several visits we made to eighteenth and nineteenth century Baptist churches, including my first ever visit to Barton in the Beans, laid much of the groundwork for this present study. Muriel organised a sponsored walk and cycle ride of the Derbyshire Baptist churches back in 2002 which provided many people with a glimpse into the wider Baptist family in the county. She would have eagerly lapped up the contents of this book and been one of its most excited advocates. I hope that in some small way this book honours the work she did at Pear Tree for over fifty years.

Sketch map of the county of Derbyshire and Burton on Trent showing the geographical distribution of Baptist witness in the late twentieth century.

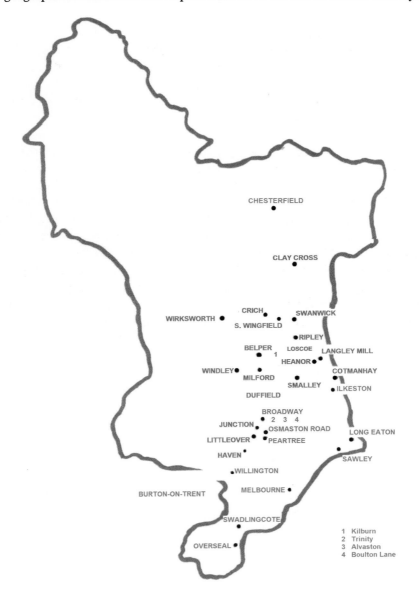

CHESTERFIELD

CLAY CROSS

WIRKSWORTH
CRICH
S. WINGFIELD
SWANWICK
RIPLEY
BELPER
LOSCOE
LANGLEY MILL
1
HEANOR
WINDLEY
MILFORD
COTMANHAY
SMALLEY
ILKESTON
DUFFIELD

BROADWAY
2 3 4
JUNCTION
OSMASTON ROAD
LONG EATON
LITTLEOVER
PEARTREE
HAVEN
SAWLEY
WILLINGTON
BURTON-ON-TRENT
MELBOURNE
SWADLINGCOTE
1 Kilburn
2 Trinity
3 Alvaston
4 Boulton Lane
OVERSEAL

CONTENTS

INTRODUCTION

The History of the Baptists of Derbyshire has proved very difficult to tell. While some of the story has been told and retold many times (the Barton preachers, for example), much of the story is contained in Church Meeting minute books which have rarely seen the light of day. Most churches have some secondary sources which have attempted to relate and condense the story of a particular chapel. These are usually in the form of centenary booklets or brief histories, and they form a veritable gold mine of information helping both to tell the story of a people, and place it in some kind of context.

Part of the difficulties entailed in pulling this wider history together is connected with the variation in primary sources. Some churches have copious notes and minute books often going back to the very earliest stages of their church's history. Other churches have no minute books whatsoever. This might be the result of carelessness and neglect; books were kept but were allowed to get in a terrible condition. This is the reason why the Barton Church tragically has no minutes available from those early years. Some churches had their minute books stolen. Other churches lost their minute books to sabotage. There are also stories of bonfires being lit in gardens as a means of clearing away grandad's old rubbish! Thankfully many churches have availed themselves of the services of the County Record Offices in Matlock and Leicester, and have found them a wonderful place to deposit and safeguard these priceless documents.

The variation in material available for each Church means that in this book some churches have more written about them than others. This is regrettable and is in no way intended to say anything about the relative importance of one Church against another. It seemed a shame not to include some exceptional material simply to ensure that the same coverage was given to each Church. My real dread, of course, is that having put pen to paper in this way, someone will come forward with a case full of old minute books which have been gathering dust in a loft and which flatly disproves some of the connections I had made, or provides some wonderful illumination to an otherwise obscure aspect of the history of Derbyshire Baptists.

The real difficulty, however, in telling the story is that it isn't an easy story to tell. It certainly isn't a smooth story. The problem lies in the very different types of Baptists that were to be found. It is only just about possible to speak of the Baptists as a single denomination from 1892. Prior to that there were two very distinct strands which were two completely separate denominations.

The Particular Baptists, as their name indicates, adhered to a strict Calvinistic outlook that maintained a limited or particular view of salvation. Christ died for the elect. Origins of these ideas can be traced back to the Puritans in this country, although continental influence ultimately played a significant part.

The General Baptists, by contrast, maintained that Christ died for all, and upheld a more Arminian position on the exercise of Free Will. Human beings ultimately could shape their own destiny and that of others too. The composition of the true Church was not simply the product of a predetermined decision on the part of God, but was open to the response of human minds and wills.

So, while agreed on such issues as the importance of believers' baptism, General and Particular Baptists could in many other matters differ enormously. The fact that Derby's first General Baptist Chapel on Brook Street was built in the adjacent street to an existing Particular Baptist Chapel on Agard Street indicates the differences quite markedly. At no point was it considered that the two churches should join forces.

There was some fluidity between Generals and Particulars. J.G.Pike, for many years the minister at Brook Street, was always a welcome preacher at Agard Street. And when Pike was looking for ministerial training for his son he chose the Particular Baptist Academy at Stepney. Relationships between Generals and Particulars changed and improved during the nineteenth century. Andrew Fuller's version of moderate and Evangelical Calvinism was not only the inspiration

9

behind the formation of the (Particular) Baptist Missionary Society, but also drew the Particulars into a closer orbit with the New Connexion General Baptists, themselves a product of the Evangelical Awakening of the mid eighteenth century. It was this realignment of both Generals and Particulars which was to pave the way for a subsequent convergence of these Baptist cousins[1].

But even that paragraph needs explanation. By the late eighteenth century there were two sorts of General Baptists. While the majority of General Baptist churches in Derbyshire were the product of the New Connexion grouping that formed under the auspices of Dan Taylor in 1770, there were older groups of General Baptists already in existence. These were much more plentiful in Lincolnshire than in Derbyshire. Some of the older General Baptist Churches joined the burgeoning New Connexion; others refused to do so and stood outside.

In Derbyshire, the presence of General and Particular Baptists means that there isn't just one story to tell but two. The stories overlap, and, inevitably have different origins. This makes the movement and progression in the story both clumsy and repetitious. We seem to be going back over the same historical period again. In Derbyshire (though not in the country as a whole) the Generals were far more in abundance than the Particulars so that their story could be said to form the Majority Report.

The story becomes even more complex because of geographical boundaries. In seeking to compile a history of Derbyshire Baptists[2] I begin in Leicestershire, wander into Yorkshire, dabble in Nottinghamshire and am required to deal with Staffordshire. No history of Derbyshire Baptists could begin without taking these other counties into consideration. Such was the evangelistic endeavours of the eighteenth century General Baptists that they were always eager to plant churches in far distant places, and county boundaries never stopped them. Barton in the Beans planted Kirby Woodhouse near Mansfield; Kegworth planted Ilkeston, and Gamston in Nottinghamshire serviced Ashford in the Peak some forty miles away! In a quest for origins of Baptists in Derbyshire one is compelled to trace roots back to the surrounding counties. What started out as a relatively simple task began to grow into something much larger.

The complexity of the task is compounded by the fact that there was no overall system or planning to what happened. There was no overall Baptist Church; there were only Baptist churches. These were autonomous and self governing. They acted as they saw fit. Their missionary enterprises were not controlled in any way by an external organisation. Indeed the churches themselves were frequently not the initiators of preaching and congregational planting. Invariably a few zealous individuals took it upon themselves to start preaching in a certain location. With persistence a regular congregation gathered; sometimes demand for a meeting place arose and at that point the Church was brought in to normalise proceedings. The beginnings of Cauldwell Baptist Church and Junction Baptist Church, Derby both bear this out.

Baptists are just one branch of religious Dissent (or Non-conformity) as it is sometimes called. They refused to conform to the worship and the requirements of the state Church. Along with many forms of older Dissent[3] (like Presbyterians and Unitarians), and to a lesser extent newer Dissent (Methodists), they were persecuted (see appendix 1), discriminated against, and denied basic rights because of their religious convictions. Educational, political and even employment opportunities were denied them. They were even officially denied a place in the after life. Graveyards feature very prominently in most of the early Baptist communities in the county. For the present generation these are a nightmare to maintain and a puzzle as to why we had them in the first place. Graveyards, however, were a practical necessity. Those who refused to be baptised through the state Church were denied burial rights in the Church of England. The case of the infants at Smalley in 1779 (page 78) is a case in point. Baptist Churches needed graveyards, and often went to extraordinary and costly lengths to ensure they obtained an adequate site.

The dissenting nature of Baptist churches was expressed through their deliberate disregard of the observance of festivals recognised by the Church of England and the general public. Nowhere is this more

11

obvious than the use of Christmas Day as the occasion not only for Church Meetings but in many churches for their Annual General Meeting. Junction Baptist Church held an 8.00am breakfast on Christmas Morning for many years, followed by their AGM. They were still having 110 people to breakfast on Christmas Day 1896, although they appear to have moved their AGM to another date. The North Derbyshire Conference regularly held its meetings on Christmas Day and also on Good Friday. In doing so they were trying to make a statement: that Christmas Day was like any other day, and that Baptists resisted the ways of the world. Wirksworth Baptist Church were certainly no fans of Christmas (see page 136).

Perhaps some perspective might help at this stage. This book is about Baptists in Derbyshire. A reading of the book might well give the impression that Baptists were in plentiful supply in the county. That would be misleading. Baptists were and always have been a minority among the Christians of Derbyshire. The 1851 Religious Census revealed that just under 50,000 Anglicans were at worship on Sunday 30th March. On the same day there were 33,000 Wesleyan Methodists, 20,000 Primitive Methodists, but only 6,000 General Baptists and 2,000 Particular Baptists at worship. Large swathes of the county had no Baptist presence at all. As the century progressed, the Baptists advanced, but percentage wise they remained a significant minority. Should my enthusiasm for this subject run away with me, then these statistics should at least provide some perspective into the wider ecclesiastical picture.

A few explanatory points should be made at this point. Statistical information appears throughout this volume. Such information is culled sometimes from national sources such as the Baptist handbook, at other times from regional sources such as Association Annual Reports. At times these statistics are at variance with each other. One entry could be based on out-dated information, or a variation in the point of the year data was acquired could account for the differences. (National figures tended to be based on statistics compiled at the end of the previous year: Association figures were often compiled mid summer). All these figures pertain to the number of people who were classed as Church Members. Only the 1851 Religious Census dealt with the number of people actually present in the congregation. This latter figure would provide a much more accurate gauge of the strength of a Church, since there were always going to be more people in the congregation who were not (yet) Church Members[4]. While membership figures, therefore, only tell us part of the story, they still remain the only consistent tool to measure an individual church's progress, and to compare that progress with other churches.

I have not been consistent in use of the terms 'pastor' and 'minister.' This may reflect my own clumsiness, but it also reflects the confusion that existed at the time. Some churches preferred one term rather than the other. There again, some individuals preferred one term rather than the other. While some churches flung either phrase around with abandon! This again reflects a continued problem over the subject of ordination. In the late eighteenth and early nineteenth century ordination was something that only happened after perhaps years of faithful and consistent ministry. J.G.Pike was ordained in August 1830, some twenty years after commencing his ministry at Brook Street, Derby. Some men fulfilled a life time of Christian ministry and never received ordination. Still others were refused ordination by their Church but continued to exercise ministry in that same situation. Baptists were ambivalent about ordination. The use of the term 'Rev' was slow to catch on among churches that advocated the priesthood of all believers. The term was often adopted as a means of gaining parity, status and acceptance with other denominations.

Finally, a word about 'The College,'[5] which features quite regularly in the pages of Baptist Church minute books in Derbyshire.

General Baptist College, Chilwell, near Nottingham
Source: The General Baptist Magazine 1862

Dan Taylor had established an Academy for training men for the General Baptist[6] ministry at Mile End, London, in 1798. When he retired in 1813 a new tutor needed to be identified to take the institution forwards. Joseph Jarrom was regarded as the most suitable minister, and since he was serving in Wisbech, the College moved to Wisbech. A second General Baptist College was formed in the Midlands (1825) under Thomas Stevenson, minister at Loughborough Baptist Church, but following Jarrom's retirement in 1837 the two colleges merged to form, 'The Midland Baptist College.' Thomas Stevenson died in 1841[7]. The nomadic College moved to Leicester until 1857, and thereafter to Sherwood Rise, Nottingham under the stern hand of Dr William Underwood. In 1862 Underwood took the College to Chilwell. He was succeeded in 1873 by Thomas Goadby who had been serving as minister of Osmaston Road, Derby. In 1884 the College moved back to Nottingham where it remained until a decision was reached not to reopen at the close of the First World War.

The Midland College trained 300 ministers during its existence including some of the leading figures in the denomination. For the Derbyshire Baptist Churches it proved an even more valuable resource. It provided a fertile ground for preaching supply in some of the smaller churches with no ministers, and in some of the larger churches during periods of pastoral vacancy. Students would often serve placements in Derbyshire churches, and not a few churches in the county invited students to become their ministers after prolonged trials.

Derek Meller of Barton reminds me that people don't know history any more. He is absolutely right. The problem with that is that it becomes very difficult to understand who we are or what exactly we believe without some recourse to where we have come from. An understanding of the history of Derbyshire Baptists will, I hope, serve to consolidate faith and perhaps inspire the present generation as they comprehend the energy expended as well as the sacrifices and rigours endured by that earlier generation. As such I hope that this volume won't just be of antiquarian interest but will have a contribution to the resurgence of vital Christian faith to day.

Stephen Greasley
September 2007

1. Peter Shepherd: 'The making of a northern Baptist college' page 11
2. In truth I have not attempted to cover the whole of the county of Derbyshire in this study. Areas around Glossop and Chapel en le Frith as well as Dronfield could have been covered but time and space have prevented any assessment of Baptist work there. Dronfield does appear under the Derbyshire entries in the Baptist Handbook and some scant information can be found in some statistical tables.
3. Margery Tranter's helpful 1974 MA dissertation on Rural Dissent in Derbyshire makes much of the distinction between Old and New Dissent.
4. Sheila Spendlove in her own study of the Baptist congregations of Derby estimates that in the early days of Brook Street "the number of Church hearers seems to have been about as many as the number of Church members."(p.17) My own rule of thumb is that in an established and settled Baptist Church the official membership size is

probably about two thirds of the congregational base.   Not that everyone turns up at Church every week!

5.   Again, I am indebted to Peter Shepherd's study for this information.

6.   The Particular Baptists were much further ahead with ministerial training.   A College had been established at Bristol before the 1770s. John Fawcett was training men for the ministry at Hebden Bridge, and within a few years Academies had been set up at Stepney and Bradford.

7.   One of the saddest features of the period under investigation is the plight of Baptist Ministers in an age before pension provision.   It was not uncommon for ministers to die in harnass as with Stevenson here. Equally it was common to hear of ministers being compelled to resign or move to another Church on the grounds of ill health.   Few ever enjoyed the opportunity of retirement as such.   Most had to struggle on until they dropped or became too decrepid to function.

PART ONE

1650's - 1914

21st Century Map of Derbyshire Peak District
Source: Google Maps

18

CHAPTER 1

THE EARLIEST BAPTIST CONGREGATIONS

About a mile out of the village of Ashford in the Water, on the B6465 heading towards Wardlow, is a cemetery[1]. It is a rather small cemetery, very overgrown and broken down; access to it is difficult and parking is highly dangerous. But this is all that remains of the Baptist cause in the Derbyshire Peak District.

The origins of this Baptist cause are difficult to trace, but Adam Taylor is almost certainly correct when he states that it was "probably founded during the Protectorate of Cromwell."[2] The English Civil War (1642-49) and the ensuing Protectorate of Oliver Cromwell (1653 – 1658) was a period that gave free expression to religious opinions that had been suppressed for many years. For many of those who took up arms against King Charles 1 the war was a holy war. Aspirations to be rid of the rule of bishops were often displayed on banners being carried into battle. The ideas may have been circulating for some time, but it was the Civil War and the Protectorate that allowed them to surface.

In some parts of the country the spread of Non-Conformist religious views can clearly be linked to the movement of Parliamentary Officers.[3] There is some evidence of this in Derbyshire, but perhaps the main source of Independent religious opinions was to be traced to the rank and file of the New Model Army.

Derbyshire saw its fair share of activity during the Civil War. The main Parliamentary military leader in the county was Sir John Gell, of Hopton Hall. Sir John's own religious beliefs were understood to be Presbyterian, and he certainly seems to have encouraged and at times sponsored clergymen who held firmly Presbyterian as opposed to traditional Anglican views.[4] During the course of the War South Wingfield Manor was occupied and besieged by both sides, and was eventually torn down by Cromwell's army in 1646. Bolsover Castle and Tutbury Castle were also places of intense military activity, although not quite sharing the same fate as South Wingfield. Other skirmishes took place at Ribbleton Moor, Swarkestone Bridge, and Boylestone. Derby was a main garrison of the parliamentary forces in the region.

Evidence of Baptist presence in Derby and Burton at this time is thin. A loyal address was sent to Oliver Cromwell, Lord Protector, in 1654, "From the Baptized Churches in Northumberland etc."[5] The address was signed by representatives of the Baptist Church in Hexham; Wharton in Bradford; and by Robert Holpe and William Tomblinson "of the Church of Christ at Derby and Burton on Trent." William Hutton, a prominent Derby citizen in the later eighteenth century, records how his grandmother, Elinor Jennings (1657 -1727) lived in St Alkmund's churchyard with her father, who "was a Baptist preacher one day in the week and a shoemaker the other six."[6] However, no corroborating evidence for these Baptist congregations has survived.

We have much better evidence for Baptist activity in the Peak District. One of the most fascinating accounts of the religious diversity that was prevalent in the Derbyshire Peak District at this time comes from the Quaker, John Gratton (1642 – 1712). "A Journal of the Life of that ancient servant of Jesus Christ" was written towards the end of Gratton's life. He was born in Tideswell, but spent the largest part of his life in Monyash some six miles from there, and only a few miles from Ashford in the Water. This whole area now looks quaint and rural, but in the seventeenth and eighteenth centuries it was the centre of a major lead mining industry which attracted and supported a very resilient population. The Journal deals with Gratton's quest for a form of religion that met his Biblical and spiritual viewpoint. In 1660 he had thrown in his lot with the Presbyterians, but was disappointed by the way the clergy abandoned their congregations when the Restoration of Charles the Second took place. Then he encountered a group of Baptists around Monyash (about 1668). He liked their Biblical ideas and decided to join with them. The stumbling block for him was their insistence on Believers Baptism. The idea that baptism was equivalent to a death meant that baptism should only be undertaken by those who were dead to sin, Gratton maintained. Since he didn't seem to be dead to sin then he couldn't bring himself to baptism, although he confesses to having come very close. He witnessed his sister's baptism in the river Wye, and that of some other people too. He attended their meetings regularly, but was again disappointed by their response to the Conventicle Act (1670) which limited to five the number of non-Anglicans meeting together for worship. Gratton believed they should have flouted the rule, whereas the elders and preachers of the Baptist cause (Humphrey Chapman, William Blackshaw, and a man called Brume) were very nervous about being caught and risking a £20 fine. Gratton abandoned the Baptists of Monyash and instead found the Quakers more to his liking, spending the rest of his life as a roving evangelist/ambassador for the Quakers, and enduring at least one prolonged spell in Derby Prison.

On good authority, therefore, we can identify Baptists in the Monyash area at the time of the Restoration. Gratton later mentions (1677) that the Presbyterians were given liberty by Charles the Second to licence places of worship, and that they obtained a barn at Ashford in the Water. A baptismal register for the Presbyterian chapel at Ashford for the period 1789 – 1826 is still accessible in the Derbyshire County Record Office. But a Baptist congregation is also recorded in the 'Minutes of the General Assembly of the General Baptists 1654 – 1728' so that there is little doubt that Baptists were active in both Monyash and Ashford throughout this period.

The most comprehensive account of the subsequent history of Ashford Baptist Church is contained in volume two of Adam Taylor's 'History of the General Baptists." Concerning that ancient society, Taylor records,

"At the close of the seventeenth century it appears to have been in a flourishing state, and extended over most of the neighbouring villages: but its principal stations were at Ashford, Wardlow, Blackwell, Monsaldale, and Puttyhill. Two burying grounds then belonged to it, one at Ashford, and the other at Blackwell, five miles north-eastward. About that time (1700) Mr Samuel White and Mr Mason, two very worthy members of the Church, began to preach, and for a long time were diligently and successfully engaged in the sacred work.[7]"

While Mason's labours seem to have been confined to Blackwell, Samuel White was somewhat liberated by being possessed of some property. He exercised this freedom by "the constant habit of riding over the bleak mountains of the Peak, to distant places, to publish the glad tidings of salvation or to transact the affairs of the churches.[7]"

Samuel White died on October 17th 1727. He was only 47 years old. After his death the cause appeared to decline markedly since the disparate congregations lost touch with each other.

"In this state of apathy, Mr Israel Cotton, pastor of the General Baptist Society in the Isle of Axholme, visited his friends on the Peak, of which he was a native. Pitying their situation he collected a few of them together and preached for them several times at a house in Monsaldale.[8]"

Israel Cotton obviously thought the cause was still viable, and he had a meaningful conversation with his colleague Joseph Jeffrey of Gamston in Nottinghamshire, a Church which will again figure prominently in chapter 3. What follows must surely constitute one of the most remarkable stories in the annals of Baptist history.

The Gamston Baptist cause was started by Aaron Jeffrey round about 1700, although it was only after his death in 1729 that his son, Joseph, registered his house for meetings and subsequently constructed a chapel. On hearing Israel Cotton's account of the plight and potential of the Ashford cause, Joseph Jeffrey decided to make the 40 mile journey to assess the situation for himself. Impressed by the reception he received, Jeffrey agreed that the Gamston Church would take a monthly service at Ashford, and he and his assistant, John Dossey, took this between them without any remuneration.

"Work prospered, but there was no place of worship. So a piece of ground was purchased ajoining the burying ground in Ashford Lane, nearly a mile from town. On this ground a small meeting house was erected, almost wholly at the expense of Messrs Jeffrey and Dossey: the former advancing in the first instance £30 and the latter £40. Mr Jeffrey had the pulpit and pews prepared in the neighbourhood of Gamston and employed his own wagon in conveying all the materials to the building.[8]"

The chapel was completed in 1760 and was opened by Gilbert Boyce. To complete the work, Mr Jeffrey bought three acres of land "contiguous with the meeting house" and built a house which was designed for the accommodation of the minister.

The first minister was supplied by the Gamston Church (Benjamin Fox). He served for five years after which William Kelsey settled (1766) from Lincolnshire. He stayed for twelve years, but was unpopular and the work declined drastically. By the time the Ashford Church joined the New Connexion in 1782 they were down to 10 members. Regular preaching was still maintained at Ashford and Wardlow, but there were great difficulties getting people to supply the pulpit given the great distance from any other General Baptist cause. Eventually in 1788 William Pickering from Castle Donington spent five months with the folk at Ashford. He went down well and baptised five people during his time with them. He accepted a call to the Church and settled there in 1789, although not receiving ordination until April 1794. "Symptoms of revival contrived to appear." As well as the regular preaching at Ashford and Wardlow, a new cause was started at Bradwell, eight miles to the north of Ashford. At first the Baptists borrowed the Methodist Church; then hired a barn; eventually opening a meeting house in October 1790. People started coming from Abney, a village two miles from Bradwell, and preaching started there. All along the work was handicapped by the distance Mr Pickering had to travel. One nineteenth century source records Pickering walking 60 miles and preaching eight times on any given week[9].

In 1796 eighteen people were added to the Church at Ashford by baptism, and the membership rose to 43. Sadly, it was to prove a false dawn.

"Disputes among themselves and the disorderly conduct of too many of the members soon reduced their numbers and thinned their congregations, especially at Bradwell.[10]"

By 1800 membership had reduced to 23, and that same year William Pickering decided to leave the Peak on receiving a call from Ilkeston. He left Ashford on August 14th.

23

Adam Taylor records that Mr Robert Bradbury, one of their members endeavoured to serve the Ashford – Bradwell – Abney – Wardlow group of churches, having already sensed a call to the ministry. For a while they even started preaching at Lingston, near Ashford. But there were huge difficulties servicing these outposts, with the result that in 1811 Abney and Bradwell formed their own Church with 9 members while Ashford and Wardlow had 20. Mr Bradbury carried on at Ashford while ministers from the Sheffield area apparently tried to keep Abney and Bradwell going.

Adam Taylor's study was written in 1818 before the final chapter in the Baptists of the Peak was complete. When J.H.Wood wrote his 'History' in 1847 he simply informs us that the work at Ashford became extinct in 1839.

But this is by no means the end of the tale. Association Minute books for 1828 record that a 'brother Bramwell' of Ashford had to give up taking public services because of nervous trouble. One of the gravestones in the Ashford cemetery is to William Bramwell of Ashford who died in 1845 aged 87 years. There is another gravestone for Grace Bramwell 1830-1878 and Robert Bramwell who died in 1904 aged 74 years. Clearly the graveyard was still in use well after the Church had closed.

It wasn't just the graveyard that lingered on. For the next quarter of a century the cases of Ashford and Bradwell continued to vex the General Baptists in their Association life. Gathered in the North Derbyshire Conference (formed in 1839) or the Midland Conference, the fate of the buildings of these chapels severely exercised the Baptists of their day.

On April 17th 1840 Mr Wilders, Secretary to the North Derbsyhire Conference, informed the assembled brethren that the chapels of Ashford and Bradwell were in danger of being lost to the Connexion. Brother Ingham was asked to go and preach there and visit the neighbourhood.

Mr Ingham's report at the next meeting (Smalley, 3rd August 1840) explained that the Independents were meeting in Ashford Chapel and that Bradwell was let to the Primitive Methodists. On 7th August 1842 the Derbyshire Conference meeting at Crich was informed that six new trustees had been appointed for the Bradwell Chapel (popularly referred to as "Pickering Chapel"). Mr Burrows updated the meeting on his recent visit to the village. On Christmas Day 1843 the Derbyshire Conference meeting at Belper heard a full report from brother Kenney. Given the "dilapidated state of the (Ashford) Chapel, and the difficulty supplying it" it was agreed to let the chapel to the Independents on a 20 year lease. The deeds of the Bradwell Chapel meanwhile were signed at the meeting by those Trustees who were present.

Things never run smoothly. At the next meeting (Ilkeston, April 5th 1844) it was reported that because the burial ground was so fully occupied the Independents had decided not to continue with Ashford Chapel, but to build their own place instead. The Bradwell case was referred to the Midland Conference (April 9th, Burton on Trent) at which it was determined to continue with the lease to the Methodists until its expiry in January 1846, "but we are not disposed to renew the lease or sell the place."

On Christmas Day 1844 (Belper) Mr Kenney, chairman to the North Derbyshire Conference) informed the meeting of the possibility of a minister moving into the Ashford – Bradwell area with a view to reviving the two churches. The person in question was Mr Birley[11] of Wardlow, a village equidistant between Ashford and Bradwell. Nothing came of the scheme.

Today there is no evidence remaining of the meeting house or the manse that Messrs Jeffrey and Dossey paid to be constructed. Only fields surround this isolated cluster of graves.

There is, however, one further interesting snippet of information. In 1912 Seth Evans, a member of the Derbyshire Archaeological Society, put together a collection of articles on aspects of 'Bradwell: Ancient and Modern.' An enlarged facsimile of this book was printed and published in 2004. The book contains a photograph of the old Baptist Chapel which subsequently became the Primitive Methodist Sunday School. He also pens the following words:

"The Baptists had a cause here (in Bradwell) in the latter part of the eighteenth century, and built a chapel. But the adherents were never very numerous, although there was a regular minister. Those who joined the cause were immersed in the waters of Bramwell Brook down the Holmes, and not long ago there were persons living who could well remember these "dippings" as they were termed.[12]"

Seth Evans tells us that the cause never prospered and that by 1841 services ceased and the chapel was abandoned. "By this time the Primitive Methodists had established a Sunday School, and occupied the old Baptist Chapel, which they acquired, improved and enlarged." "There was a small burial ground attached to the Baptist Chapel, containing a few graves, over one of which is an old headstone still remaining.[12]"

A visit to Bradwell Chapel today is still possible. It is no longer used as a place of worship, but acts as a recycling centre for old newspaper. The graveyard is quite extensive and is still in use. But there are no obvious gravestones before the 1840s.

1. I am grateful to the Rev Arthur Bonser for first drawing to my attention the existence of this graveyard. Arthur kindly made available to me his correspondence with Dr Margaret O'Sullivan and Rev Douglas Sparkes going back to 1996 which identified the site as a Baptist graveyard. Interestingly the Bakewell Historical Society believe the Baptists may have opened up the graveyard to Quakers as well. As well as members of the Bramwell family the graveyard also contains headstones of Samuel Shaw, Joseph Birch (d.1803), George Brushfield (d.1825), John Birley of Bradwell (d.1831), Josiah and Hannah Birley of Wardlow.
2. Adam Taylor – History of the General Baptists vol.2 p.261.
3. See David F Neil – The Baptists of North East England p.8
4 Sir John Gell appears to have sponsored Rev John Hieron to the parish of Breadsall in 1644. Hieron was subsequently ejected from his parish in 1662 for refusing to abandon his Presbyterian views.

5. The document is found in E.B Underhill, Confessions of Faith and other Public documents of the Baptist Churches of England in the 17th Century (1854)

6. The reference is in L Jewitt, 'The life of William Hutton' (1872). I am very grateful to Mrs Sheila Spendlove who drew my attention to this reference and the previous one.

7. Taylor p.261ff

8. Taylor p.264

9. This information is found in 'Memoirs and remains of Rev J.G.Pike' (1855) p.114

10. Taylor p.269

11. George Birley submitted the entry in the 1851 Religious Census. Other members of the Birley family have headstones in the graveyard.

12. Seth Evans – Bradwell Ancient and Modern p.25

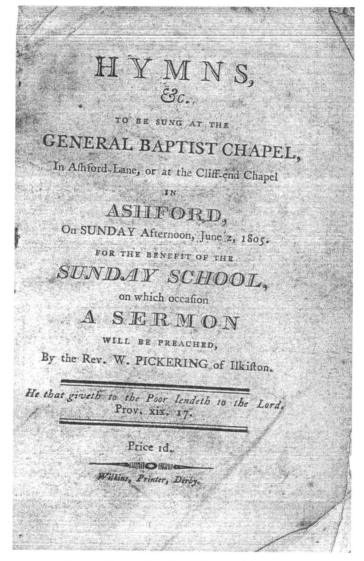

HYMNS,
&c.

TO BE SUNG AT THE

GENERAL BAPTIST CHAPEL,

In Aſhford-Lane, or at the Cliff-end Chapel

IN

ASHFORD,

On SUNDAY Afternoon, June 2, 1805.

FOR THE BENEFIT OF THE

SUNDAY SCHOOL,

on which occaſion

A SERMON

WILL BE PREACHED,

By the Rev. W. PICKERING of Ilkiſton.

He that giveth to the Poor lendeth to the Lord.
Prov. xix. 17.

Price 1d.

Wilkins, Printer, Derby.

Source: Local Studies Library, Matlock

Ashford in the Water Baptist Cemetery

Bradwell Primitive Methodist Chapel, formerly Bradwell Baptist Chapel

CHAPTER 2

THE BARTON PREACHERS

The General Baptists of Derbyshire are a product of the Evangelical Awakening of the 1730s and 1740s, a movement that is synonymous with the work of John Wesley and George Whitfield. Their rediscovery of 'justification by faith alone' re-invigorated Christianity in Britain at a time when it had grown stale. A new passion for outdoor preaching accompanied a message of good news for ordinary men and women. While this new enthusiasm was not welcomed by many in the Established Church, it found a warm response in some quarters. One of the most loyal supporters and defenders of evangelicalism was Selina, Countess of Huntingdon. From her home at Donington Hall she readily welcomed Wesley and Whitfield, and it was there, in the second week of June 1741 that John Wesley made his first appearance in the Midlands.

Wesley preached at Melbourne and Markfield where the countess had property. His words clearly affected some of those who gathered, one of whom was David Taylor, a servant of the countess.

Traditional Baptist hagiography has it that the countess encouraged David Taylor in his itinerant preaching ministry around Glenfield and Ratby[1]. A more recent and scholarly assessment, however, has seriously questioned that analysis. While the countess appointed David Taylor to read prayers and devotional books to people in their own homes, Taylor took it upon himself to preach outdoors, something that did not have her approval. "His activities soon became a source of distress to Lady Huntingdon and the Wesleys because he refused to surrender control of the societies he had formed."[2] By April 1842 the countess had quite despaired of him and refused to give him any further encouragement.

David Taylor was more of a maverick and a loose cannon. But his preaching seemed to be effective. Preaching a message of liberation in the villages of Glenfield and Ratby, it was in the latter venue that

Taylor made a profound and lasting impression upon Samuel Deacon snr. (1714-1812).

At the same time several other people came into a similar experience of evangelical awakening including Joseph Donisthorpe, a blacksmith and watchmaker of Normanton on the Heath; Stephen Dixon; and John Taylor, a schoolmaster at Markfield, one of Lady Huntingdon's schools. For a while John Taylor assisted David Taylor in an itinerant preaching ministry.

"In 1743 John Whyatt, carpenter, and John Aldridge, farmer, of Barton, heard the new preachers at Osbaston: they invited them to preach at Barton, and John Taylor delivered the first sermon in Mr Whyatt's house."[3]

On one of John Taylor's visits to Whyatt's house, they were attacked by a mob of several hundred people headed by the constable of Nailstone. They were accused of being Methodists. The door was broken down, Aldridge's parents were treated with "great brutality," John Aldridge himself was thrown into the fish pond and Joseph Donisthorpe was seized by the hair, hung over a gate and threatened with death. Both John Taylor and John Whyatt subsequently were brought before the Leicester Quarter Sessions, ultimately (1744) being vindicated of the charges brought against them. John Taylor left for London not long after this.

Stephen Dixon meanwhile had joined with a community of Moravians in Pudsey, West Yorkshire. Returning to Barton in 1744, he brought with him a colleague, William Kendrick, who had previously had links with both Whitfield and Wesley.[4] It was at Kendrick's suggestion that the small group of like minded believers in the village should join themselves together into a society. So, in 1744, seven people formed the first congregation at Barton in the Beans. These were: John Whyatt, John Aldridge, William Adcock, Stephen Dixon, Mr & Mrs Kendrick, and probably David Taylor (although he was to disappear to Yorkshire soon afterwards).

The Moravian influence was seen again the following year (1745) when they decided to build a Meeting House in the village which was in the Moravian style, with a large rostrum at the front with room for many preachers or leaders, instead of a pulpit.[5] The local population nicknamed those who attended the Church as "ravens." The Meeting House was built, opened and paid for (£170) by the end of the year. Mr William Collins from London preached at the opening and stayed for several weeks.

Dixon and Kendrick exercised the principal leadership of the new fellowship, although Dixon was subsequently expelled for promoting views of universal restoration. He left for Annesley Woodhouse in Nottinghamshire, and subsequently pastored churches in Leicestershire and Lincolnshire by which time he had become a Particular Baptist.[6] Other people, however, joined the new cause including Joseph Donisthorpe; Samuel Deacon, the farm labourer and grocer from Ratby; Francis Smith from Melbourne; Mr. Ault from Leicester; and John Grimley from Donington. Not content with being passive recipients of the Good News, they each in their turn became preachers, taking the message to villages throughout the area. In 1747 Francis Smith invited Joseph Donisthorpe to preach in Melbourne, and from that early beginning a chapel was eventually constructed in 1750. The "Barton Preachers" continued their work of evangelism throughout the area.

Until this point the congregation at Barton had simply called themselves, "Independents." Gradually, however, their views on baptism began to change. In the earliest period of the Barton in the Beans Chapel infant sprinkling was practiced. A concentrated study of the New Testament indicated that sprinkling with water was not a biblical pattern. They subsequently brought a tub into the centre of the chapel and baptised their infants by immersion in the tub. This practice was also soon discontinued in favour of Infant Presentation, and along with that came the corollary of Believers Baptism. "Donisthorpe baptised Kendrick, and Kendrick, Donisthorpe, and then both set to and baptised the remainder. Thus it came to pass that ten years after their first formation into a society they became a Baptist Church."[7] Between 60 -70 of them were baptised on that occasion in

November 1755. Others remained in the fellowship but did not feel comfortable with the practice of believers' baptism. Alan Betteridge suggests that the practice of believers' baptism had been seriously considered several years earlier while William Allt was part of the group. Allt was a convinced Baptist and his group in Hinckley were Baptists by 1752. The Barton group delayed believers' baptism for fear of being seen to imitate Allt.[8]

The geographical range of the Barton Preachers was astounding. As well as the surrounding villages in Leicestershire, preaching was taken into Derbyshire, Nottinghamshire, Staffordshire and Warwickshire. All of this was done on foot. Samuel Deacon and Francis Smith thought nothing of walking 20 miles to preach on a Sunday, taking two or three services and then walking the same distance back again, often arriving home at 3.00am. A full day's manual work would follow the next day. But eventually the huge area covered by the Barton Church began to prove difficult to manage. Two events brought this to a head.

The only places that the Lord's Supper was observed were Barton and Melbourne. It was observed once a month in each place alternately. The members at Barton and Melbourne regularly made the 28 mile round trip. Part of the gatherings involved the provision of hospitality for those who had made the long journeys. In 1759 the trustees of the two chapels were fined £50 for breach of the Excise laws. This was a financially crippling blow and helped precipitate the division of the Barton Church.

The second event which heralded this next phase in the life of the churches was the departure of William Kendrick. Kendrick had been joined by Francis Smith as joint Ruling Elders following the removal of Stephen Dixon. Kendrick ran a Boarding School near Barton which required him to be tied to the Barton end, while Francis Smith had charge of the Melbourne side of things. In 1760 Kendrick was excluded from the Church after allegations of immoral conduct were substantiated.[9] It was the absence of the man who had hitherto masterminded the whole Barton enterprise that forced the Barton Church to take a radically new step.

John Grimley and Abraham Booth are linked with the idea of dividing the Barton Church into five separate and independent churches in 1760 each with their own pastors to oversee the work:

Barton under John Whyatt of Barton, Samuel Deacon of Ratby, John Aldridge of Hugglescote

Melbourne under Francis Smith and Thomas Perkins

Kegworth under Nathaniel Pickering of Donington and John Tarratt of Kegworth

Loughborough under Joseph Donisthorpe of Normanton and John Grimley of Donington le Heath

Kirby Woodhouse under Abraham Booth

The division might not have been as neat as this would indicate. J. J. Goadby in a circular letter to the 100th Annual Meeting of the New Connexion in 1869 indicated that Melbourne first separated from Barton in 1759 before Kendrick's departure. The other churches separated within the following twelve months.

The fact remains that by 1760 there were five churches formed out of the one. In 1766 Barton divided again releasing the branches at Hinckley and Longford to form their own Church. By 1770 there were 900 members spread across the 6 churches. Relationships between the churches remained good. They still had monthly ministers' meetings, and quarterly conferences at each Church in rotation.

The Barton Church, therefore, found itself with three ministers once the Hinckley and Longford Church had departed in 1766: Samuel Deacon, John Whyatt and John Aldridge. Within a few years both Whyatt and Aldridge had left the ministry. In 1767 Aldridge became embroiled in a theological dispute concerning the active and passive righteousness of Christ, and doubted his continued call to the ministry, although he stayed on as a member until his death in 1795. Whyatt was excluded for immorality in 1769.

The burden was too much for Sam Deacon to carry alone. As well as the Barton Church there were other preaching stations attached to Barton: Hugglescote, Stanton under Bardon, Markfield and Ratby. Several faithful members of the Church continued to help out with taking services. William Adcock, for example, had been one of the original founder members of the Church, and served as a deacon for 60 years. (Adcock is buried in the graveyard at Barton and his headstone pays tribute to his faithful years of ministry at the Church). Clearly, however, the Church needed additional ministerial assistance. This arrived in 1772 through Mr John Yates of Hugglescote, formerly of the Particular Baptists in Shepshed. Yates proved to be an excellent preacher, but sadly he died very suddenly in December 1773 aged 36 leaving a widow and five children.

Friends from other churches helped out, but the final solution came with the appointment of Samuel Deacon jnr. as assistant minister at Barton. Born in 1746 Sam Deacon jnr. had been sent into service when aged 11, eventually (1761) becoming apprenticed to Joseph Donisthorpe the watchmaker. Samuel attended services at Packington and also at Loughborough, eventually offering himself for baptism and Church fellowship at Barton in 1766. He continued his apprenticeship in Loughborough and Leicester, but never missed a Church Meeting or the Lord's Supper at Barton in the five years he was away. In 1771 he married the daughter of William Adcock, founder member of the Barton Church, and a few weeks after the marriage Samuel Deacon jnr. moved into his father in law's house in the village. Samuel began preaching in 1777 and on 25th September 1779 he was ordained as co-pastor with his father. Nathaniel Pickering led the service, Dan Taylor performed the ordination, and Francis Smith gave one of the addresses. Samuel Deacon jnr. established his own clockmaking business in Barton, a business which not only thrived but grew in reputation. Deacon clocks became highly sought after and the family business carried on in Barton right up until the Second World War. 'The Lilacs' was the family home and is still present in the village today.

Samuel Deacon's ministry proved highly successful. He was possessed of far greater abilities than his father, and consequently he had a breadth to his preaching that appealed to many people. The Church grew. Membership which had stood at 139 in 1785 had risen to 215 by 1795. Three years later the Hugglescote Church separated from Barton. 150 members stayed at Barton but 100 parted with Hugglescote. Mr Orton took charge of the Hugglescote congregation. But still Barton continued to grow, the membership rising to 305 by 1810. Sam Deacon jnr. himself helped to pioneer preaching in new villages: Ibstock (1788), Barlestone (1793), Market Bosworth (1794), Whitwick (1796), Bagworth (1796). In 1797 Mr Jacob Brewin, a member of the Church, was appointed assistant to Sam Deacon jnr. In 1809 the chapel at Barton was enlarged by the addition of two schoolrooms.

Samuel Deacon senior died in 1812 aged 98. He had still been walking up to 30 miles on a Sunday when 80, but in later years he became quite enfeebled. Samuel Deacon jnr. did not enjoy the same longevity as his father. His first wife, Elizabeth had died in 1803, aged 50. He remarried in 1805, by which time he was already conscious of his own declining health. Throughout the 1790s he had made impassioned pleas with the Barton Church to invest more in the ministry than in the buildings, and ensured that the Church took seriously the need to set ministers free from secular employment in order to give themselves fully to the ministry. Sam Deacon himself never received a penny for his labours from the Church, but did establish a principle and a fund to ensure that future ministers faired better.

On February 8th 1816 Sam Deacon jnr. resigned his office. He preached his last sermon on his 70th birthday (February 18th). He died on March 2nd, his body being interred in the Barton Chapel. In some 27 years of pastoral ministry at Barton he had baptised 512 people. During his years in the ministry he had produced several short works, some of which are on display at the Barton museum, along with a myriad of hymns most of which disappeared from congregational usage not long after his death. Samuel and Elizabeth Deacon had no children.

Jacob Brewin died a few weeks before Sam Deacon (February 23rd 1816). He was aged 60. The following year, Mr John Green, a student from the Wisbech Academy, took up the pastorate. He stayed until 1823 after which John Derry became minister. He was still minister in 1845 when the centenary services were conducted. More chapels were constructed amongst the village preaching stations: Congerstone (1821), Newbold Vernon (1833). By 1840 the Church reached its highest mark with 420 Church members; this in a village with a population even then of little more than 200. John Derry "laboured with ardent zeal and rich success until 1852."[10] During this time the old chapel was taken down and the new and present building was erected. Towards the west side of the field at the rear of the old and new churches is a stream which was dammed to make an open-air baptistry. Today the stream and the dam are overgrown and inaccessible, but this was the place where countless hundreds of people demonstrated their Christian faith and commitment.

1. "David Taylor left his secular services at the Hall with the prayers and good wishes of the pious countess and itinerates as a preacher in Charnwood Forest." J.R.Godfrey Historic memorials 1891 p.5
2. Edwin Welch Spiritual Pilgrim 1995 p.49 &50
3. J.H.Wood Condensed History p.159
4. Alan Betteridge B.Q 36 page 73
5. Percy Austin B.Q 11page 417
6. Alan Betteridge B.Q 36 page 77
7. J.R.Godfrey Historic memorials 1891 p.15
8. Alan Betteridge B.Q 36 page 76
9. "What rendered the business still more distressing, he had artfully secured the possession of the deeds of several meeting houses, nor could they, but by a sum of money, induce him to surrender those important documents." 'Preacher, Pastor, Mechanic: a Memoir of Samuel Deacon' p.5
10. J.R Godfrey Historic memorials p.93

Samuel Deacon Senior
1714 – 1812

Samuel Deacon Junior
1746 - 1816

John Derry, Minister Barton in the Beans
1824 - 1852

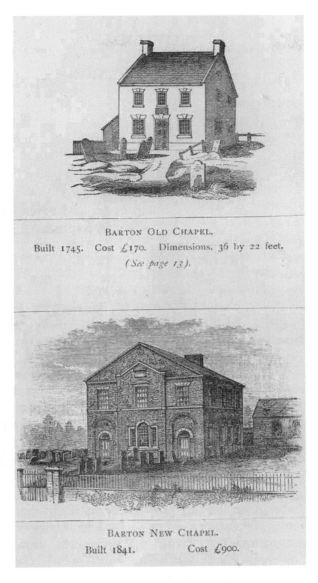

BARTON OLD CHAPEL.

Built 1745.   Cost £170.   Dimensions. 36 by 22 feet.

(See page 13).

BARTON NEW CHAPEL.

Built 1841.   Cost £900.

Drawings of the old and new Baptist Chapel at Barton

CHAPTER 3

THE NEW CONNEXION

Rev Dan Taylor
(1738 – 1816)
Founder of the New Connexion
General Baptists

In order to move the story on it is necessary to make a diversion into West Yorkshire, and to explore developments within the General Baptists in that part of the country. Once again it is the Evangelical, particularly Methodist, influence that is paramount, and especially the way that Methodist influence impinged on the life of a young man called Dan Taylor.[1]

Dan Taylor was born on 21st December 1738 in Sour-milk Hall, Northowram near Halifax. From the age of 5 he was working down the mines, an occupation with which he continued until he was 24. Unusually, however, Taylor was a voracious reader, even smuggling books down the mine and reading by what little light was available to him.

From the age of 15 he listened attentively to local Methodist preachers, and at 20 he formerly joined the Methodist communion. He was urged to preach, and he delivered his first sermon at Hipperholm, near Halifax in September 1761. But Dan Taylor soon became dissatisfied with the Methodists. His own broad reading had given him a wider theological grasp than many of his peers, and he was unhappy with some of the answers to theological questions coming from his Methodist teachers. He apparently was also unhappy with the Methodist system of Church discipline which Wesley had imposed on his followers. Taylor withdrew from the Methodists in 1762.

At approximately the same time four other people in the area of Heptonstall also left the Methodists for more or less the same reasons. They were John Slater, John Parker, William Crossley and an unnamed woman. Although they lived nine miles away from each other, their similar stories eventually connected, and the Heptonstall four invited Taylor to preach to them throughout the summer of 1762. They met in the open air under a tree at a place called The Nook, a mile from Halifax. In the winter they hired a house in Wadsworth Lanes which doubled as a school room during the week where Taylor gave lessons.

This informal gathering slowly attracted a few more adherents. Topics ranged far and wide, but the issue of the nature of the Church constantly arose, and, along with that the subject of baptism. The group came to the conclusion that there was no scriptural basis for infant baptism and that as a result they were all unbaptised believers. In order to correct this anomaly, Taylor approached some nearby Particular Baptist Ministers to request Believers Baptism. The Particular Baptists refused, being unhappy with the Wesleyan and Arminian theological emphasis that the group espoused – Christ died for all – a view which Taylor tenaciously defended. The Particular Baptists were good enough, however, to mention that there were other General Baptists with similar views in Boston, Lincolnshire. Perhaps they might like to make the 120 mile trip to Boston!! On Friday 11th February 1763 Dan Taylor and John Slater set off to find the General Baptists of Boston.

By the Saturday night, however, they were told about a group of Baptists much nearer to them, in Gamston, Nottinghamshire. Taylor and Slater tracked down the cause on Sunday 13th February, and met the assistant Minister, Mr Dossey. He in turn introduced the pair to Mr Jeffrey the senior minister, and it was after Jeffrey was satisfied with the sincerity of the two men that he baptised Dan Taylor in the river at Gamston on February 16th. Slater refused to be baptised by Jeffrey insisting that Taylor himself perform the ceremony once they returned to Yorkshire.

Taylor and Slater carried on their journey to Boston, meeting William Thompson the General Baptist minister in the town. Thompson in turn introduced Taylor to the Lincolnshire General Baptist Association of which Taylor formerly became a member (May 1763).

It was William Thompson who then made the pioneering next step agreeing to return with Taylor and Slater to Wadsworth where he subsequently baptised several people, forming fourteen of them into a General Baptist Church and ordaining Taylor as their pastor in the Autumn of 1763.

The Wadsworth congregation grew, and by 1764 they began to construct a new building in a rugged terrain known as Birchcliffe. Funds for the new building were needed, so Dan Taylor decided to return to Lincolnshire to renew his acquaintance with the General Baptist Association there. He attended their meetings in summer 1764, and, still trying to raise funds for the Birchcliffe Chapel, made a visit into the Midlands. Taylor stopped at Loughborough, and spent time with Mr Hutchinson, one of the leading figures of the General Baptist Church there. Hutchinson in turn acquainted Taylor with the work of the Barton preachers and the Baptist Churches in that area.

Taylor was keen to discover that the views of the Barton group of churches were so similar to his own. In subsequent contact he attempted to persuade the Leicestershire churches to join the Lincolnshire Association. But such an idea was fiercely rejected by the Leicestershire group.

The problem stemmed from the nature of the Old General Baptist Churches and their Association. While starting off in the late seventeenth and early eighteenth centuries with firm Trinitarian and evangelical viewpoints, by the mid eighteenth century the General Baptists had become quite a disparate and theologically divided group. Many of them espoused views that were nearer to the Unitarians with the result that those General Baptists that had experienced the Evangelical Awakening felt they could not have fellowship with those who diverged so fundamentally on the essentials of the faith.

In 1765 and 1767 Dan Taylor, still representing the Lincolnshire Association, attended the national General Baptist Assembly in London. By 1769 it was clear that there could be no rapprochement with the older General Baptists, and no likelihood of the newer Leicestershire churches associating with them. The result was that at Michaelmas 1769 a meeting was held in Lincoln with a view to the formation of a New Connexion of General Baptists. They resolved to meet again in June 1770 at the same time as the General Baptist Assembly.

So, on 6th June 1770 the following Midlands ministers gathered at the Meeting House, Church Lane, London:

Samuel Deacon (Barton, Leicestershire); John Tarratt & Nathaniel Pickering (Kegworth, Leicestershire); John Grimley (Loughborough, Leicestershire); William Smith & George Hickling (Longford, Warwickshire); and Francis Smith and Thomas Perkins (Melbourne, Derbyshire).

Along with these men were the ministers from General Baptist Churches currently belonging to the Assembly who had decided to withdraw from the Old Connexion:

Dan Taylor (Wadsworth, Yorkshire); William Thompson (Boston, Lincs); John Brittain (Church Lane, London); William Summers (Park, Southwark); John Knott (Eythorne, Kent); James Fenn (Deal, Kent); J.Stanger (Bessel's Green, Kent); David Wilkin (Halstead, Essex); Charles Parman (Castle Headingham, Essex); R.French (Coggeshall, Essex); H.Poole (Fleet, Lincs).

A deputation was sent to the General Assembly then meeting informing them of their decision to withdraw. The following morning, 7th June 1774, Dan Taylor addressed the new meeting from 2Timothy 1:8. In the afternoon Taylor was appointed chairman of the "Assembly of Free – Grace General Baptists".

The new group established Six Articles of Faith concerning:

1. The Fall and depravity of the human race
2. The abiding relevance of the Moral Law
3. The person and work of Christ – Jesus Christ is God and Man united in one person; he suffered to make a full atonement for all the sins of all men, and thereby has wrought a complete salvation.
4. That Christ should be offered to all
5. The regenerating work of the Holy Spirit naturally produces holiness in heart and life.
6. That it is the "indispensable duty of all who repent and believe the Gospel to be baptised by immersion in water" and that "no person ought to be received into the Church without submission to this ordinance."

Gilbert Boyce, the Lincolnshire Association Messenger, worked very hard to prevent the separation. On February 10th 1770 he wrote to Dan Taylor pleading with him not to precipitate the schism: "Think, O think again, what will be the consequence of separation." And even after the split had taken place Boyce and William Thompson tried to find common ground between the two groups based on the Six Articles. But to no avail. In 1770 "The New Connexion of General Baptists"[2] was formed "with a design to revive experimental religion or primitive Christianity in Faith and Practice." There was no going back.

It was the New Connexion that flourished. As the Midlands churches grew and multiplied so did the membership of the New Connexion movement. Many of the old General Baptist churches eventually were subsumed within Unitarianism, while others, like Friar lane, Leicester were revived through membership with the New Connexion. In reality the New Connexion became the new General Baptists. The impetus was with them and so too the drive and the missionary enterprise.

Dan Taylor's own Church at Wadsworth (Birchcliffe) had grown to a membership of 69 by 1770. In 1783 he moved to take over the pastorate at Halifax just a few miles further away. But in 1785 he was urged by his friends to rescue the cause at Church Lane, London, which had been declining under the ministry of the now visibly ageing Mr Brittain. Recognising the strategic nature of this Church in London, Dan Taylor accepted the call and was inducted there on 8th June 1785.

Taylor's pivotal role in the life of the General Baptists was re-enforced a few years later over the matter of educating ministers for the Baptist ministry. Both Dan Taylor and John Fawcett, his Particular Baptist neighbour in Yorkshire, had been concerned about the need to train those who would assume the pastorate of churches. There was residual suspicion about learning among many Baptists but eventually Taylor's arguments were accepted and it was agreed to form such an institution. It quickly transpired that the man to lead this educational establishment was the man whose vision it had been all along: Dan Taylor. So, in 1798, the self taught miner from Yorkshire became head of the Mile End Road Academy in London. He was 59 years old. Taylor continued in charge of the Academy until failing health forced his resignation in 1813, whereupon the College moved to Wisbech where Joseph Goadby, the local minister, was identified as the man to lead the College into its next phase of life.

1. The biographical details on Dan Taylor and subsequent developments are culled from J.H.Wood's 1847 'Condensed History of the New Connexion' and Peter Shepherd's history of Northern Baptist College (2004).
2. Frank Rinaldi was awarded a PhD (Glasgow 1996) for his research into the history of the New Connexion General Baptists. The title of his work was "The tribe of Dan" – an ingenius play on words between the Old Testament tribe, and the group which took its origin from Dan Taylor.

CHAPTER 4

MELBOURNE

The Baptist cause at Melbourne is inextricably linked with Mr Francis Smith. He was born on July 3rd 1719. His parents were "industrious and creditable" and were attenders at the Parish Church. According to Smith's own testimony, produced at the launch of the New Connexion and reprinted by his son Robert in the General Baptist Magazine for Summer 1798, his parents died when he was aged 16 and he went somewhat off the rails. How much credence should be given to this is hard to say. At the age of 23, Smith tells us, he was spiritually awakened by listening to some Methodist preachers. He continued in some anxiety for a number of years, conscious of his unworthiness but failed to obtain the peace that came through belief in Christ's all sufficient sacrifice. Helpfully, Smith tells us that his conversion "May be compared to a misty and dark morning which gradually became clearer and clearer."

During his period of religious searching he attended meetings for prayer and bible study held at Donington Hall at which the Countess of Huntingdon dubbed him "Little Timothy." It was in 1746 or 1747 when, according to Robert Smith, his father began his public labours in the work of the ministry. His first sermon was delivered in the home of Mr William Allen of Kirby Woodhouse, Nottinghamshire. His text was Luke 2:10 "Behold I bring you good tidings."

Lacking confidence in his own abilities, Francis Smith decided that he was not the person to bring the Good News into Melbourne, and so invited the six foot blacksmith and watchmaker from Normanton-le-Heath, Joseph Donisthorpe, to carry out this task. In 1747 Donisthorpe arrived in the market place, then known as Green Hill, and began to preach, being in effect the first person to bring what was to become the 'Baptist' cause into the town.

A ready group of hearers were soon assembled. At first they met in cottages, but eventually they looked to build a meeting place. Between

1749 and 1750 a chapel was built on the present site, this becoming the second chapel to be built by the Barton Society. According to Thomas J. Budge, "The work at Barton and Melbourne was one, and in 1747 William Kendrick and Francis Smith were ordained Ruling Elders of the society. Francis Smith had particular, though nor exclusive, charge of Melbourne."

On August 20th 1753 Francis Smith married Elizabeth Toone. Perhaps at other times this event would not have warranted much notice. But these religious dissenters were very mindful of the opposition they faced both from sections of the public and also the powers that be. Although the law permitted dissenters to be married in their own places of worship John Aldridge had needed to face a lengthy legal challenge to the validity of his marriage a short while before Smith's wedding. In the light of that experience Francis Smith and Elizabeth Toone drew up a marriage covenant which set out their intentions and commitments to live together in Christian marriage. The covenant and the marriage was witnessed and signed by 22 people. William Kendrick conducted the service. The following year (1754) the right of Dissenters to marry in their own places of worship was withdrawn (with the exception of Quakers and Jews), and wasn't restored until 1836.

Francis Smith and Elizabeth Toone had a very happy marriage which tragically was cut short. The Barton Centenary history says that Elizabeth died of consumption (tuberculosis) on October 17th 1768. She left seven children. Francis Smith subsequently remarried in 1776 to a member of Melbourne Baptist Church called Mary Hucknall. The Barton Centenary politely tells us that she "proved a valuable partner." Robert Smith, on the other hand candidly remarks that, "an unhappy disposition rendered this union not so agreeable as might have been wished."

When the division of the Barton Society took place in 1760 Francis Smith and Thomas Perkins were ordained to the pastoral office. They had charge not only of Melbourne, but also of the two main branches at Packington and Measham with smaller satellites at Swannington and Ticknall. The charge to the two ministers was given by Abraham

Booth of Kirby Woodhouse and was based on Acts 20:28. Others taking part in the ordination were John Grimley of Loughborough, John Tarrat of Kegworth, Joseph Donisthorpe who prayed and John Aldridge who announced the hymns.

Perkins and Smith were a good complementary team. Perkins had a reputation for being a hell fire preacher while Smith was more noted for his gentle, pastoral work. The team were, however, very effective. Numbers increased. In 1760 there were only 40 members in the Church. By 1770 this had risen to 160; by 1775 there were 258 members; and in 1781 the membership reached 281. In 1768 the chapel had to be enlarged. Fourteen years later they had to add on a gallery. In 1785 the Church membership stood at 305.

None of this happened without a lot of hard work. Robert Smith records how his father spent the first 20 years of his ministry without receiving a penny from the Church. He earned a living as a journeyman and had to pack much of what needed to be done in the Church into the spare time available to him. Francis Smith would walk up to eight miles on a week night evening to take a service at one of the outlying villages. On Fridays he would walk to the ministers' conference at Barton, 14 miles way. The meetings started at 6.00pm and rarely ended before midnight. And on Sundays his preaching could take him upwards of 20 or even 30 miles from home. The fact that his first sermon was delivered at Kirby Woodhouse near Mansfield illustrates the point very well. In 1770 Smith and Perkins both walked to London to attend the inaugural meeting of the New Connexion General Baptists.

Hard work and sacrifice were key elements of some of these pioneering ministers. Smith himself was known to have paid the workmen involved in the various building extensions at the chapel from his own meagre income. But it wasn't just the ministers who demonstrated this spirit. The chapel enlargement in 1768 cost £120. In order to play her part in reaching that target, Mrs Elizabeth Pegg famously sold her wedding ring.

Until 1785 Smith and Perkins preached alternately at Melbourne and Packington (the principal preaching station). The meetings at Packington were first held in the house of Richard Thompson but in 1762 a large barn was adapted for public worship. In 1800 an upper room in "The Malt Shovel" yard was obtained and licensed for public worship, and in 1802 they bought a house in Mill Lane and fitted it for public worship.

The Melbourne Church Meeting minutes are available from April 4th 1774. They make it clear that meetings were held alternately between Melbourne and Packington. The meeting held on April 4th was at Packington, and members debated the subject whether women had the right to vote in the Church Meeting. "It was decided in the negative by the votes of men and women both with a majority of seventeen." The Church Meeting went on to debate the same topic on future occasions. On December 25th 1784 (meeting held at Melbourne) it was conceded that women could vote when it came to choosing officers to serve the Church "but in no other cases". It wasn't until April 1790 that it was decided "by a large majority" that women had the same right to vote as men.

Thomas Mee, along with Job Burdett and John Smedley, assisted Perkins and Smith in the preaching ministry. They were all rigorously tested before being released for this vital work. Mee spent 18 years working in the Packington branch.

Early Church Meetings were involved in discussing the issue of the separation of the growing Melbourne group of churches. But it was Cauldwell, not Packington that made the first move. The work at Cauldwell was started by Joseph Norton, a young man from the village who persuaded some 20 people from Cauldwell to join him for worship at Packington. Joseph's father, a prominent landowner in the village, was suspicious of the Barton preachers so his son, eager to get some preaching in Cauldwell, applied to Sutton Coldfield for help and a group of preachers from there supplied the early work. Eventually, Mr Norton senior mellowed in his resistance to Joseph's new found faith and in 1778 he gave a plot of land for a chapel to be built. In anticipation of this the Christmas Day Church Meeting in 1777 (held at Packington) discussed how they would finance the new building. Eventually on Christmas Day 1784 the Church Meeting (held at Melbourne) recorded the following:

"Our Cauldwell friends had united together and expressed in writing their desire that on account of the inconvenience of attending our Church Meetings, and especially on our ordinance days, that they might be a separate Church from the main body and that brother Job Burdett might be appointed over them as their pastor." The Meeting agreed to this request and in 1785 some 40 members left the Melbourne membership to constitute themselves a Church at Cauldwell.

Job Burdett was one of several able preachers who served the Melbourne Church and who supported Perkins and Smith in their work. Sadly Job Burdett died two years later from consumption (tuberculosis). He was only 27 years old. In 1788 Joseph Norton's son, Charles, was called to the pastorate of the Cauldwell Church, a position he held until his own premature death in 1800.

Joseph Goadby[1] became the first pastor of the Packington Church. He was born in 1774 at Market Bosworth; was baptised and received into membership of the Barton Church in December 1793; started preaching in 1797 and spent six months at Dan Taylor's Academy in London during which time the Barton Church supported his wife and children. Goadby was given charge of the Packington branch of Melbourne Baptist Church on his return and the work flourished. In 1799 he started the cause at Ashby and Measham; in 1802 preaching began at Austrey (7 miles south of Ashby), and in 1806 at Warton in Warwickshire. In 1807 the Packington Church became independent of Melbourne and in its first report to the Association the following year reported that they had 105 members. Austrey became independent of Packington in 1808. In 1810 a gallery had to be added to the Packington chapel; in 1811 a new chapel was built at Measham; and in 1817 a new chapel at Ashby was needed as well.

Joseph Goadby dedicated the whole of his ministry to the work at Packington and the surrounds. His declining health caused the Church in 1836 to call an assistant, Mr Barnet, who had oversight of the Measham branch. In 1839 the number of members reported to the Association by the Ashby – Packington Church was 297. Goadby passed away in 1841 having declined invitations from several other churches over the years. Mr Pike of Derby preached his funeral address from 2 Tim. 4:7&8. Joseph Goadby's grandson, Thomas, subsequently became principal of the Midland Baptist College when it came to Nottingham.

In 1785 Thomas Perkins retired from the ministry at Melbourne. Most accounts are silent as to the reason for this, but J.H.Wood was candid enough to explain: "Circumstances connected with an imprudent marriage in his old age occasioned Mr P's retirement from the ministry." He and Smith had enjoyed an extremely fruitful partnership which had seen churches planted and congregations grow. Perkins died in 1792.

Francis Smith carried on with great energy. He had always been keen to spread the Gospel as far a-field as possible. (He is attributed with baptising 16 people in Sutton Coldfield and forming a Church there which subsequently went on to evangelise and plant into the whole of Birmingham) But it was Derby that proved to be one of his major areas of mission.

Dan Taylor appears to have been the first to preach in Derby (May 31st 1789) as he passed through the town. Nathaniel and Thomas Pickering from Castle Donington carried on with both preaching in the open air and in hired rooms, but when they couldn't carry the work on it fell to Francis Smith from Melbourne to take up the mantle. Smith was aided by another of the able Melbourne preachers, John Smedley, along with John Goddard, the minister from Ilkeston. Preaching carried on with mixed results throughout 1790. Eventually a regular Conference of the General Baptist Ministers held at Cauldwell that Christmas decided to persevere with the work which led eventually to a small group of believers being formed in Derby. On July 5th 1791 the Conference held at Smalley decided that it would be better to form the group into their own distinct Church rather than see them as a branch of one of the surrounding Baptist churches. (No one Church seemed keen to take overall responsibility). Consequently on August 21st 1791 Francis

51

Smith, John Smedley and Thomas Pickering conducted a baptismal service in the river Derwent near the Morledge at which 9 people were baptised and formed into a Church. According to the minutes of the Brook Street Church in Derby, which eventually emerged from this group, several subsequent baptismal services were held. Six people were baptised in the Derwent on October 30th 1791; 8 more on April 22nd 1792; and 5 more on June 28th 1794. The hand writing in these minutes is that of Francis Smith. When, in 1803, a building was constructed in Brook Street, Derby, it was made a condition of the Trust Deed that a minimum of three of the new (and subsequent) Trustees should be appointed by the Melbourne Baptist Church. Wisely, Melbourne always chose Derby people to serve in this capacity.

John Smedley later became minister at Retford. Apparently Smedley was one of five men who the Church was keen to invite to the pastorate. To decide which of the five should be invited the Retford Church fell back on the methods used in Acts chapter 1 and asked the five to draw lots! In this way John Smedley was invited to Retford.

In 1793 Mr Harpur was appointed to assist Francis Smith. He turned out to be something of a fraud; was banned from preaching and was made to leave the town in November. Edmund Whitaker settled from Burnley in 1794 and within a year 45 people had been added to the Church.

On Saturday 19th March 1796 Francis Smith died. The previous Sunday he had preached and administered the Lord's Supper at Packington; preached there again in the afternoon, riding out to Ticknall for the evening where he preached his last sermon on Isaiah 1:18. Smith was 77 years old and he had pastored the Melbourne Church for nearly fifty years. John Tarratt of Kegworth preached the funeral address from Acts 20: 25 "Ye all… shall see my face no more". Francis Smith was awarded the rare privilege of being buried underneath the Communion Table in Melbourne Baptist Church.

The Church went through a very difficult patch. Edmund Whitaker soldiered on for a period but after three years his health broke down due to his asthma. Unsuitable preachers were brought in; some people in the Church seemed to drift towards Unitarianism. John Pegg, John Earp and Joseph Scott were deacons who battled for the old doctrines. But the Church Meeting minutes reflect the divisions:

10 April 1803: to meet together in a fortnight "To renew and openly profess our love one to another, and if possible to put an end to our animosities."

1 June 1806: "sadly deficient in peace and love."

7 February 1808: "does this Church desire a union of all its members?"

Outside ministers were called in to arbitrate.

Edmund Whitaker died on 10th July 1808. He was only 41. A succession of short ministries followed: James Gilchrist (1809-1811); J. Smith (1812-1814); J. Preston (1815-1823); John Winks (1824-1826); J.G.Naylor (1827-1832). Through it all the Church began to experience resurgence. The work at Ticknall was going well. A chapel had been built in 1795, and in 1817 it was necessary to enlarge it. Preaching stations were established at Hartshorn, Breedon and Chellaston. Melbourne's Church Membership was 305 in 1785. It dipped to 218 by 1790 with the departure of the Cauldwell friends, but rose again to 300 by 1795. The membership figure in 1810, following the loss of 103 members to the Packington Church, stood at 210. But by 1835 that figure had risen to 280, and so encouraging things appeared at Melbourne that a complete new chapel was built in 1832. It cost £800, and over £500 was collected at the opening alone. In 1833 Thomas Yates from the Loughborough Academy was called as the minister. In his seven years at the Church there were 108 baptisms.

1. Joseph Goadby was part of what Margaret Wombwell refers to as a 'Baptist dynasty' in the East Midlands. Joseph and Thomas Goadby's abound throughout the Nineteenth century. Margaret has provided a very helpful Family Tree of the Goadby clan which explains their complex interconnectedness.

Francis Smith 1719 - 1796

Melbourne Baptist Chapel

Marriage Covenant of Francis Smith and Elizabeth Toone 1753
This copy was taken from 'A charge to keep' by J. Brian Radford who had
received permission from Rev Thomas Budge of Melbourne Baptist Church

Former Ticknall Baptist Church, Main Street, Ticknall

CHAPTER 5

KEGWORTH AND DISEWORTH

The Kegworth group of churches emerged out of the five-way split of the Barton Group in 1760. The group consisted of Diseworth, Kegworth and Castle Donington.

The Castle Donington Church had been started in 1750 by Samuel Fellowes; the Diseworth Church two years later in 1752. Two young men, Mr J. Bradley and Mr William Holmes had been travelling from Diseworth to hear the preaching at Castle Donington. They decided eventually to set up meetings in Diseworth and invite some of the Barton preachers to the village. The meetings took place in a weaver's home now known as Lilley's cottage. A licence for Dissenting preaching was obtained from Leicester Assizes in 1751 and the building on Ladygate was constructed in 1752. The Diseworth Chapel remains the oldest General Baptist building in Derbyshire.

Both Holmes and Bradley subsequently moved to Kegworth. Bradley inherited some money, purchased a piece of ground at Kegworth and gave a portion of it as a site for a chapel. William Jarrom's 1866 'History of Kegworth Baptist Church' says that there were only six or seven members of the Kegworth congregation at this time, but they raised the money necessary, and on June 15th 1755 a Meeting House was opened. Sermons were preached by Joseph Donisthorpe. Holmes himself wasn't baptised until the summer of 1756 back at the mother Church in Barton.

The Kegworth cause flourished rapidly with reported congregations of up to 500. But doctrinal difficulties, compounded by "intellectually and morally unfit preachers"[1] led to the collapse of the Kegworth Church. It had re-emerged again, however, prior to 1760, and at the separation of the Barton group Nathaniel Pickering was put in charge of the Castle Donington branch and John Tarratt of the Kegworth – Diseworth branch. The two men were ordained as joint pastors. By 1770 the two pastors were working alongside three ruling elders, six deacons and 180 Church members. According to Adam Taylor's account "The increase of the cause rendered more labourers necessary." In 1771 Benjamin Wootton, one of the Kegworth members, was called to the work of the ministry, and in 1775 William Corah was encouraged to start preaching. At the same time preaching was also introduced into Belton, five miles north-west of Kegworth, and the following year a dwelling house was licensed in Thurgaton. By 1781 membership had reached 282.

In 1782 an unfortunate set of circumstances caused a major set back for the Kegworth Church. Benjamin Wootton was beginning to espouse views which were generally considered Unitarian. Several people tried to lead him away from views which were unorthodox, but in the end Dan Taylor had to be brought to the Church and spent the best part of a day in public dispute with Mr Wootton. In the end Wootton left the Church and took 17 members with him.

All this needs placing in the context of a cause that was still robust and moving forwards. In 1782 John Goddard from Little Hallam near Ilkeston was called to the work of the ministry within the expanding Kegworth Church. The following year Sawley (a branch of Castle Donington) opened its new Meeting House. John Tarratt preached the first sermon in the building in the Autumn of 1783. More preaching stations were started at Hathern and at Sutton Bonington. And in 1784 "The Meeting House at Little Hallam was taken down and a more substantial and commodious one erected in its stead at Ilkiston; a considerable town a mile northward of the former place."[2]

William Jarrom's 'History' is very informative:

"The Church had assumed by 1785 such large proportions and covered such a considerable area of country, extending from North to South 20 miles. There were included in it Ilkeston, Smalley, Donington, Sawley, Kegworth, Diseworth, Belton, Whatton and Sutton Bonington."

With preachers having to travel 20 -30 miles each Lord's day, it was becoming too unwieldy to handle. It was John Goddard who came up with the idea of dividing this large society into distinct and independent churches. The chief difficulty arose from the heavy debt which remained on the Ilkeston Meeting House. The congregation there was considered too weak to be able to service the debt on their own, so it was decided that the other branches of the Church would take "the greatest part of the burden on themselves."[3] With that sticking point worked through, on 22nd May 1785 an amicable separation was agreed upon. Ilkeston, including Smalley, formed one Church under Mr Goddard. They had 50 members. Castle Donington, including Sawley, formed a second Church under Nathaniel Pickering. They had 70 members. And Kegworth formed the third Church (along with Diseworth, Belton, Long Whatton and Sutton Bonington) under John Tarratt and Mr Corah. They had 109 members.

The Leicester County Record Office still has available the Register of Births for Kegworth Baptist Church. It began in 1785 and ran through (with a brief gap) until the national registration system was introduced in 1837. John Tarratt was the Protestant Dissenting Minister registering the births until 1799 by which time he had been pastor virtually 40 years. The Register of births is interesting because it highlights the broad catchment area of the Kegworth Church even after the separation had taken place. The bulk of Baptist children being registered up until 1797 were from Sutton Bonington and Long Whatton and only changed after that year when a preponderance of Kegworth and Diseworth children feature. This reflects the fact that Sutton Bonington became independent of Kegworth in 1797 with Mr W. Smith as their minister, and Long Whatton became independent of Kegworth in 1799 with Mr Corah as their minister. Neither of these separations were carried out amicably.

The membership of the Kegworth group had risen to 184 by 1797. With the breakaway of Sutton Bonington and Long Whatton this left only 78 members in the Kegworth – Diseworth pairing, "many of whom were old and sinking into their grave."[4] The Kegworth Church Meeting minute book starts on November 10th 1799 "at its establishment distinct from Long Whatton." Subsequent Church Meetings alternate between Kegworth and Diseworth.

At this point John Tarratt, who had pastored the Kegworth group for 40 years, and was still only 62, was effectively made to resign. Adam Taylor paints a very lurid account of the demise of John Tarratt:

"His mental powers began early to decay, his youthful vivacity disappeared; his intellectual furniture was already exhausted; his public exercises became only the shadow of what they formerly had been."

J.H. Wood, however, in his Condensed History of the New Connexion paints a slightly different picture. Tarratt, who had been born in Kirk Ireton in 1737, had come to Ratcliff on Soar for employment and had subsequently entered into a lively evangelical faith. His 40 years ministry at Kegworth concluded following some unpleasant circumstances. He went to Kent where he had ministries at Deal and at Hythe before returning to Kegworth where he joined the Sutton Bonington Church and assisted both Mr Smith and Mr Wilders in the ministry. He died in 1817. It seems hard to imagine Tarratt exercising two further ministries if his intellectual furniture was quite as exhausted as Adam Taylor tried to make out.

William Felkin was called to Kegworth, a prosperous village by that time, with a population of 1,400. Felkin had been pastor at Ilkeston for a brief period having previously studied at Dan Taylor's Academy in London. He settled in April 1800 and was ordained in June 1801. Dan Taylor issued the charge to the Minister.

According to Felkin's son (himself a William), Rev Felkin was a good preacher.

"Few men, originally un-taught in the dialectics of the schools, could reason more closely, clearly and convincingly. His illustrations were apt, remarkably homely, and sometimes, on that account, very striking ….. He loved and valued the souls of men, wept over their lost estate, and often moved his hearers to weep also."[5]

The Kegworth Church responded well to Mr Felkin's ministry. Membership rose to 118 by 1805 and to 122 by 1810. Sadly dissensions again afflicted the Church forcing Mr Felkin to resign in 1811.

The disputes appear in part to be about money. Felkin had been obliged early in his ministry at Kegworth to open a boarding school in order to augment his meagre salary from the Church, but the Church "either through some dissatisfaction or sheer sloth"[6] frequently compounded his difficulties by paying him late.

Felkin stayed in Kegworth, believing that it was better for his family that he should stay put. He declined the offer of the pastorate at Archdeacon Lane, Leicester.

For three years the Church had no pastor until finally in 1814 Mr Felkin was invited to return. By this time membership stood at 83. No Church minutes were produced for the years 1810-1814, although intriguingly there are a set of shorthand notes in the minutes which try to summarise the period. By 1818 the Church was again unable (or unwilling) to pay Mr Felkin his salary and he felt obliged to conclude his ministry in 1819 by which stage the membership had risen to 96. The Church Meeting on September 19th 1819 referred to Mr Felkin's "carnal appetites."

William Felkin never took on pastoral charge of a Church again. He continued with his school and with itinerant preaching until his premature death in 1824. One of his sons, William, became a successful business man and in 1851 was Mayor of Nottingham. A second son, John, trained for the Baptist ministry and was at one time minister at Smalley.

A new chapel was built at Kegworth on the present site in 1815 and was opened on December 26th by Mr Orton of Hugglescote and Mr R. Smith. The building cost £450. That the Church could afford this was in no small measure due to Mr Holmes who started the cause back in 1750s. He had bequeathed the sum of £200 in the event of a new chapel being required along with a further bequest of £200 for the maintenance of the General Baptist cause in Kegworth.

But the Church was not in good heart, and the Report to the Association in 1819 lamented the decline of the cause. No minister was found for over four years. A succession of ministers (Butler 1824-1827; Jones 1827-1829; Wilders 1830-1844; Taylor 1846-1858) consolidated the Church, but membership remained fairly constant, rarely rising above the 120 mark. Mr Butler had several tussles with the Church over his salary, and left before they could be resolved. Mr Taylor relied upon his wife to supply the money needed to construct a baptistery in the Church. The June 1851 Church Meeting was informed of the necessity of the baptistery so that the women candidates might have a suitable place to dress and undress, "without being exposed to the filth and indecency of the places hitherto used near to the river." Mrs Taylor had written to Sir Morton Peto asking him to supply £10 to cover the cost of the work. He had agreed to her request, but the Church warned her that if the baptistery cost any more than £10 she would have to pay for it herself.

William Felkin's son lamented the worldliness of many of those involved in the leadership of the Church in his father's day. It may have been a similar problem 50 years later.

The Diseworth side of the Church ticked over. The affairs of Diseworth were subsumed into the Kegworth minutes until 1870 when the Church produced its own books. In 1821 the Kegworth Report to the Association stated that "Our school at Diseworth flourishes and we have built, to accommodate them, convenient rooms communicating with the chapel."

By 1850 the name of Nathaniel Gayton becomes prominent in the Diseworth records. He was born in Diseworth in 1787. In 1805 he was baptised and received into the fellowship of the Baptist Church. In 1813 he married Elizabeth who sadly died less than a year after their marriage.

Gayton was schoolmaster in Diseworth and census enumerator. He was noted as the only person in the village to receive a newspaper and he provided the residents with national information.

In 1854 he told the Kegworth Church that the financial affairs at Diseworth were in a very discouraging state; that the tenants occupying the cottages belonging to the chapel were backward in paying their rent and that little had been paid. A committee was appointed to address the problem.

In 1861, Nathaniel Gayton, now old and deaf, wrote in his diary that he had been unsuccessful in obtaining the job of schoolmaster in the new school being built in the village.

1. William Jarrom's 1866 'Brief history'
2. Adam Taylor, 'History of the General Baptists' vol.2
3. Adam Taylor, 'History of the General Baptists' vol.2
4. William Jarrom's 1866 ' Brief history'
5. J.D Chapman M.A Thesis 1960 'William Felkin 1795 – 1874'
6. J.D Chapman M.A Thesis 1960 'William Felkin 1795 – 1874'

Diseworth Baptist Church
Source: PN Hening

Kegworth Baptist Chapel Ca. 1865
Source: Roy Chaplin

The Weaver's Shop – the first meeting place of Diseworth Baptists

William Felkin's Short hand notes 1814
Source: Leicestershire County Record Office
Reference Number: N/B/159/1

CHAPTER 6

CASTLE DONINGTON AND SAWLEY

According to T.F. Marriott's 'Brief History' of the Castle Donington Baptist Church, the present Church building was erected in 1774. Nathaniel Pickering had been the pastor of the Church from its inception in 1766 and only resigned his pastoral office in 1790. Membership of the Church had grown to 100 members by 1788. There is a wonderful account of Nathaniel Pickering's early attempts to bring the Baptist cause across the river to Sawley (See appendix 2).

Inspite of this early setback, Nathaniel Pickering's ministry was very fruitful. The first Sawley Meeting House was built in 1783 and attracted people from 20 miles away. It soon became too small for the people attending. In the Sawley Baptist Church papers is a copy of a deed of enfranchisement of a piece of land within the manor of Sawley which was to be the plot for the present chapel. The deed transferred the land from the Earl of Harrington to Mr Oldershawe and others and is dated 19th August 1793.

The new Sawley Chapel was completed in 1801. Thomas Pickering had succeeded his father to the pastoral office, and his work blossomed. In 1792 some 30 people were baptised, and between 1804 and 1806 a further 85 people were baptised. So successful had Thomas Pickering's ministry been that the Sawley Chapel needed to be enlarged. Tragically, the first occasion the newly enlarged premises were used was for Thomas Pickering's own funeral. He died on 15th November 1807, aged 50.

Back over the Trent at Donington things likewise were going well. The Castle Donington Baptist Church had opened its first Sunday School in 1804. By 1810 they couldn't cope with the numbers attending so the teachers hired a large clubroom at "The King's Head" public house. It served as the Sunday School until 1820 when new school rooms were built in the burial ground. The Castle Donington

Church itself had to be expanded in 1824 to cope with increased numbers. Between 1812 and 1834 a further 90 members were added.

Of particular interest in this period is the continued missionary zeal of the Castle Donington Church. While the Sawley congregation had its own building it still remained an official branch of Castle Donington, and they shared ministry. But not content with this one satellite congregation across the Trent, Castle Donington was eager to commence preaching stations in other villages as well.

The Castle Donington minutes for July 14th 1811 (held at Sawley) include reference to a "preaching place at Shardlow." The March 1815 minutes have an extended discussion on "preaching at Shardlow." The Castle Donington minister was to preach once a fortnight in the week day, and once in two months of a Lord's Day evening, and once in two months of an afternoon. Several other preachers including Messrs Bullock and Turner, were to supply the said place once a month on a Lord's Day. They were to receive the same allowance for preaching at Shardlow as they would for preaching at Castle Donington or Sawley.

In May 1821 there is a reference to "the Chapel at Shardlow." The minutes for September 12th 1830 state that:

"As the new chapel at Shardlow is to be opened next Lord's Day it was agreed that Sawley Chapel be closed all the day and Donington in the morning, and Donington friends to be consulted relative to closing in the evening also."

The minutes for the meeting held on August 11th 1831 contain a list of 11 trustees for the new Meeting House at Shardlow. In April 1832 the Castle Donington Church Meeting was held at Shardlow.

As well as the planting initiative at Shardlow, the Castle Donington Church was, at the same time, instrumental in starting a cause at Weston on Trent. At a Church Meeting on 20th November 1815 a committee was set up "to form a plan of preaching at Shardlow and at Weston." In January 1816 the Church Meeting noted that "a deficiency

67

of about ten pounds in the last year's accounts to be made up by public collections at Donington, Sawley, Shardlow and Weston."

Relatively little appears regarding the Weston cause in the subsequent minutes. It is possible that the silence means that the cause did not take off. Nevertheless, by April 17th 1836 the friends at Weston were still in business albeit without a building of their own. The Lord's Supper was to be administered at Weston "if a suitable room can be obtained."

By June 1838 they were still struggling to get things established at Weston. The Church Meeting agreed to send a petition to Sir R. Houton signed by several friends at Weston, stating that they have been "prohibited to maintain public worship in any of his cottages in that village, and request the restoration of the privilege so long enjoyed." In July that same year, "G.Wright and T.Soar to see Sir R.W. Houton's steward relative to the obtainment of a place at Weston in which to maintain worship."

They still seemed to have been unsuccessful. On January 3rd 1842 the minutes note that "Bro. Soar is respectfully requested to see if any room or building can be procured suitable for a preaching place."

It wasn't until 1845 that any good news was forthcoming from Weston. The January Castle Donington minutes refer to the appointment of Trustees for "our projected Weston Chapel". In February a committee of management for the projected Weston Chapel were appointed. Finally, in May it was announced that "the Weston Chapel be opened for Divine Service on the 18th and 22nd June."

Amazingly, however, Shardlow and Weston were not the only Church planting initiatives launched by Castle Donington in this period. At a Church Meeting held at Donington on March 14th 1813 reference is made to the "Long Eaton friends." The following meeting (April 11th 1813) records that a "Meeting House at Long Eaton to be rented." The July 1813 Church Meeting was dominated by a fascinating incident. John Turner, John Shepherd and John Henson (or Stenson) had gone on strike because the Church hadn't remunerated them for preaching.

The Church argued that it had only taken them on as official "servants of the church" in December 1812. Prior to that any preaching opportunities they were given were to be considered as practice and honing their skills. Consequently the Church Meeting agreed that the three men should be paid for the preaching they had done since December 1812 at Long Eaton and at Castle Donington.

The minutes subsequently go on to report that "Long Eaton is now going from us" and that the Church at Beeston is "re-taking" responsibility for supplying preachers for Long Eaton. The Castle Donington Church appointed one of their number to go round to Long Eaton and get the money owed to the three brethren.

This particular attempt to plant a Church in Long Eaton failed. It was to be a further 50 years before the Sawley Church successfully planted in their satellite village.

Quite clearly the Castle Donington Church, along with its major branch at Sawley, was growing during the first half of the nineteenth century. (In June 1838 the membership figure is given as 294). However, not everything was going smoothly, and the Church did in fact experience some very difficult and painful times particularly with reference to its ministers.

In February 1815 the Church Meeting had a major discussion about the "temporal concerns of our minister, Mr Brand." Apparently, due to the decline of the worsted spinning industry trade in which Mr Brand was engaged "he found it necessary for the support and comfort of his family to engage in manual labours 6 days a week and 12 hours each day." The friends at Castle Donington and Sawley agreed to see what "could be done to set him more at liberty."

One idea was to recommend him for ordination which would then allow him more scope for pecuniary advancement. Unfortunately this idea did not chime well with everyone in the Church because when, in October 1815, a proposal to recommend him for ordination came to the Church Meeting, only 45 people voted for it, while 53 voted against.

In January 1817 a second attempt to recommend Mr Brand for ordination was made, this time with more success. (111 in favour, 79 against, 2 abstentions). Unfortunately the minority wouldn't accept the decision and heated words were exchanged in the following weeks. Finally, in March 1817, the minority group produced a list of 12 grounds for not ordaining Mr Brand, including such charges as "too fond of filthy lucre", "too self willed", "some think he does not preach the Gospel and the Law clear enough." Mr Brand dropped the idea of his ordination. He did, however, continue to exercise his pastoral ministry among them. In March 1818 the Church decided to reduce Mr Brand's salary from £65 to £55 a year.

The following year he was in trouble again. He had been accused of hitting a lad who worked for him across the face with a leather strap. Accused of bringing the Church into disrepute, a canvass of the Church members resulted in his apparent vindication. (122 desired him to stay on; 26 against; 39 abstentions). However, the minority opinion again refused to accept the decision. They stopped meeting at the Baptist Church and even set up a rival cause in Castle Donington (September 1820). Mr Brand bowed to the inevitable, and gave notice of his intention to resign at the end of March 1821.

In June 1838 the Church began another crisis over its minister, Mr Stocks. He was accused of appearing dishevelled at a prayer meeting "as if he had had too much to drink," "also that his breath had been observed to smell of liquor." The Church Meeting investigated the accusations twice over the summer and found him "not guilty". But the minority refused to accept this verdict and decided to take matters into their own hands reporting Mr Stocks to the Midland Conference.

The three-man enquiry from the Conference concluded that while Mr Stocks could carry on in the Baptist ministry he couldn't carry on at Castle Donington. In point of fact he did soldier on for two more years, but these were not happy times with references to the "strife and bitterness of feeling" and the need to work for reconciliation in the fellowship.

While the cause at Weston on Trent had been very slow to become established, the opening of its own chapel meant that the work there could move into a new phase. Sadly, while the cause at Shardlow had quickly taken off, with its own chapel in a few years of commencement, by the 1840s the cause was running into trouble through in-fighting and mutual recrimination.

The Castle Donington minutes for September 10th 1844 note that the Church "feels grieved" that there is so much dissension among "the few friends" belonging to the Shardlow branch. There is also a hint of some financial irregularities in the branch. A note from June 1843 observed that as a result of "some differences amongst the Shardlow friends as to pecuniary affairs" they would request brother Soar "to act as treasurer for this branch of the Church."

The cause at Shardlow limped along but in April 1853 it was reported to be in "a very low state." Castle Donington decided to send some of its own congregation along to the Sunday services at Shardlow as a means of encouraging them. However, the following July the officers at Castle Donington were to visit the members at Shardlow "to ascertain their disposition as to keeping up the cause there." In 1855 they changed the time of the Shardlow service from evening to afternoon to see if that made any difference.

In 1856 it was noted that the Wesleyans wanted to purchase the Shardlow Chapel which the Castle Donington Church were keen to pursue. They were finding it increasingly difficult to get preachers to supply the pulpit. Thomas Soar, who had invested so much of himself in the Shardlow mission, tried one last time to revive the cause, but to no avail. The 1857 Report to the Association recorded that the work at Shardlow "is nearly extinct." When, on 1st May 1857, Thomas Soar himself passed away, so too did the Shardlow Baptist cause. The 1859 Report to the Association tersely records that "Shardlow has been given up and the chapel sold to the Wesleyans."

The Midsummer Reports to the Association, summaries of which are preserved in the Church minute books, are very informative sources of information. This is especially so in the case of Castle Donington and

71

Sawley, because the membership figures are given separately for the two principal congregations.

Castle Donington			Sawley		
1854	175	+	97	=	272
1855	174	+	94	=	268
1856	170	+	88	=	258
1857	176	+	83	=	258
1858	176	+	98	=	274
1859	183	+	99	=	282
1860	175	+	116	=	291
1861	191	+	117	=	308
1862	190	+	136	=	326
1863	177	+	137	=	314
1864	172	+	129	=	301
1865	173	+	122	=	295

Clearly the Sawley branch was strengthening. From 1844 Sawley started to keep its own Church Meeting minute books. They continued to share a minister with Castle Donington, but clearly felt able to make their own decisions and assert their own independence from time to time. Thus when new Trustees were appointed for Sawley in September 1859 the Sawley branch rejected Castle Donington's request to have two of their members included in the list.

Castle Donington and Sawley tended to work well together. Occasionally, however, they did have a difference of opinion over calling or retaining a minister. In December 1852, for example, the Sawley branch was greatly distressed to hear that their pastor, Mr Nightingale, felt the need to leave the Church. The Sawley branch wrote to Castle Donington to ask them "to remove obstacles which interrupt the comfort and usefulness of our esteemed pastor." The Castle Donington Church did nothing to rectify the situation and Mr Nightingale left for Staffordshire in 1853.

In November 1855 the Castle Donington Church Meeting recommended accepting a student from the College, Mr Burrows, to be their minister. This was vetoed by a canvass of the Sawley members.

The main bone of contention between the two churches, however, was over money, and chiefly over how much Sawley should pay for their part of the ministry costs.

The minister of Castle Donington-Sawley had a hard job. In September 1856 Mr Needham became pastor. As part of his terms of employment he was expected to preach twice each Sunday at Castle Donington and once at Sawley. In addition he was to preach midweek at Sawley and midweek at Castle Donington and occasionally at Shardlow and Weston. For this he was to receive £90 each year (£60 from Donington and £30 from Sawley). The two churches also argued about who should pay the costs for conveying the minister to and from Sawley, which often involved the hiring of a horse.

Little wonder that Mr Needham struggled with his workload, and in 1859 he left for a simpler task at Ripley. Mr Taylor, who succeeded him, came from the college, but he too had to resign in 1862 on the grounds of ill health.

It isn't clear what the problems were with Mr Cockerton, who came in 1864, but in April 1866 the Church agreed to pay him "the sum of £20 beyond his salary provided he cease preaching after the next Lord's Day, and leave the town on or before the 2nd July."!! Mr Johnson, who came next, seemed most acceptable but stayed only four years (1866-1870).

It took the arrival of Dr Underwood in 1873 to bring matters to a head. After labouring for a year preaching three times each Sunday, he indicated his intention to no longer accept the arrangement. He would no longer take the weeknight service at Sawley and would preach there only on alternate Sunday afternoons. The Sawley Church clearly felt that this was not good enough.

73

"We were unanimously of the opinion that taking into account the welfare of our Church branch of the cause it will not answer to retain the Dr. as our pastor under such circumstances and feel that we shall be compelled to make some new arrangement for ministerial supplies."

The reason for such defiance from Sawley was because of the rapid improvement in their fortunes. From a membership of 99 in 1859 they had grown to one of 164 by June 1874. This growth was in large measure a result of the emergence of their own satellite congregation in Long Eaton.

Shardlow Wesleyan Methodist Chapel (now redundant): formerly Shardlow Baptist Chapel. It is located at The Wharf behind the Malt Shovel Pub.

Sawley Baptist Church

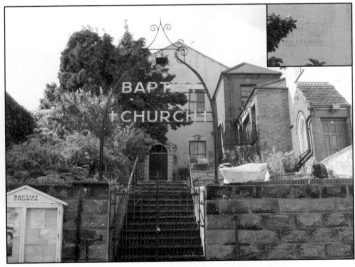

Castle Donington Baptist Church

Source: Margery Tranter

The former Weston Baptist Chapel in Trent Lane

CHAPTER 7

ILKESTON, SMALLEY, HEANOR, LANGLEY MILL

It is tidy and simple to say that the Ilkeston – Smalley Church emerged out of Kegworth Baptist Church in 1785 at the separation of the Kegworth group. It was a suggestion made by John Goddard, one of the members at Kegworth who lived at Little Hallam. History, however, is rarely tidy or simple.

The oldest minutes of Ilkeston Baptist Church declare: "The Church at Ilkeston first established distinct from <u>Castle Donington</u> May 22nd 1785." There follow the names of 53 founder members, the first five being:

John W Goddard, Minister
Richard Kerry, Ruling Elder
Christopher Harrison, deacon
Joseph Harrison, since chosen deacon
William Greasley

Smalley, although part of the Ilkeston Church, also kept a set of records for this same period. Their earliest minute book is a set of deacons meetings, the first one being 5th June 1786. All these deacons meetings are simply financial balance sheets with income and expenditure, but the first entry states: "Expenses since 22nd May 1785 which was the time of our first establishment as a distinct Church from Castle Donington Church."

Clearly the Ilkeston-Smalley Church regarded itself as part of Castle Donington rather than Kegworth. The reason for this must simply be that the pioneer missionary to Smalley and Ilkeston was Nathaniel Pickering who, along with John Tarratt, was joint minister of the Kegworth group but whose primary responsibility was for Castle Donington. The Ilkeston friends would have perceived Pickering as an ambassador from Castle Donington even though the latter was technically only a branch of Kegworth.

Baptist presence in the Smalley area was noted in Kerry's 'History of Smalley.' In the year 1779 an epidemic of smallpox hit the community with devastating consequences. Many children died, but a significant number were unable to be buried in the parish of Smalley because they were from dissenting families and had not been baptised by Anglican rites. Instead they had to be taken to Little Hallam where they were interred in a field used by the Baptists for burials.[1]

Dale Moor was the earliest site of Baptist witness in that area[2]. But when it came to erecting a Meeting House it was Little Hallam that was chosen. Colin Hargreaves, who produced a very comprehensive history of the Ilkeston cause back in 1958, records that "Little Hallam was a distinct hamlet within the Ilkeston parish, important enough to have its own main street, known as Town Street (now called Little Hallam Hill)." An application to register the place of worship was lodged with the Derby Quarter Sessions on 13th January 1767, and was signed by John Bakewell, Jacob Kirby and Edward Briggs[3].

The precise whereabouts of the Meeting House and the graveyard in Little Hallam have been lost in the mists of time.

The cause clearly prospered and there was need of larger premises. According to Adam Taylor, "In 1784 the Meeting House at Little Hallam was taken down, and a more substantial and commodious one erected in its stead at Ilkeston, a considerable town a mile north west of the former place." This was the Meeting House that still stands on South Street with the Foundation date clearly marked. It wasn't until 1790 that the Smalley side of the Church had its own building constructed. The building was smaller than the present one and was roughly square. In or around 1820 the roof was made higher and the chapel lengthened, enabling the gallery to be constructed.

Both the Smalley side of the Church and the Ilkeston side of the Church only had one Service each Sunday. This was partly in recognition of the distance its members had to travel; partly too in recognition of the fact that they shared a minister who couldn't be in two places at once. But Hargreaves is probably right when he says that they only had one service at each place in order that they could engage in outdoor preaching in the surrounding areas.

This becomes very evident in the Ilkeston minutes. In June 1786 they were still preaching at Dale Moor. In July 1788 they began preaching at Mapperley once in two weeks Lord's Day evening. In April 1790 they were engaged in preaching at Derby (or it could be Denby). In June 1791 they began to preach at Stanton once in two weeks Lord's Day evening. In April 1796 "began to preach at Cotmanhay on Lord's Day evenings occasionally." Quite often the preaching was seasonal, often desisting in September and beginning again in April. But these early Baptist pioneers were evidently filled with a real missionary zeal.

Commencing with 53 members in 1785, the Ilkeston-Smalley Church had added 72 more men and women by baptism within five years. Baptisms inevitably took place outside. At Ilkeston they took place in the river Erewash at "Gallas Inne." At Smalley they took place at a variety of places including the Mill Dam, Mr Radford's Water and Kyte's pond at the back of the Bell Inn. One fascinating insight can be gleaned from the early deacons' minutes at Smalley. Basically a set of quarterly accounts, the list of expenses for September 1799 includes 3 quarts of wine, bread (celebrating the Lord's Supper), but also a pint of gin (1 shilling) which comes under the heading 'baptising'. In August 1809 they spent 2 shillings and 8 pence on a pint of rum. Presumably with no means of heating the water they could at least attempt to heat the person being baptised!

The first Minister at Ilkeston-Smalley was John Goddard. His name appears at the head of the members roll at Ilkeston on their formation as an independent Church. Goddard was a member of the Ilkeston Church who was recognised as possessing requisite gifts for the task. He was formally set apart for the Gospel by Dan Taylor and B. Pollard at the request of the Church in June 1789. Goddard had been responsible for the division from Castle Donington – Kegworth, and also played a key role in supplying the preaching at the new General Baptist cause in Derby. He had oversight of the construction of the Meeting House at Smalley and formally opened the building in Michaelmas 1790. Unfortunately, Goddard's ministry came to an end

79

in 1795 after an unspecified crisis led to both the Minister and his daughter being put out of the Church. Even though the Church had great problems finding supply preaching (relying heavily on brethren Kerry and Twills the ruling elders), they still declined to take Mr Goddard back when he wrote to them in 1797 offering his services again.

The solution for ministry once again was to come from within the fellowship. In August 1797 the Church agreed to send William Felkin to Dan Taylor's London Academy for some instruction, "that he may be better qualified for the work of the ministry."

Felkin was born in Bramcote in December 1772. He had been converted while hearing William Corah expound, "For God so loved the world," and he had been baptised at Ilkeston in 1790. He married Sarah Harrison, one of the Ilkeston members in 1794.

Felkin went to London in February 1798 and returned in June. His family were paid 12 shillings a week in his absence. By July 1798 the minutes record that "Mr Felkin to preach at Cotmanhay once in a fortnight" on Sunday evenings. In March 1799 the Church meeting discussed the question of his ordination to the pastoral office. Adam Taylor records that his ministry was very fruitful. In one year alone the Church had twenty baptisms. By 1800 membership had risen to 149.

At this point Felkin sensed the need to make better provision for his growing family. In October 1799 he set out some extremely exacting terms for staying at Ilkeston-Smalley. It specified the number of services he was willing to take; agreement that he could work two days a week on his own business; (he was a frame-work knitter); to be paid 45 guineas a year; and, "to have a little red wine kept in the vestry at Smalley that I may have one glass before and after preaching when I please."

The Annual General Meeting that year (on Christmas Day as usual) agreed to his terms, but it subsequently transpired that very few people had turned out to the meeting because they did not want him as their

Minister. Consequently at Easter Mr Felkin left Ilkeston and took up the post as Minister of Kegworth Baptist Church. He was obliged to repay the money the Church had given to his family while he was training at the College.

The Ilkeston-Smalley Church did not have to wait long before their next Minister arrived (their first appointment made from outside the fellowship): Mr William Pickering from Ashford in the Water. Pickering arrived in the August with his wife, Jemima, and their three children, Mary, Sarah and George. All three had been born at Ashford, near Bakewell, although their births were only registered when the family arrived in Ilkeston. William Pickering was to remain as minister at Ilkeston for 15 years.

Pickering, as we saw in his Peak District days, was mission-minded through and through. He was a keen believer in the new method of reaching the young known as Sunday School. Originating with Robert Raikes in Gloucester in the 1780s, the movement quickly spread, and it found in William Pickering an enthusiastic advocate. On 15th May 1802 he is noted to be taking the Sunday School Anniversary service at Quorndon. In 1804 the Ilkeston-Smalley Church discussed the establishment of a Sunday School in earnest. Smalley set up a Sunday School almost straight away (using a vestry as a class room). It took Ilkeston longer to get round to it, in part for lack of space. It wasn't until 1807 that they managed to erect a lean-to at the side of the South Street Chapel in Robey's yard. It seated 80 scholars.

It didn't take Pickering long to get into his stride and to carry on the evangelistic preaching work of his predecessors. The Ilkeston minutes record (January 1802) that preaching at Coxbench was to be supplied from Ilkeston once a month and from Smalley once a month. Joshua Stevenson assisted him in his work and in 1802 the Church agreed to send Stevenson to Dan Taylor's Academy for twelve months.

Chilwell became another preaching out-post for William Pickering and the Ilkeston Church. Two of the Ilkeston members lived at Chilwell and they did so well at inviting their neighbours to hear the preaching that eventually thirteen of the villagers of Chilwell were baptised and joined the Ilkeston Church. Tragically preaching at Chilwell ceased when Mr Twells, a mining engineer and Ruling Elder at Ilkeston who held some responsibility for Chilwell, died in a mining accident. Joshua Stevenson had already departed for ministry in Coningsby.

Preaching at Beeston had been carried out by Thomas Rogers, assistant minister at Stoney Sreet, Nottingham. So successful was his work in Beeston that on one day he baptised twenty people! Ilkeston were reluctant to release their thirteen Chilwell members to the new Beeston cause, but eventually the demands of geography came into play, and the transfer did take place.

A more fruitful Church planting initiative for Ilkeston took place at Newthorpe. After several years of regular preaching in the village it was formally agreed (July 1817) that the friends at Newthorpe could "enter into a subscription amongst themselves towards building a chapel." It was slow progress. Only in 1822 was a plot of land purchased and it was 1828 before a chapel was built. Once Smalley had separated from Ilkeston in 1822 Church Meetings were held alternately at Ilkeston and Newthorpe.

William Pickering's ministry at Ilkeston was crowned with success. Adam Taylor records that 65 people were added to the Church through baptism in just three years. Sadly, "disorder and bitterness" broke out in the Church resulting in Pickering's departure for Staley Bridge in Yorkshire (1815). Following his departure "twenty disaffected members left and peace was restored."

Mr Pickering's sojourn in Yorkshire did not last long. By 1818 Ilkeston still had not found another Minister, and Mr Pickering, already seeking to move on from Staley Bridge, entered into negotiations with Ilkeston with a view to coming back to his old job. In November 1818 he was requesting letters of support from key people, the Ilkeston Church Meeting already having given their approval for his return. But then all went silent. No reply from Mr Pickering had been received by February 1819, and when he did finally reply in the March it was to inform them of his decision to decline their invitation. Instead, William Pickering took over the pastorate of Stoney Street, Nottingham.

In 1819 Mr G.N. Purcell became Minister of the Ilkeston-Smalley Church. At a Church Meeting held on April 16th 1822 it was formally (and amicably) agreed that the two sides of the Church should separate and become independent of each other. Some complicated manoeuvres had to be entered into to divide up the monies of the joint Church (and the debts owed on their respective buildings). But once that had been safely negotiated Mr Purcell left the Ilkeston Church and became the sole Minister at Smalley. According to the New Connexion General Baptist Minutes for 1823, Smalley had a membership of 96 and Ilkeston had a membership of 83.

Smalley continued the same missionary spirit that had dominated the early history of the joint Church. Preachers were sent out to Kilburn, Denby, Morley Moor and Langley Mill. But if the focus of Ilkeston's missionary endeavours had been Newthorpe, then the focus of Smalley's missionary endeavours was Heanor, or Tag Hill as it was called.

In 1825 the Smalley Church reported to the New Connexion: "At Tag Hill, Heanor, we preach twice every Lord's day. Hearers increase and we are now contemplating the purchase of a piece of ground with a view to building a chapel." This optimism was somewhat misplaced.

The cause at Tag Hill, Heanor, seemed to move from house to house. In 1824 they were meeting in John Ealy's house. This proved unsuitable and in May 1825 they moved to the house of Richard Woodhouse. Benjamin Soar of Tag Hill kindly offered to sell the Church a plot of land to build on, but for whatever reason the offer was never taken up. In 1827 they were meeting in a room made available by Mr Soar. A Sunday School was started and a deacon (brother Wilkinson) was appointed for the Heanor side of the Church. But by 1830 the Tag Hill friends had run into financial difficulties; commitment seemed to have waned and in April 1830 it was resolved "that Mr B.Soar's room which we have occupied for preaching be given up."

Rev Chapman, who produced a useful history of the Heanor Baptist Church in 1947, indicates that the cause at Heanor was effectively given up by Smalley at this time. But that is not borne out by the reports which Smalley submitted to the New Connexion. By the 1830s Smalley was in a much healthier state than Ilkeston. "A spirit of disunion has crept in," Ilkeston reported in 1829. By 1835 its membership had fallen to 70 whereas the membership at Smalley stood at 107. In 1832 Smalley reported to the Association that "We have built a chapel at Kilbourn..... We have preaching in five places, Smalley, Denby, Heanor, Horsley and Kilbourn." So clearly, even though they had given up Mr Soar's room at Tag Hill there was still a Baptist presence in Heanor. In 1834 they reported to the Association that "We have opened a new place of worship in the Parish of Heanor."

Tag Hill may not have featured in the minutes of Smalley Baptist Church during this period but clearly behind the scenes plenty was happening. It wasn't until 1847 that a plot of land was secured for building a Baptist Meeting House at Tag Hill, and Heanor Baptist Church sets its foundation date to that year. In 1851 it was agreed by the Smalley Church that Tag Hill should be placed on the same footing as Kilburn, with Quarterly Church Meetings and a status as a Branch Church rather than simply a Preaching Station.

The old chapel at Kilburn: it was opened in June 1832 by Rev J.G.Pike.

The painstaking but fruitful work at Kilburn and Heanor was also joined by success at Langley Mill. By 1833 nine people were worshipping in a house in Heanor Lane (now known as Station Road)

Langley Mill[4]. The Smalley Church's returns to the Association in 1839 recorded, "At Langley Mill we have begun to build a chapel." A fulsome description of the Opening Ceremony for the Langley Chapel is provided in the General Baptist Repository for 1840. The Opening services had taken place on 27th and 28th October 1839. Mr Pottenger from Swanwick was the preacher in the afternoon. The building work had only been made possible through the generosity of Mr Stanhope who had contributed £100 towards the building costs; had superintended the building work; and had committed himself to raise the outstanding amount owed on the premises. Mr Stanhope was elected the first deacon of the Church. The cottage where the first meeting had been held was retained as part of the Church premises, being used as an institute and later by the Good Templars[4].

In 1840 the Association 'state of the churches' recorded against Smalley's name, "At Langley Mill we have erected a commodious chapel, and both there and at Kilburn we have commenced Sabbath Schools." But Langley Mill's identification with Smalley was to be short lived. The 1846 Association 'state of the churches' has the following statement from Smalley: "The Langley Mill friends have withdrawn from us having taken offence at the discipline of the Church." No specifics are given. In 1847 Langley Mill approached the North Derbyshire Conference for support for their cause. The advice that was provided (April 2nd) was that they should unite with another local Baptist Church. Not until April 1849 did the Conference finally agree to accept them in their own right.

Langley Mill did not submit their own returns to the Association until 1852 when they record having just 20 members. But the departure of the Langley Mill members left a more substantial hole in the Smalley membership returns. From a total of 168 members in 1847 they fell to 128 members in 1848, and never really recovered from that. They were down to 102 members in 1851, and from 1847 – 1861 they only had 2 pastorates both of approximately one year each. Langley Mill meanwhile had grown to 55 members in 1858, falling back to 32 members by 1861.

South Street Baptist Church, Ilkeston, meanwhile was on the up. Three successful ministries came in rapid succession: Mr J.Peggs (1841-1846); Mr Caleb Springthorpe (1847-1853); Mr T.R.Stevenson (1854-1859). Baptisms were plentiful. On 1st May 1842 the Ilkeston minutes record that, "The seven friends were baptised in the Erewash – about 1500 spectators, who behaved very orderly." Three years later we read, "Baptism .... at Mitchell's Bridge between Ilkeston and Newthorpe. Thirteen candidates ... a good day." The growth of the work led to crowded conditions and in 1842 a substantial enlargement of the South Street premises took place. In 1844 Ilkeston reported to the Association that they had just built a chapel at Babbington, and in 1846 they followed that up by reporting: "At Babbington there is quite a revival, 8 persons added to the Church from that place this year." In 1851 it was the cause at Newthorpe that was reported to be doing so well that they had to construct a gallery.

Church Membership was rising. From 113 members when Mr Peggs came in 1842, it had grown to 141 by 1845 and to 181 by 1851. Despite the enlargement of the South Street premises in 1842 it was becoming abundantly clear that the Church needed larger premises. Following the arrival of Thomas Stevenson in 1854 the Church actively began fund-raising for a new chapel. In October 1856 permission was given to the Committee charged with finding a new site to purchase lots owned by the late Mr Lowe. They eventually purchased lots 12 and 14, and Trustees were appointed. In February 1857 it was agreed to appoint Mr Booker of Nottingham to be the architect of the new chapel, (he had recently completed the work on the General Baptist Chapel in Burton), and in June the contract was awarded to Mr Wigley. The stone laying ceremony at the new Queen Street site took place on November 23rd 1857, and the building was officially opened on Tuesday 22nd June 1858. The South Street premises were retained as a Sunday School.

There is always a tendency to eulogise the construction of an imposing place of worship. It actually took 23 years before one Ilkeston newspaper felt confident enough to write what many others had probably been thinking for years: "Of the many places of worship which have sprung up in our town this is certainly the least attractive;

some people think it positively ugly and repellant, and we have heard it likened to an engine shed."[5]

What should have been the crowning glory of Mr Stevenson's ministry at Ilkeston in fact paved the way for his quick exit. The official line reported to the Association was that Mr Stevenson's decision to leave was,"owing principally to a division amongst some of the members of the Church respecting its management." But in the Church minutes it reads much more about a shortage of money. Four months after the new building had been opened, Mr Stevenson asked for a pay rise. The Church refused on the grounds that they had to service a heavy debt taken out on the chapel. Mr Stevenson left for Burnley. His departure caused something of a rift in the Church with a significant group spending twelve months worshipping back at South Street until eventually a reconciliation was made possible.

Money continued to dominate events at Queen Street. Decisions about a new Minister were put on hold. When eventually they did actively look for a Minister they had to prize assurances of financial support from the congregation. Mr Anderson was appointed Minister in 1862. Financial pressures, however, persisted, and the following year, with money still desperately short, Mr Anderson tendered his resignation. The Church refused to accept it (July 27th 1864), and promised to be more ardent in the cause of Christ. But in August they conceded that they couldn't increase his salary and reluctantly accepted his resignation. In 1865 Home Mission agreed that they would provide £25 towards the salary of any new Minister appointed at Ilkeston.

Ilkeston were not the only Church to have overstretched themselves financially through major capital expenditure on building work. At a Church Meeting held at Smalley on July 23rd 1854, Thomas Cresswell and Robert Fletcher came to ask if Tag Hill Chapel could be sold. Before this could be pursued, in September, a committee consisting of Smalley members and the Trustees of Tag Hill Chapel were appointed to investigate the financial matters and also "to know why Robert Fletcher has sold the Chapel without the consent of the Church or Trustees either." Some definite arrangement appears to have been entered into with the Congregationalists without the consent of the

Church. When news leaked out there was such ire and indignation that immediate steps were taken to halt the process, one Hannah Bircumshaw walking with several others all the way to Belper to prevent the sale proceeding.

The North Derbyshire Conference meeting in Ripley on Christmas Day considered the Tag Hill case first on its agenda in 1854. It was confirmed that two trustees had indeed tried to sell the building. The meeting resolved that if Smalley were still of a mind to keep the cause on then Conference would arrange for regular pulpit supply. William Hanson and Edward Turner took oversight of Tag Hill which subsequently became a Home Mission cause and never looked back. In November 1860 a deputation from Tag Hill made a request of the Smalley Church Meeting that they "be allowed to go to themselves and have the deeds." The North Derbyshire Conference were uncertain as to the wisdom of this move, but Smalley did eventually agree to the separation which accounts for a further drop in the Smalley membership, from 105 members in 1860 to 77 members in 1861.

Footnote on Rev William Pickering

Following successful ministries at Ashford in the Water and Ilkeston, and a brief period at Staley Bridge, Yorkshire, William Pickering took over as Minister at Stoney Street, Nottingham in 1819. He was 51 years old. In 1824 Stoney Street had a membership of 387. By 1827 it was 458. Thereafter membership of the Church rose year on year:

1828 – 491 members	1838 – 622 members
1829 – 498 members	1839 – 680 members
1830 – 517 members	1840 – 698 members
1831 – 529 members	1841 – 836 members
1832 – 542 members	1842 – 917 members
1833 – 563 members	1843 – 955 members
1834 – 584 members	1844 – 966 members
1835 – 635 members	1845 – 1000 members
1836 - 671 members	1846 – 1083 members
1837 – 704 members	1847 – 1238 members

The membership fall in 1838 was a result of three of the branch churches (Old Basford, Hucknall, and Bulwell) becoming independent of the mother Church. A similar process happened after 1848 when the Stoney Street membership reached its peak of 1344 members.

Stoney Street's reports to the Association trace the often precarious health of William Pickering. In 1831 they recorded their deep gratitude to their beloved pastor "who amid personal affliction and domestic sorrows continues to preach to us the unsearchable riches of Christ." The Church decided to appoint an assistant to help Mr Pickering. Hugh Hunter came that same year, and the two of them made a remarkable team. In 1844 it was reported that "both our pastors have been severely afflicted." The junior pastor was making a good recovery, but "we greatly fear that we shall not often be favoured with the labours of our venerable and senior pastor, Mr Pickering."

Pickering died on Saturday 19th February 1848 after "a long and painful affliction." He was in his 82nd year of life. Hugh Hunter compiled a memorial tribute to him in which he outlined his extraordinary ministries at Ashford and Bradwell in the Peak as a young man; his solid work as pastor of Ilkeston for 15 years in his middle age; and finally his outstanding work for over a quarter of a century at Stoney Street, Nottingham in his old age. He was "beloved and honoured by his people, both for his piety and his talents, and regarded by all parties, political and religious, as one of the best of men."

Rev William Pickering
Source: General Baptist Repository 1834

1. Rev Charles Kerry wrote his 'History of Smalley' in 1905. This particular reference is found in volume 1 and page 40. The information was provided by the Rector of Smalley in 1779, one Robert Wilmot.
2. This detail and several others pertaining to the origins of the cause were recorded in a series of articles in the 'Ilkeston Pioneer' in June 1908 by Frank Burrows. The articles can be located in the Ilkeston Local Studies Library.
3. A copy of this application can also be found in the Ilkeston Local Studies Library.
4. See www.heanorhistory.org.uk/langleymillbaptistChurch.htm
5. The quote is found in Hargeaves' "One hundred Years of Queen Street" page 27.

THE OLD BAPTIST CHAPEL, SOUTH STREET. (1785)
South West view from the site of Robey's Yard, showing original Schoolroom. (*See page 8*).

QUEEN STREET CHAPEL. (1858)
South East view.

The old South Street Baptist Church in 2007

Smalley Baptist Church

Langley Mill Baptist Chapel
Source: Heanor and District Local History Society

Langley Mill Baptist Chapel 2001

CHAPTER 8

BROOK STREET AND ST. MARY'S GATE, DERBY

We have seen already (pages 51-52) that the General Baptist cause in Derby started as a result of Dan Taylor's preaching on Willow Row on 31st May 1789, and was sustained by the ministers from Melbourne, Castle Donington and Ilkeston. The decision of Conference meeting at Smalley on 5th July 1791 determined that the cause should be independent from the word go, and shouldn't be regarded as a branch of any one of the outlying churches. The first nine people were baptised by Francis Smith of Melbourne on 21st August 1791. Subsequent baptismal services took place on October 30th 1791 (5 people); April 22nd 1792 (8 people); Sept.9th 1792 (6 people); May 26th 1793 (4 people); and June 8th 1794 (5 people). The last four baptisms were conducted respectively by J.Goddard of Ilkeston, Benjamin Pollard of Loughborough, John Tarratt of Kegworth, and Thomas Pickering of Castle Donington.

Those first nine people baptised by Francis Smith were: Gilbert Dallison, Joseph Barrow, John Etches, Joseph Johnson, Samuel Hill, Mary Porter, Jane Porter, Rachel Etches, Margaret Pipes.

John Etches in particular had an interesting story. He had been a sailor and lost an arm in a naval battle in 1782. He returned to Derby with a pension of £8. He was a keen and active footballer. He met and married Rachel Johnson, and it was partly through her influence that he started to attend evangelical preaching. It was while listening to the preaching of the "dippers" on Willow Row that he decided to become baptised. On the day in question John Etches stood by the water's edge in his full sailor's uniform to much abuse from the surrounding crowd. Etches became a deacon of the fledgling Church in 1795 and maintained an honourable Christian profession for 47 years. He died in October 1838 aged 85. His naval pension was given each year to the Church.

The congregation met in various rooms in the early years. Membership grew to 40 by 1796 but then doctrinal differences set in and the numbers fell back to 29 by 1799. It has to be said that some of those who made professions of faith were very short lived in their commitments. Will and Ann Plant both came into membership through baptism in October 1791. By the August of the following year he had been excluded for "drunkenness and justifying himself in the act." She was excluded in January 1793 for "scolding and brawling with her neighbour."

The Midland Conference felt that they could not allow the General Baptist cause in such a populous area to collapse. Consequently they engaged as Minister Mr James Taylor (Dan Taylor's nephew) to come from the Academy in 1800. Slowly the work began to pick up. Preaching was undertaken at several outlying villages including 'Alverston', Burniston, 'Allestry', Windley and Duffield. On July 20th 1802 the Church opened its first Meeting House in Brook Street, Derby. The event was advertised in the Derby Mercury. Preaching was undertaken by Messrs Felkin, Whittaker and both Thomas and William Pickering.

James Taylor was supported in the preaching ministry by several of the members, perhaps the most prominent one being Joseph Barrow who was especially active in the Windley and Duffield area. By 1807, however, James Taylor was clearly finding the work hard going, and at a Church Meeting on 13th September 1807 it was agreed (with 3 abstentions) that "brother Taylor was at liberty to remove from Derby if he thought proper." In October he moved to his new Church at Heptonstall Slack in West Yorkshire. Brook Street set about a search for a new Minister.

The man who replaced him as Minister in 1810 was John Gregory Pike[1]. Born on 6th April 1784 in Edmonton, Middlesex, Pike was the son of a Dissenting (though not a Baptist) Minister. From childhood he was eager to serve God and become a Minister of the Gospel. "This probably arose from my parents having a desire that in that sacred occupation my life should be spent."[2] Pike had no dramatic conversion experience and in his 'Memoir' he helpfully tells us that, "In meeting with me the Lord was not in the whirlwind, not in the fire or the storm, but in the still, small voice."

He entered Wymondley Academy in 1802, a Protestant Dissenting College but with no Evangelical credentials. He spent four years at the College and valued enormously the opportunity to study. It was while in College that he came to a view on Believers Baptism and was subsequently baptised in August 1804 by Mr Evans of Worship Street Chapel. Pike did not at that stage join a Baptist Church, but he did become an active supporter of the British and Foreign Bible Society, and it was the Secretary of this organisation that eventually brought him into contact with Dan Taylor. Pike became a member of Dan Taylor's London Church in May 1808 and by the October had been called by that Church into a preaching ministry.

Pike was a deeply conscientious man. On his 21st birthday (April 1805) he drew up a sacred covenant in which he pledged himself wholeheartedly to God's service. He signed and sealed the covenant and ratified it by receiving the Lord's Supper. Subsequently Pike used his birthday every year to take stock of his own spiritual progress (which he usually regarded as minimal) and reaffirmed his commitment to Christ. While at Wymondley he drew up 14 resolutions of discipleship including never allowing himself the luxury of more than six hours sleep, and never wasting his time with an amusing book when he could be engaged in serious study. Even Pike's godly mother became anxious that he was becoming too serious!

Pike came to be linked with Derby through a strange and fortuitous set of circumstances. In the early summer of 1809 Pike was attending the Annual Association of General Baptist Churches at Quorndon in Leicestershire. Apparently he missed the coach back to London after the meetings and fell into conversation with Rev John Deacon of Leicester. Deacon arranged for Pike, who by this time had been anxiously looking for an outlet for service, to preach in some of the Midland churches. He was well liked and at one time he was being touted for the pastorate at Castle Donington. But it was in Derby and the surrounding villages that he entered into a trial of several months which led to the Derby Church inviting him to become their minister in November 1809.

Pike loved the Derbyshire countryside. On September 9th he wrote to his oldest sister from Quarndon, near Derby, waxing eloquent on the beauty around him. The same letter also describes his excitement at the experience of conducting an open air baptismal service:

"The river Derwent is here the only baptistry, and on its banks, and on the bridge which crosses it just at the place, several thousand spectators can accommodate themselves with stations for observing the impressive ceremony. I know of none more impressive. It is so when administered in a confined building and you may suppose it much more so when 16 or 20 persons are baptized in the view of hundreds or thousands of spectators, and thus profess to renounce earth for heaven."[3]

Pike was first introduced to village open air preaching at this time, and became quite expert at delivering extempore sermons. His father was appalled, fearing that his son's learning would go to waste and that he would simply degenerate into a ranting preacher. But Pike was warming to the thrill of seeing men and women respond to the Gospel.

Pike's love of the countryside and the excitement and responsiveness of the village communities led to his being drawn not to Derby but in fact to Duffield. His 'Memoir' (page 60) contains another extract from one of his letters at that time:

"Duffield was at first considered a branch of the Derby society, but now mention is frequently made of separating from it. Should that be the case, and I should stop in this neighbourhood, I should much prefer Duffield to Derby. I prefer the country and the people, while the prospect of usefulness is much greater. Last night I preached at Milford, about a mile and a half from Duffield. The place was crowded."

When the invitation came, however, it was from Derby and not from Duffield. This was hardly to his liking. He regarded the building at

Brook Street quite miserable and dreary. The congregation were thinly spread out and generally of a poor, working class origin. When the invitation came he delayed making a response for nearly eight months, presumably waiting either for a better offer from somewhere else or waiting for Duffield to get its act together and constitute itself a separate Church. The latter didn't happen, although it was the calling of Pike to Brook Street and the ensuing tussle with Duffield that precipitated the separation of the two causes and the establishment of Duffield as an independent Church.

John Gregory Pike commenced his ministry at Brook Street on 10th July 1810. He was originally invited for a two year period. He actually stayed as pastor for 44 years and died in post. His ministry was to be perhaps the most significant ministry of any Baptist in Derbyshire throughout the whole nineteenth century.

Brook Street Baptist Church was poor. Pike accepted a salary of £50 a year, which was a fraction of what his counterpart at Agard Street was receiving. To supplement his income Pike had to open a Day School and take in pupils. On 22nd June 1811 he married Miss Sarah Sandars, the daughter of Mr James Sandars of Derby. Children quickly followed and with that came further financial demands. The Pikes were struggling so much financially that at one time they contemplated starting a business and even emigrating to America.

Pike made considerable personal sacrifices, out of which the work at Brook Street simply took off. When he arrived the Church had a membership of 63. The same month he arrived he baptised 6 people using the baptistery at Agard Street. In September a further 10 people were baptised at Agard Street and in the October a further 10 were baptised in a brook at Alvaston. By the middle of 1811 membership had risen to 114. Not all of these people worshipped at the Brook Street premises. A considerable number were attached to the preaching stations around the town which sprung out of the itinerant preaching from Brook Street. Members were found in Alvaston (15), Weston (11), Darley (29), and Littleover (13). Pike himself recorded having preached at virtually all the villages within a 12 mile radius of Derby within his first 2 years at the Church.

There was, however, significant growth in the Brook Street congregation to the extent that even in 1811 they were looking at purchasing a site in Silk Mill Lane for a larger chapel. Lack of money prevented this from happening. Instead the Church erected a temporary gallery in the Brook Street premises. Within two years even this arrangement was proving unsatisfactory. As numbers grew Mr Pike was making it clear that he was not prepared to stay unless the Church made efforts to substantially enlarge the premises. But again they seemed unwilling or unable to contemplate the undertaking.

In a letter dated May 19th 1813 Pike wrote: "Anything respecting the chapel seems about at a standstill. If all poorness of spirit was acceptable to God the General Baptists would stand very high in his esteem, for most of them, as far as zeal and activity are concerned, are poor enough. I like the zeal of the Methodists."

In the end Pike realised that if he wanted to see the premises enlarged he was going to have to do something about it himself. Consequently he resigned himself to the inevitable, and decided to subject himself "to all the annoyances and drudgery, the slights and rebuffs, the denials, civil and uncivil, which in days of yore were the usual portion of those who perambulated the country with a 'begging case'. A more irksome or thankless errand cannot well be imagined."[4]

For the first six months of 1814 Pike left Derby, and, making a base with his mother in London, he set to raise the funds needed to substantially enlarge and renovate the Brook Street premises. Personal sacrifice again came into the equation because it meant he had to give up his employment as a school teacher in Derby. After six months perambulating the country appealing for funds for the chapel he returned to Derby with £400, a colossal amount of money at that time.

From the summer of 1814 building work commenced on the chapel. Eventually, in April 1815 the new sanctuary was opened with a proper gallery and a seating capacity of 600. There were also two moderate size school rooms. The total cost was £1000 with some £600 coming from loans from members and friends of the Church. There were those who scoffed that they would never see the building (three times the size of its predecessor) filled in their life time. Within four years numbers had grown so extensively that the Church for the third time had to expand the building by the addition of side galleries to seat a further 150 people. In 1817 the membership of the Church stood at 154. By 1826 it had increased to 256.

Adam Taylor points out that the rapid growth of the congregation and membership outstripped the Church's structures and ability to provide pastoral and spiritual support. Neglect of Church discipline had "a baneful effect." They divided the Church into classes "and proper persons were appointed to superintend their conduct and religious improvement."

Being a Baptist Christian in those days was no easy thing. Expectations were extremely high, and discipleship was very demanding. Among the archive material of Broadway Baptist Church is an undated "Baptismal Covenant and rules of the Baptist Church, Brook Street, Derby." The document gives a flavour of evangelical life at the beginning of the nineteenth century.

"In coming forward to be baptized and join the Church of the Lord Jesus you are taking a step of unutterable importance...... Into this solemn covenant you are now about to enter, and it is highly important that you should do this with a clear understanding of the sacred engagements you contract."

Those expectations included: "Incur not debts which you have not a probability of discharging."

"Shun on the Sabbath worldly conversation. Let no work that should be done on the Saturday night be left for Lord's Day morning. Let there be no cleaning of knives and shoes upon the Lord's Day. Let there be no sending to a bakehouse, or fetching liquor..."

"Indulge not the disorderly habit of coming in after worship has commenced, and thus of disturbing others that have been more timely in their attendance."

"Avoid a sinful conformity to the world by vain extravagance in apparel or other respects. Love of dress is in many professors of the Gospel a besetting sin. And totally abstain from the sinful amusements of the world, such as wakes, races, dances, playhouses, cards, and the reading of plays, novels, romances etc."

The Covenant concludes: "If we should ever be so wretched as to forsake these engagements to God and Christ, and should turn back to the world .... We acknowledge that the Church is bound in duty to Christ to exclude us from Communion, and thus to give us up to Satan (1Cor.5:5) and confess that that exclusion would be confirmed in heaven."

John Gregory Pike's fame did not merely extend to his role as minister of Brook Street, Derby. He became quite a prolific author. In 1816 he produced the first of his publications, "A Catechism of Scriptural Instructions for young persons." It reflected his deep concern for the spiritual nurture of the young that he was pioneering at Brook Street. This publication was followed the next year by "The consolations of Gospel Truth" (a collection of death bed spiritual testimonies). It was very popular and went through several editions. In 1818 Pike produced the work for which he became most famous, "Persuasives to early piety." It was an encouragement again to young people to follow the Way of Christ. Over Pike's lifetime he received a string of letters from people all over the world (especially America) whose lives had been changed through reading "Persuasives." Such was its fame that it was specifically mentioned on his tombstone. Other works followed including "Guide to Young Disciples" (1823), "The Christian ministry contemplated" (1839), and "Anti Christ unmasked: or Popery and Christianity contrasted." (1843).

Pike's major achievement, however, came from neither his pastoral ministry nor his written prowess, but from his role as pioneer, founder and first Secretary of the General Baptist Missionary Society.

Pike had always had a passionate interest in missionary work. In 1809, when doors were not opening for him in this country, he seriously considered candidating for missionary service overseas. Along with his older contemporary, William Pickering, he was a keen advocate of the British and Foreign Bible Society, and in the early days at Brook Street he harangued his congregation for their insularity and their inability to grasp the global dimension of the Gospel.

But Pike's fire and passion was reserved for the General Baptist family as a whole. In an appeal to the broader constituency given on October 6th 1815 he reminded them in no uncertain terms that 500 million people existed in the world who had no knowledge of Christ:

"It almost makes one's blood run chill to repeat the words – FIVE HUNDRED MILLIONs of immortal beings involved in the deepest night – a night almost as dark and hopeless as the eternal night of hell …. were towns to be peopled by them, fifty thousand considerable towns would arise. Were villages to be planted, one million respectable villages would appear. O ye who weep over the inhabitants of <u>one</u> city, who mourn the depravity of <u>one</u> town, who lament the state of <u>one</u> village, weep here! Our hearts are ice, or these views would call forth floods of sorrow."[5]

The Particular Baptists were already well ahead of the game, and as early as 1792, prodded by William Carey, had formed the Baptist Missionary Society. Pike developed a keen interest in the work, and when a disastrous fire broke out at Serampore in India, destroying the printing presses, Pike was quick to get his own Church and the Association to raise funds for the restoration. But he was mindful that it was difficult for General Baptists to wholeheartedly engage in the work of the Particular Baptists. He explored the possibility with Andrew Fuller, Secretary to the BMS, of forming a General Baptist Auxiliary of the BMS. Fuller felt that such a move would be unworkable, and instead encouraged Pike to press ahead with plans to form a wholly separate General Baptist Missionary Society.

At the Annual Association Meeting held in Boston in 1816 Pike launched his plan. In this he was again well supported by William Pickering. Pickering wrote the Annual Letter to the churches that year and took as his theme, "Christian Zeal." But Pickering deliberately set his theme in a global and missionary setting. There could be no true

Christian zeal that did not express itself in action for the benighted heathen. Pickering went on:

"The Christian contemplates with an aching heart the vast empire of Satan, the millions who are destroyed by lack of knowledge. He feels a holy ambition to extend the cause of Christ, and to be an instrument of saving immortal souls from death ...... The establishment of missionary societies and their wonderful success; the translation of the scriptures into so many languages, the increase of missionaries ... should stimulate every Christian to put his shoulder to the work."[6]

By the time of the First Annual Meeting of the Missionary Society at Castle Donington on Tuesday June 24th 1817, Brook Street's Missionary Auxiliary Society had raised more than £42, an amazing accomplishment given their general impoverishment, a sum of money almost equivalent to the total salary paid to their Minister. Over 38 years Pike's Church gave an average of £100 a year to the Society.

It soon became clear that Pike was the driving force behind the GBMS, and if it was going to work then it required his personal commitment and energy. Almost by default, therefore, Pike became the first Secretary of the GBMS, a position he held until his death. In 1822 the GBMS decided that Orissa, in India, was to be the focus of its early missionary endeavours. Pike subsequently had a hand in preparing prospective missionaries for service overseas. Several generations of missionaries stayed with him in Derby and received training in preaching and theology from the great man.

As the work of the Society expanded and Pike's workload increased he eventually received a salary for his extra work. But in the early years he did everything on a voluntary basis and did it all for the shear love of what he believed in.

An indication of the amount of work the Society generated for Pike can be deduced from a letter he wrote to one of the missionaries, Mr Peggs, on 5th March 1824.

"I hope to get a little more leisure, but I assure you the Mission takes up much of my time. Last year I had to attend between 40 – 50 missionary meetings. Some of these, besides the time expended on them, required one or two days additional for travelling. This work, apparently, will increase, rather than lessen, as new associations are formed."[7]

The Church at Brook Street was by no means tolerant or understanding of their minister's commitments throughout the length and breadth of the country. The Church's Annual Report to the Association in 1825 reads quite pointedly: "We regret the frequent absences of our Minister, and believe that could we enjoy more of his friendly visits our prosperity would be increased." They were still complaining about his absences in 1838; and in 1839 the Annual report records: "We have still cause to complain that the claims of the Foreign Mission occasion the very frequent absence of our Minister." That same Annual report recorded a membership figure for Brook Street of 384. They had witnessed 32 baptisms that year!

Brook Street was bursting at the seams. Even with three Services each Sunday there was difficulty accommodating everyone who wanted to attend. By January 1841 the Church was seriously exploring yet another enlargement of the Brook Street premises and the work had been placed in the hands of "a respectable architect of Chelmsford." Suddenly, quite unexpectedly, another opportunity presented itself.

On 24th April 1841 Pike jotted down a scribbled note: "This morning I was summoned at ten to go and inspect Mr Evans' premises; this occupied us more than two hours. There is a deal of property and land. He states that he meant his price to be £4,500, but he offers it to us for £4,000. I am to meet the deacons again about it at 9 tonight."[8]

The premises in question were often described as a 'mansion' on St Mary's Gate, in the centre of town. Events moved at an incredible pace. On 5th May the Church had given its approval to the purchase of the property. It would need substantial adaptation to become a place of worship, but by the October Pike was writing to one of his sons that the workmen were putting in the beams and joists in the floor and the main timbers in the gallery and roof. Before that, however, (22nd August 1841) the Church met to celebrate its Golden Jubilee. Predictably, Brook Street was packed with people for the occasion, and "about 750 took tea in the grounds of the mansion recently purchased in St Mary's Gate."

On Sunday May 15th 1842 they held their last Service at Brook Street. Josiah Pike, one of the Minister's sons, preached in the morning on Haggai 2:9 while the Minister himself preached in the evening from Psalm 115:1. On Wednesday May 18th they walked to the new Sanctuary in St Mary's Gate. Several sermons were delivered including one from "the venerable Rev W. Pickering of Nottingham." The following Sunday evening Pike preached at the new chapel "with thrilling power and effect" from 1Cor.2:2, "I determined not to know anything among you, save Jesus Christ and Him crucified." The total collection that day yielded £425. The new chapel could accommodate 1200 people. The building work was carried out by Mr Henry Winterton, an active member of the Church. The total cost of the venture, which included some cottages in Walker lane and a new Minister's house was £7,233. Mr Evans allowed £2,000 to remain on mortgage and none of this amount was paid until 1860. The final instalment of the debt was not paid off until 1878. At first the basement of the new chapel was used for schoolrooms. But in 1852 two spacious rooms were added to accommodate 600 scholars.

Pike now decided he should devote more of his time to the pulpit ministry. He curtailed his journeys and devoted more time to study and preparation. "The congregations rapidly increased, and in the course of a few months were twice as large as the old chapel could have accommodated ... In the first year 51 members were added to their number by baptism."[8] The Church membership in 1842 stood at 426. In 1847 it was 542 and in 1849 it reached 571.

From that point on, however, things became more difficult. Pike had been complaining of weariness in the body from 1846. Reports describe him as becoming 'enfeebled'. His wife, Sarah, who had been in poor health for many years, died in the spring of 1848. This, along with the untimely death of one of his grandchildren, had an adverse effect upon him.

The Church had been badgering Pike to have an assistant minister since 1838. But Pike was clearly not at ease with the idea, and dragged his feet. Throughout 1845 and 1846 the Church tried to get Pike to agree. Eventually, in February 1847, it was agreed that "Mr William Stevenson be invited (as assistant minister) at the close of his studies, to spend a year at Derby"[9] with a view to a more permanent settlement. In November they drew up a plan whereby one of the ministers would preach in the morning and the other in the afternoon and evening. They would alternate each week. Mr Stevenson seems to have gone down well because in November 1848 the Church invited him to become permanent by a majority of 456 votes to 8.

The real trouble began in 1850 and concerned the superintendence of the adult Girls Class. The Sunday School teachers felt it was right for this branch of the Church to come under their control. But Mr Pike adamantly refused. He had established the group himself shortly after arriving in Derby. It had met at his home and had never been connected with the Sunday School. Only recently had the group needed to use a room in the Church to meet in, but he saw no reason why it should be considered outside of his jurisdiction. The Sunday School teachers in protest had gone on strike and a new set of teachers had been drafted in to cover the emergency. Eventually the matter was resolved with the old teachers coming back and the new ones staying on, but clearly the Minister's moral authority had taken a severe knock.

None of the minutes regarding this episode mention Mr Stevenson, and the Church was perfectly happy with his conduct since in September 1850 the Church Meeting agreed "by a large majority" that he was to be ordained. Mr Pike, however, refused to take part in the ordination service. Without the support of the senior Minister Stevenson had little alternative but to resign, the Church accepting his resignation on February 11th 1851.

Pike's sons, who compiled the 'Memoir and Remains,' acknowledge (pages 345-346) that the arrangement between their father and the assistant minister didn't work. Stevenson should have shown more respect for Pike, and the latter should have been more mindful of the aspirations of his younger colleague. Had Stevenson not resigned, Pike had himself drafted a letter of resignation which he would have submitted.

By 1852 Pike's health was deteriorating. Surgeons decided that they could not operate on the cataract in his left eye which made it harder for him to carry out some of his work. His journeys outdoors in 1854 dramatically reduced, although he did manage to preach one sermon on 12th March for the opening of the new organ. He was persuaded to take a holiday to Scarborough and on his return it was generally agreed that he seemed much renewed in health.

On Sunday 3rd September Pike presided over the Lord's Supper. On the morning of Monday 4th he attended a United Ministers meeting in Derby, and later in the afternoon he retired to his study to deal with his correspondence. Failing to respond to his daughter's calls for him to come to tea, she entered into the study to find the great man collapsed at his desk, pen still in hand[10]. He was in the 71st year of his life. The 'Derby Mercury' on 6th September contained an article announcing Pike's death. The inquest delivered the verdict, "Died by the visitation of God."

The funeral of John Gregory Pike was one of the largest public gatherings the town had ever witnessed. It took place on Saturday 9th September at 3.30pm. The time was deliberately chosen to allow as many of the factory workers as possible to attend. Queues formed in the adjacent streets long before the doors of St Mary's Gate Chapel opened. The Service was conducted by Rev J. Gawthorn from Victoria Street Chapel and Rev W. Underwood, the Baptist Minister at Sacheverel Street. The deacons of the Church were the pall bearers. An impressive procession was formed with nearly a dozen of the town's Anglican clergy joining with the Dissenting ministers on the three quarters of a mile march to Uttoxeter Road Cemetry. The head of the procession was taken by the Committee of the Bible Society. Crowds lined the streets as the procession walked past. Once at the graveside a short address was given by Rev J. Buckley after which the procession re-formed and made its way back to the Church.

On Sunday 10th September a funeral address was given at St Mary's Gate in the evening by Rev J. Goadby of Loughborough. He spoke from Matthew 25:21, "Well done, good and faithful servant." As many people stood outside the building as were gathered inside, so afterwards the Rev Underwood gave an impromptu sermon from Psalm 116:5 to those assembled in front of the building. Pike left behind four sons, three of whom were in the Baptist ministry and two unmarried daughters.

The Church at St Mary's Gate agreed to pay for the funeral of their late pastor. A substantial monument was subsequently erected in Uttoxeter Road Cemetery which is still impressive today. Designed by J.B. Robinson, sculptor, the monument lists Pike achievements as Pastor of St Mary's Gate Chapel for forty four years, founder of the General Baptist Missionary Society and author of "Persuasions to early piety" and other valuable works. The monument also contains the words of Daniel 12:3:

"They that be wise shall shine as the brightness of the firmament, and they that turn many to righteousness as the stars for ever and ever."

Following Pike's death the Church at St Mary's Gate had a difficult decision to make about its future direction. In April 1855 they invited Rev John Stevenson to become their Minister, but behind that call and Stevenson's acceptance was a great deal of soul searching. The deacons recommended Stevenson as early as the January, but he was not the only candidate in the frame and there was a sizable number in the Church who were keen to see Rev John Baxter Pike, son of their late pastor, take on his father's mantle. The Church Meeting in April 1855 was a complicated affair. There were 121 votes cast for Stevenson and 117 for J.B.Pike. But this was only to have Stevenson for twelve months. Stevenson accepted the offer only after consulting with his rival and gaining his approval to the appointment. Twelve months later when the Church had to decide again about Mr Stevenson the votes were 129 in favour of him staying and 63 against.

Many Ministers faced with such a divided Church, and recognising the enormous challenge of following a colossus such as J.G.Pike, would probably have declined the offer. But Stevenson didn't and was proved justified in accepting the call. St Mary's Gate, in Pike's later years had seen an unprecedented fall in its membership. From a peak of 571 members in 1849 it had declined to 516 members by the time of Pike's death in 1854. But thereafter the Church once more began to flourish. There were 589 members in 1857; 625 members in 1859; and 676 members in 1861. One of the features of the ministry of John Stevenson at St Mary's Gate was the establishment of the branch Church at Parcel Terrace which subsequently became Junction Baptist Church. Stevenson also oversaw the sale of the old Brook Street Chapel to the Methodists which generated sufficient funds to repay some of the outstanding debt that was still crippling even this wealthy Church.

Stevenson's ministry ended on a sad note. Not only did the Baptist ministry not enjoy any pension scheme in those days, resulting in aged ministers having to carry on into their dotage, but no sickness scheme operated either. John Stevenson became very unwell in early 1863. In July the Church gave him an ultimatum that unless he was able to return to work within two months they would have to terminate their arrangement with him. With little prospect of a recovery to full health at that time, Stevenson submitted his resignation to the Church on 20th September. A week later the Church accepted his resignation. An amendment NOT to accept his resignation was defeated by 57 votes to 70.

1. Pike's full name was John Deodatus Gregory Pike, and occasionally there is reference to him as JDG Pike. But most of the contemporary and subsequent accounts simply refer to him as John Gregory or J.G Pike.
2. 'The Memoir and Remains of Rev J.G.Pike' page 7. The book was edited by two of Pike's sons, John Baxter (J.B) Pike and James Carey (J.C) Pike. The work was based on first hand accounts from Pike himself along with correspondence and biographical gleanings. The work was published in 1855.
3. 'The Memoir' page 57
4. 'The Memoir' page 89
5. 'The Memoir' pages 107-108

6. 'The Memoir' page 114
7. 'The Memoir' page 176
8. 'The Memoir' chapter 20
9. Church Meeting minutes
10. William Wilkins was a long standing friend of Pike and also deacon of St Mary's Gate Baptist Church. A diary he kept meticulously for all his adult life contains interesting and additional detail regarding the events of 4th September 1854. Mr Pike "ate a hearty dinner of ham and peas and rice pudding, and afterwards slept in his easy chair." When his daughter found Pike slumped in his chair she "immediately sent for me in great haste; I was there as soon as possible. When I saw him I felt convinced the spirit was departed. I requested that a surgeon or two should be immediately obtained, which was done, and they pronounced that he had been dead some time."

Footnote: In 1937 St Mary's Gate Baptist Church received an offer of £12,000 for their site from Messrs Kennings Ltd. The Church accepted the offer. They bought a new site on Broadway. The Stone Laying Ceremony took place in September 1938 and the Church was opened in September 1939. The gates that proudly hung at the entrance to St Mary's Gate Baptist Church subsequently took pride of place outside Derby Cathedral.

Bust of
John Etches

1754 - 1838

Brook Street chapel 1826.

Brook Street Chapel 2005
The Masa Restaurant

St Mary's Gate Baptist Chapel

Rev J.D.G. Pike 1784 – 1854

Pike's grave and Memorial:
Uttoxeter Road Cemetery, Derby

CHAPTER 9

DUFFIELD, WINDLEY AND MILFORD

Preaching began in Duffield during the Spring of 1807. Mr Joseph Barrow, one of the original nine members of Brook Street, Derby, had been recognised as a preacher by the Brook Street Church as early as June 1804, and by 1807 he felt inclined to commence public services in Duffield. He had already made the acquaintance of John Taylor, a business man and landowner of Duffield, and sympathetic to Barrow's cause Taylor invited him to come and preach in Duffield. On March 21st 1807 Mr Barrow came and preached from John 3:16.

In actual fact preaching at Windley had commenced at least a year before this. In the Brook Street minutes for January 1806 it is recorded that "brother Taylor[1] and Dallison to assist brother Barrow in preaching at Windley." On May 11th 1806 an entry in the Brook Street minutes records that "brother Taylor[1] to go to Windley next Lord's Day." While at the Brook Street Church Meeting on 10th January 1807 it was agreed that collections should be taken quarterly at "Derby, Alvaston and Windley." Not until March 1807 is there a reference to preaching at Duffield which at the same time mentioned preaching at Windley and "Allestry".

Windley may have been regarded as a branch of Duffield for most of the nineteenth century, but in point of fact it pre-dated Duffield as a preaching station and a centre of Baptist witness.

Mr Barrow's meetings at Duffield soon attracted considerable numbers of people. A room was hired that would accommodate 200 people, but finding even that too small John Taylor made available one of his unoccupied factories which was opened for public worship on April 23rd 1809. It could seat 400 people. The previous year (June 1808) John Taylor's request for baptism was noted in the minutes of Brook Street Chapel, and he was subsequently baptised at Duffield in the Derwent. By the end of 1809 some 40 people from Duffield and surrounds had joined the Duffield branch of the Derby Church.

In 1810 there was a significant disagreement between Duffield and Derby. Correspondence still existing indicates that this was in part the result of Duffield acting without reference to Derby in the matter of baptisms. But the clash also centred upon the differing protocol preferred by the two groups regarding the calling of a minister. Duffield were convinced that any candidate had to be sanctioned by Conference, a position which Brook Street thought impaired the autonomy of the local Church. More specifically the clash centred on the struggle to obtain one Minister in particular, John Gregory Pike.

In May 1810, Barrow and Taylor wrote to the Brook Street Church urging a separation which was eventually agreed. On 21st May 1810 they formed themselves into a distinct Church of 47 members, and in October they successfully obtained a Licence from the Bishop of Lichfield and Coventry to maintain a Dissenting Church in the village. In March 1811 John Taylor offered the members a room on a twelve year lease. The room was in a building "adjoining to the dwelling house of the said John Taylor."

Joseph Barrow left Duffield in 1812 to concentrate on a new cause in Shottle and Wirksworth. Mr Richard Ingham, a student from the College, was called as Minister. The Church at that time had 90 members. Ingham was ordained to the pastoral office in June 1819, and remained at the Church until 1822. There were then 203 members of whom 43 had been baptised the previous year.

These 203 members were based not just in Duffield but in the other neighbouring villages where preaching was maintained. These included Windley, Milford and Belper. (Shottle and Wirksworth had separated in 1818). There were also preaching stations at Quarndon, Holbrook and Heage.

Not everything went well for the Duffield Church. In the Church's own archive is a surviving report from an Association team who visited Duffield (about 1824) to deal with a severe dispute that was tearing the Church apart. The report, under the chairmanship of William Pickering, doesn't make clear what the unpleasantness was or who it was between, but it refers to "the present crisis" and refers to the

114

"baneful effects of which have spread their influence over a considerable part of the Church." The report also observes that matters haven't been helped by Church Meetings being taken up with frivolous cases which engender strife.

The site for the Baptist Chapel in Duffield was purchased by John Taylor in 1826 for £100. By 1830 the new chapel was completed in brick and stone, the cost being met largely by John Taylor, whose initials are engraved over the main chapel entrance, and in whose memory a memorial plaque was erected in the chapel which describes him as an "honourable deacon of the Church assembling here, and the chief contributor to this place of worship." John Taylor died on 12th December 1837, but several months before his death he transferred the chapel to a group of seven Trustees including George Malin the elder, a farmer from Shottle; George Malin the younger, a farmer from Ashley Hay; and George Houlgate, a farmer from Hazelwood.

The Belper branch of the Duffield Church separated in 1822. This depleted Duffield's membership so that in the Association returns for 1823 they were reduced to 91 members. This total fell still further so that in 1833 there were 74 members. Mr W. Crabtree served the Church briefly in 1834, and from 1836 – 1845 Stephen Taylor served as Duffield's minister.

There is a rather delightful account of a baptism at Duffield recorded in the General Baptist Repository for 1840:

"On Lord's Day April 5th at Duffield a packed Church service was held at which brother Taylor preached. We then repaired to our old baptistery, the river Derwent. The bridge was lined, and the banks on each side of the river were fairly studded. (It is supposed there were between 2,000 – 3,000 people.)"

Five men and two women were baptised by brother Barton: "The sun shone bright, the water was very clear, the voices of the people in their singing thrilled through the air."

The Association report for 1837 mentioned that while Duffield's congregations remained about the same, those at Milford were much better. The 1838 report repeated that Milford's congregations were good, but also observed that "At Windley – things are much as they were." Intriguingly, the report also states that, "We have lately introduced our cause into Little Eaton, a person there having very kindly furnished us with a Chapel." The 1839 report says that the work at Milford is "retarded for want of a larger place to worship in." Some disquiet among the Milford brethren was reported the following year, while in 1843 the Church recorded that "our cause at Windley is in a prosperous state." It was still described as 'prosperous' in 1845, the year the Church had to record the resignation of Stephen Taylor following a paralysing stroke. In 1848 Duffield were proudly able to announce, "We have been able to erect a neat and commodious chapel at Windley."

Brief details of the Windley Chapel Opening are found in the General Baptist Repository for 1848. The ceremony took place on May 16th. Sermons were delivered, in the afternoon by Rev J. Burns D.D. and in the evening by Rev E.Stevenson of Loughborough. "On Lord's Day May 28th Rev J.G.Pike of Derby preached two very impressive sermons." Collections at these special services raised nearly £26.

The following year (1849) "Milford friends commenced building a chapel." It was opened in October, Rev J.G.Pike again delivering "two deeply impressive sermons" to formally open the building in this "populous village." By the time that Milford had been granted independence (1855) there were only 40 members left at Duffield and Windley. By 1861 this figure was 39.

The letter from the deacons at Milford (Charles Bainbridge, Robert Bell and William Parkinson) formally requesting separation from Duffield was long over due. As it gently pointed out, they had been functioning separately to all intents and purposes for years. The reply from Duffield (Nov. 29th 1854) recognised the inevitable. "We feel in duty bound to accede to your resolution, as in our weak state we cannot do much for you...."

116

The cause at Milford was a product of the Industrial Revolution. Jedediah Strutt (1726 – 1797) was the founder of the Milford Cotton Mills, and turned a very small hamlet that was recorded in the Domesday Book into a bustling centre of industrial production. Strutt himself was a Unitarian and ensured that a Unitarian Chapel was built as part of the Mill complex. He was also a man of very broad sympathies and under his and his family's patronage several non-conformist chapels were constructed in Milford. The Baptist Chapel on Chevin Road was first built in 1824 and the new chapel in 1849. Apparently, the land for the new chapel was sold to the Baptists by the Strutt family for £13. An extension for a school room was added in 1857.

An appeal for funds (dated August 7th) towards this extension appeared in the General Baptist Repository for 1857.

"The Chapel on most Lord's days is filled to overflowing; and frequently, after seats have been placed along the aisle, many persons have been obliged to go into the school room or to return home."

The Church explained their desire to enlarge the premises but having an outstanding debt of £120 they could not afford to. All donations were to be sent to Mr W. Parkinson the senior deacon.

The influence of the Mill on the life of the Baptist Chapel can be measured from the Church Members Roll. An unusually informative document here at Milford, the Members Roll includes a section for 'profession' of the member. Of the 31 members whose profession is given 23 are connected to the Mill complex. There are six people described as 'Stockinger', six "Millhand", three people who work "at the bleach mill", one "at the dye house", three "overlooker Cotton Mill" and one "Superintendent of the Cotton Mill". This was William Parkinson.

In 1856 the Church received 30 people into membership mainly through baptism. Of these 30 people, 18 were millhands, 1 was a stockinger and 1 a dyer. Equally revealing and informative was the section (not always completed) "presumed age at baptism". Again, of the 30 people baptised in 1856, 12 were in their teens (the youngest being 15), 10 were in their 20s, 6 were in their 30s and only 2 were aged 55.

Milford very rarely had any form of settled ministry. Between 1852 and 1854 Mr Joseph Townend came over from Nottingham each weekend, while for 15 months in 1857-58 Rev G. Rodgers served the Milford Church while he was residing in the area on health grounds. With those two brief exceptions Milford relied on a regular supply of local preachers to conduct services for them.

The first independent entry for Milford appears in the Association records for 1855 when 73 members are attributed to the Church. This figure grew to 96 members following the remarkable year 1856, and peaked at 107 in 1858. By 1861 membership at Milford had again fallen back to 74, but this still represented almost double the membership of the mother Church in Duffield (39 members).

1. I am assuming that the 'brother Taylor' referred to here is James Taylor, the Minister at Brook Street.

Duffield Baptist Chapel

The Bridge over the Derwent at Duffield

Milford Baptist Chapel

Windley Baptist Chapel: drawing by D. Litchfield

CHAPTER 10

BELPER AND CRICH

The decision to start a Baptist cause at Belper emerged from a question posed at the Duffield Church Meeting in August 1817. "Can we not introduce preaching into Holbrook? Can we not begin preaching at Belper?" It was decided to postpone attempts to start a cause in Holbrook but on Sunday Evening August 17th the Duffield Church Meeting agreed to hire a room at the 'George and Dragon' in Belper, and on Sunday August 24th 1817 it was opened for public worship by the Duffield Minister, Richard Ingham.

A good congregation started to emerge, and an appeal for a Church building and burial ground was launched at the Church Meeting held at Cowhouse Lane on February 16th 1818. The Association gave its blessing to the venture (provided they did not incur too large a debt) and shortly afterwards a Mr Hardy sold them a 480 yard plot of land off Bridge Street for 5 shillings a yard. In order to raise funds for the new chapel Mr Ingham the Minister went on a begging campaign in Yorkshire. He returned with £27.18 shillings towards the new chapel. In all 32 Baptist Churches contributed towards a chapel at Belper. Barton gave £14, Loughborough gave £14; Heptonstall Slack gave £13; Melbourne and Ticknall gave £12; and £14 was raised from churches in Nottingham, principally Broad Street. Amazingly, the largest single donation from a Church was £30.14.6 which came from Shottle!

A Church Meeting (held at Cowhouse Lane) on June 7th 1818 made the first moves towards the division of the large cluster of churches now focused on Duffield. In response to the request from Wirksworth, "It was agreed that Wirksworth, Shottle and Cowhouse Lane should form one Church; and Duffield, Windley, Milford and Belper with all the places in those quarters another."

Appeals for more funds for the Belper Church were made, and the building would appear to have been opened sometime in March 1819.

The Old Belper Baptist Chapel, Bridge Street:
On the opposite side of the road to the current Chapel,
and down a narrow alley way
Source: Michael Mitchell

In August 1820 the Church Meeting (held at Belper) agreed to the pastor's suggestion that he should move his residence to Belper, effectively taking on more responsibility for this side of the Church. The following year, however, Mr Ingham confided in the Church that he was being approached by the friends at Heptonstall Slack in Yorkshire to become their minister, and that he was inclined to accept their invitation. Mr Ingham's last Church Meeting was in March 1822. Shortly afterwards the Duffield – Belper Church invited a Mr Smedley to become their pastor.

On January 12th 1823 Mr Smedley opened the Club Room in Heage as a place for Public Worship. The Church Meeting a week later heard that the place had been crowded to excess in the evening and "great good was likely to be done." References to prayer meetings and preaching at Heage date back to as early as 1820. Brother Sellars appears to have been the main contact person at Heage.

It was on February 2nd 1823 that the Duffield – Belper Church Meeting agreed by a large majority to separate and form two independent churches. A committee was drawn up to examine the division of money and assets. The decision was one driven by the Belper side of the Church which had seen most of the numerical growth in the previous five years. Of the candidates who were baptised at Duffield on April 26th 1818, for example, 17 were from Belper, 5 from Milford, and a few from Little Eaton. With some bitterness the Duffield Church Meeting on February 17th 1823 refused to take any responsibility for the Belper Chapel debt.

The first entry in the Association minutes for Belper is 1823 where it records a membership total of 96. Duffield had 91, and Wirksworth and Shottle had 189. Preaching was carried out beyond Belper itself and went as far as Heage, Morley and Crich where (1827) it is recorded that the congregations were large. By the 1840s's Belper also had preaching at Belper Lane, Openwoodgate and Cow Hill.

In truth the Baptist cause in Belper went through a terribly torrid time. The decision of the Crich congregation to separate from Belper does not appear to have been amicable. The 1828 Association report from Belper makes passing reference to the separation of "one branch of the Church". But the report from St Mary's Gate, Derby is most revealing: "Our branch at Crich has received 11 members who were formerly at Belper. Should an acceptable minister be found at Belper then hopefully Crich and Belper can unite again." Mr G. Pike, who had very briefly served as Belper's minister (1825-1828) had left the Church, and either as a cause or effect of this departure the Crich friends had decided to turn to St Mary's Gate for support rather than to Belper. The 1828 report notes that with their withdrawal, membership at Belper stood at 69. It also observed that "our debt hangs like a mill-stone about the neck of the cause."

By 1836 Belper had shrunk to 31 members, and in 1837 with only 28 members it was knocking on the door of extinction. "We are greatly indebted to our friends at Duffield, Derby and Wirksworth for their kind labours in keeping open our doors." But then the cause revived.

The 1839 report to the Association recorded that "Our highly respected friend, Mr Ingham, the founder of our cause, has again removed to us, and become our Minister and pastor." Richard Ingham had been minister at Duffield (1812 -22) and had opened the first meeting room for Baptists in Belper before he moved off to Yorkshire. His return now to Belper proved to be an inspired decision. In his first year at Belper there were 16 baptisms. Membership stood at 72 in 1839; 85 in 1840; 110 in 1841 (23 baptisms in the year) and 110 again in 1842 when Ingham's ministry was cut short. An inspirational and energetic member of the North Derbyshire Conference of General Baptists, Ingham had tried to revive the cause at Ashford in the Water, and start a cause at Chesterfield. He preached the first sermon of the newly formed General Baptist cause in Chesterfield in October 1842. He returned to Yorkshire (Bradford) to carry out work for the Foreign Mission that month, was taken ill and died shortly afterwards. He was 55 years old. His death was marked at Belper by a Service on October 30th conducted by 'Brother Pike' who preached from Hebrews 13:7. The Church was "crowded to excess" great numbers not able to obtain admittance.

Richard Ingham's premature death was a blow to the Baptists in the county. But it was a particular blow to the Baptists in Belper who suddenly found themselves plunged into a bout of mutual acrimony and in-fighting.

In May 1844 the Church Meeting at Belper decided that, "Owing to the unpleasant state of the Church it was thought best not to send any reports to the Association." In fact word did get back to the North Derbyshire Conference because at their meeting on Good Friday 1844 (Ilkeston), "a letter was read from this town subscribed on behalf of a number amounting to 18 or 20 persons representing a very unpleasant state of things and asking the advice of conference." A committee was appointed to arbitrate and promote peace.

In July 1846 things still had not been resolved. The Church Meeting that month recommended that "a committee be appointed ... to ascertain the cause of the declension in the Church and to investigate the unpleasantness existing with friend Tomlinson." (Mr Tomlinson was the Treasurer, and a deacon.)

Matters got worse. In June 1847 John Felkin, son of the former minister at Ilkeston and Kegworth, was invited to become pastor at Belper. Mr Tomlinson did not support the invitation and neither did the other three deacons. On August 24th 1847 the Church received the resignation of 19 members who objected to Felkin's appointment.

Mr Felkin's arrival at Belper served to make matters worse. He immediately clashed with one of the leading families in the Church (the Barton-Clays). In January 1850 a deputation from the Church had to remonstrate with Mr Felkin for making unpleasant remarks from the pulpit "injurious to the Church and congregation." Things came to a head on 28th February when Mr Felkin demanded the expulsion of the whole of the Barton-Clay family or else he would resign. The Church sided with the Barton-Clays, they accepted Mr Felkin's resignation and five more members gave notice of their intention of resigning at the same time.

With Mr Felkin ejected, the way was now clear to invite those members who had earlier seceded to return. The group attached to Mr Tomlinson had set up an alternative Church in King Street. On April 16th 1850 the Church Meeting agreed that a "letter be sent to the King Street friends to the effect that we shall be glad to receive them if they desire it ... and to bury all grievances, if any, in oblivion." In May the Barton-Clays offered to meet with Mr Tomlinson to pave the way for their return. The Report to the Association in June 1851 indicated that 25 people had been received (back) into membership, although 11 more had also withdrawn. In November 1851 Mr Tomlinson was re-apointed to his old job as Church Treasurer.

In 1852 Mr Tomlinson collided with Mr J.Barton Clay snr, accusing him of immoral conduct. The Church backed Mr Tomlinson, and insisted on the expulsion of the family from the Church. By 1854 Mr Tomlinson was chairing the Church Meetings.

Church Membership had slumped to 45 by 1855, and the North Derbyshire Conference was sufficiently concerned about the future of the Baptist cause in Belper that at its summer meeting at Kirby in Ashfield in 1855 the question was asked, "Can anything be done to revive the Church there?"

For nine years (1849 – 1857) Belper Baptist Church had been unable to attract or support a minister. Finally in 1857 sufficient pledges were received from the members to open a ministry fund, and with the Conference supplying a modest amount, the Church felt able to offer an invitation to Mr W. Shakespeare from the Loughborough College to become their minister. He accepted and settled with them in July 1857.

Mr Shakespeare gave his own appraisal of the health of the Church on taking on the pastorate:

"The state of the cause was very low. The Ordnance of the Lord's Supper had been for a long time grievously neglected. Order had not been properly maintained. Congregations were very small. Prospects seemed not very bright."

Any optimism the Church might have had with the arrival of a minister was quickly dispelled. Promises of money simply did not materialise, and by 1858 it was becoming clear that financially they could not support a minister. When the North Derbyshire Conference met at Wirksworth on Monday August 2nd 1858 they were dismayed at the lack of progress at either Belper or Crich, and concluded that, "as a Conference we think it advisable that they should unite and form one Church."

This did not happen. Belper tried to cling on to their minister tenaciously, even refusing to allow him to preach at Crich unless they sent someone acceptable in his place. Finally, with funds exhausted (July 1859) the Church had to ask Mr Shakespeare to leave. He promptly accepted an appointment at Crich! Belper have no Church minutes available for the period 1859 – 1862.

An indication of how dire things had become at Belper can be discovered from the North Derbyshire Conference minutes of August 1863. "The Belper friends desired the advice of the Conference, their state and prospects being very low and gloomy. [Belper's membership figure for 1864 is recorded in the Baptist handbook as only 19!] They were recommended to follow out the provisions of the Trust Deed relative to the disposal of the chapel etc."

In other words, the North Derbyshire Conference told them, in no uncertain terms, that they should close. Belper responded to this advice by promptly resigning from the Conference and joined the Midland Conference in April 1865.

The cunning shift to a different Conference seemed to have worked for Belper because in September 1865 the Midland Conference was recommending Belper as a Home Mission cause. Once all the history and salient facts had been reported to them, however, the Midland Conference decided (December 1865) that Belper would not be recommended as a Home mission cause, "due to the difficulties which surround the whole case."

Crich

J.H. Wood provides the most helpful account of the origins of the Baptist cause in Crich:

"Mr G. Pike, then Minister at Belper, introduced preaching here in 1826. The friends at Crich withdrew from Belper in 1828 and united with the Church in Derby of which they continued a branch until they were formed into a distinct society."

The Brook Street minutes indicate that 11 members (the Crich branch) were received into their membership on December 10th 1827

Thomas Sims	John Steepel
John Hardstone	Elizabeth Slack
Joshua Roe	Samuel (?) Slyder

Thomas Hudson   Mary Hudson
Elizabeth Fritchley   Elizabeth Potter
Sarah Sims

Thomas Hudson was excluded for drunkenness in September 1828.

Subsequent additions to the Crich Branch of Brook Street were Geo. Marshall (baptised June 1828); John Wragg and Enoch Harrison who were baptised in September 1828.

The arrangement with Brook Street didn't last long. On August 24th 1829 a Church Meeting minute records:

"In answer to the question from Crich, it is answered that the friends at Crich are advised to stay as members of Derby Church as present."

A sharp letter was sent to one of the members at Crich for having his children sprinkled. He would be allowed to stay as a member if he admitted his error.

The last reference to the Crich branch of Brook Street occurred on September 15th 1829:

"The Crich friends having baptised several candidates and acted independently to be informed that if they wish to act this way we shall consider them as having withdrawn." Their conduct was not considered orderly "and cannot be allowed in future."

J.H.Wood records that Crich Baptist Church was formed with 20 members in 1830 and was received into the Association in 1831 at which point it had 31 members. J. Garratt was minister between 1834 and 1845. Membership hovered around the mid 30s throughout most of that period, but there was a burst of progress in 1842 and 1843 when it reached 50 following 18 baptisms in the one year.

The Association reports reveal that the Church constructed its first building in 1839. By 1844, despite two good years, the Report to the Association made gloomy reading: "The state of our Church is a matter of lamentation...deficient in brotherly affection...Church Meetings and Lord's Supper indifferently attended... depressed financially." Once Mr Garratt had gone the Church did not have a minister for another 16 years. Membership slumped back into the 30s again in the later 1840s, but rose to 53 by 1855. In the Report to the Association that year Crich Baptist Church gave an interesting assessment of its position:

"The members of the Established Church are very active here now, and have in some measure affected our congregations as well as taken away a number of our Sabbath School scholars. Still, our Sabbath School is by far the largest and most efficient in the village."

Numbers fell back and by 1860 Crich's membership stood only at 38.

Once again, one of the major problems facing the Church was financial indebtedness. In March 1842 Crich asked the North Derbyshire Conference what they should do about their chapel debts. The Conference suggested a letter be sent to those churches that had not previously supported them financially. In March 1845 the following letter appeared in the General Baptist Repository:

"The General Baptist Church, Crich, beg through the medium of the Repository, to inform the Connexion that they are in great difficulties, the money borrowed on their small chapel, £145, being called in, and required to be paid without fail in a few months. We hope to be able to realise among ourselves about £50; but as their will still be a great deficiency, we are laid under the absolute necessity of making application to those churches who have not assisted us heretofore. We humbly trust that this appeal will not be in vain; as we are anxious to avoid the loss of our chapel, and the total overthrow of the cause of Christ among us."

From 1845, and for at least five years, the Conference agreed to find preaching supply for Crich for which the Church were extremely grateful.

At this point a most remarkable event took place in the life of this Baptist Church. The Church's own minute book confirms the apparent lack lustre and pedestrian nature of this village Baptist Church. Minutes begin in 1841 but rarely discuss anything more meaningful than the need for a new lamp for the gallery, selling the harmonium and purchasing a new ladder. There are very few baptisms and little evidence of the missionary fervour that marked some of the other Baptist Churches in the county. (There is one brief reference in January 1853 of an attempt to purchase land on which to build a chapel on the Moor.) Even the appointment of a new minister in 1860 (Mr W. Shakespeare who had spent the previous 18 months at Belper) gets less mention than the introduction of the weekly offering system, the sale of the harmonium and the chapel cleaning.

In December 1860 the minutes reveal plans for a missionary meeting and a members' tea meeting. They were also going to experiment by having a Morning Service for three months starting in the New Year.

On February 6th 1861 the Church Meeting explained Mr Shakespeare's plans for an address on "The great religious awakening of the Nineteenth Century." The meeting was to be followed by a prayer meeting. The minutes go on to say:

"A very deep religious feeling has, however, at this time, been extensively awakened in this neighbourhood, and the subject of the address and prayer meeting were alike adopted in order to meet the spiritual demands of the place."

On Shrove Tuesday (5th March 1861) Mr Shakespeare again made notes of the day's events. Approximately 120 people sat down for tea, and afterwards comparison was made between the religious awakening in America and the one being experienced in Crich.

"A most excellent meeting for prayer was held afterwards. It began about 8 o'clock and lasted two hours. The spirit of prayer was largely manifested. The Spirit of God was working mightily in our midst."

Meetings were held every evening (except Fridays) during that period. Mr Shakespeare was keen to counter the criticism that the extra meetings were responsible for working up the revival. "The revival came first when minister and people alike were not calculating upon it, and the extra meetings, as a matter of necessity, came afterwards." He went on to say: "The Church was remarkably quickened, nearly every member being conscious of the revival's powerful influence.... All classes out of the Church were affected."

The Report in the Association minutes was particularly striking, given the usually brief and predictable topics of discussion:

"Shortly after a remarkable religious movement began and spread rapidly all around us. Never before had we been blessed with such an out pouring of the Holy Spirit .... Sinners of every class, even some of the most hardened, were brought under the mighty influence. Drunkenness and profanity became almost unknown. Prayer and praise were heard everywhere......For four months this wonderful movement continued. Hundreds were awakened ... by baptism and restoration we have added about 40, and thus by the blessing of God we have doubled our numbers."

The Church's membership figures recorded in the Association minutes jumped from 38 in 1860 to 83 in 1861. There were 35 baptisms mentioned for that year. Curiously, the Church's own Membership roll records only seven baptisms in 1862, the same number that had taken place in the Church for the whole of the period 1843 – 58. The discrepancy might have more to do with poor record keeping than anything else.

In the General Baptist Repository for 1861 there is an account of a Baptismal Service that took place at Crich:

"On the Lord's Day, March 24th 1861 24 persons were baptised in the Baptist Chapel, Crich, being the first fruits of the great religious awakening with which God has visited this place and neighbourhood. The chapel was crowded and many were unable to gain admittance. In the afternoon they were received to the Lord's Table. It was the most memorable day in the history of the Church."

The North Derbyshire Conference for August 1861 recorded a further 12 baptisms had taken place at Crich.

The revival at Crich was clearly an amazing event. It was also very short lived. Following on from Mr Shakespeare's exciting minutes, the next minute in the Church book reads:

"It must be remembered that Mr Shakespeare was not allowed to preach after the Church became fully aware he had gone after the pastoral office of the Unitarians at Ilkeston." 7 Nov. 1861.

What exactly transpired in the life of minister and Church is impossible to guess. But it would appear that Rev Shakespeare went through something of a personal spiritual crisis. Almost as soon as he arrived as Belper's minister he was appointed as the Secretary to the North Derbyshire Conference (1858). He was reappointed to that role in 1861. At the Good Friday Conference held at Milford in 1862, however, it was agreed to accept Mr Shakespeare's resignation as their Secretary, "and regret that he should so far have changed his sentiments as to necessitate his removal from us." The Conference went on to say:

"That we deeply sympathise with our friends at Crich under the painful circumstances through which they have passed, and recommend them still to adhere to the doctrines assuredly believed among us."

The Conference also went on to appoint a committee to explore the possibilities of Crich, Belper and Milford uniting together in order to support a minister.

Following this exciting period in the life of Crich Baptist Church, the Church minutes return once again to the mundane and pedantic discussion of such matters as tablecloths and tea towels.

CHAPTER 11

SHOTTLE, WIRKSWORTH AND BONSALL

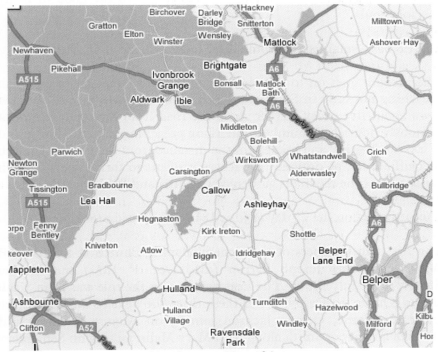

21st Century Map of Area
Source: Google Maps

"Joseph Barrow, one of the first members of the Church at Derby, extended his labours from Duffield to Shottle, Wirksworth etc. The converts here were members of Duffield Church until it was judged expedient to form a distinct society."

This is the brief synopsis of the origin of the Baptists in Shottle and Wirksworth provided by J.H.Wood in his 'Condensed History' of 1847. The earliest minute book of the Shottle and Wirksworth Church provides a little more detail.

"The General Baptist cause was first introduced into Shottle by Mr Barrow of Quarndon, near Derby, who preached his first sermon, August 12th 1812 in a house belonging to Sarah Jackson. After preaching there a few Lord's days they removed to a school room where the preaching of the Gospel was blessed to the good of many precious souls."

Shottle was a small hamlet some three miles outside of Duffield.

The account goes on to explain how Mr Barrow went on to establish preaching not only in Shottle but also in Wirksworth as well, a small town about five miles further along the road from Shottle. The work obviously flourished; numbers attending preaching in both Shottle and Wirksworth grew, and because of the distance from the mother Church in Duffield it was decided that it was prudent to form a new Church consisting of the members gathered at Shottle and Wirksworth.

"Accordingly, on the 7th day of June 1818 this division took place."

The first two members of the General Baptist Church at Shottle and Wirksworth were Joseph Barrow (died Dec. 1st 1831) and Martha Barrow (died July 1824). The next member on the role was John Slack also of 'Quorn' in Derby. After these three the next 18 members were all from Shottle, George Jackson joining on August 1st 1813, and William and Sarah Smith along with Mary Malin joining on September 26th 1813. The first members living at Wirksworth (numbers 41 – 55 on the roll) joined in 1817. Thereafter members were drawn evenly from Shottle and Wirksworth interspersed with others from Ashleyhay, Stonebridge, Ireton Wood and Cowhouse Lane. By 1818 the majority of those joining the Church were coming from Wirksworth. Between August 1st 1813 and May 1818 there were 70 baptisms.

The first entry in the Church Meeting minutes is for June 1819 and concerns the appointment of two deacons for the two halves of the Church, namely, George Malin for the Shottle half, and William Smith of Stonebridge for the Wirksworth half.

According to J.H. Wood, membership of the new Church stood at 87 by 1820.

In early 1820 the Church imaginatively called Brother Richardson from Ticknall to work with Mr Barrow, with a particular responsibility for introducing the Gospel into several neighbouring villages, namely, Middleton, Cromford and Bonsall. The work at Bonsall in particular took off. A minute for November 26th 1822 records:

"Unanimously agreed that brother Job Worthy shall go to Congleton to the owner of a piece of land situate at Bonsall suitable to build a chapel upon, and try to purchase it."

The owner of the land in Yeoman Street was Robert Woodhouse, a cordwainer from Cheshire, who had inherited it from his father in 1802. The property had fallen into disrepair which meant that the Baptists could buy the plot for just £8. Job Worthy, a miner, along with Richard Smith, a Bonsall farmer, and several other tradesmen and businessmen ensured that a meeting house was built 'for promoting the Christian Religion as professed by Protestant Dissenters of the denomination of General Baptists at Bonsall.' However, in order to build the chapel they had to take out fairly extensive loans which were to feature in the life of the Shottle-Wirksworth Church for over thirty years.

News of the new chapel at Bonsall was included in the Church's report to the Association for 1823 along with the information that they had also started preaching at Carsington.

The presence of Baptists in Bonsall can be confirmed by Bishop Butler's Visitation record of 1823 which notes that there was a Baptist chapel "but not a large congregation." Six years later, in 1829, William Tomison, the Parish Clerk or Constable noted that there was one Baptist Chapel in the village with "64 people baptized".

The membership figures for the Shottle-Wirksworth Church in 1823 (including its branch at Bonsall and various preaching stations) was 189. Little wonder that the Church Meeting Minutes for 1823 record their "thanks to brother Richardson for all his faithful labours." In March 1824 the minutes record that they were also assisting with the preaching at Ashbourne.

A brief snapshot into the life and attitudes of a nineteenth century Baptist Church can be found in a couple of minutes of Church Meetings that deal with Christmas. In February 1824 a minute reads:

"That we as a Church do disapprove and discountenance the practice of Christmas singing as being unscriptural and highly unbecoming those who profess to be dissenters."

On January 10th 1837 a similar minute records their severe disapproval of Christmas singing as being "an irreligious and unsanctified practice." They instruct their minister to publish this in all places of worship.

Joseph Barrow's links with the Shottle-Wirksworth Church seem to have ended about 1825. His wife had died the previous year. J.H. Wood records Barrow's ministry finshing in 1825, and the Association report for 1826 confirms this:

"The removal of brother Barrow to Loscoe, from whence we can seldom enjoy his labours, and the long affliction that has laid aside brother Malin from preaching most of the winter, have made it a difficulty to supply all our places of preaching."

Mr Richardson's work at the Church continued until 1835 by which time he indicated that "due to distance of residence, secular employment and imperfect health he would have to lay down his pastoral duties." He was held in such esteem by the Church that on leaving he was presented with "a valuable and beautifully embossed silver cup."

In seeking a new minister the Church contacted Mr Stevenson at the Loughborough Academy to enquire about the availability of a student. As a result Mr W. Underwood came for several Sundays, and after his studies were completed he was invited for a longer period until finally he received a call from the Church to become their minister. Mr Underwood was ordained on Good Friday (March 24th) 1837.

That same month the Church had seen the necessity of increasing the organisational strength of the Church by the appointment of more deacons. There was to be a deacon for Shottle, one for Cromford, one for Bonsall and two additional deacons for Wirksworth.

Cromford never actually obtained a Baptist Chapel. In April 1838 the Church minutes record "attempts having been made to procure ground for a chapel at Cromford but without success." A deputation from the Church subsequently went to wait upon Peter Arkwright esq. "to request permission to build a chapel on his ground." But nothing can have come of this, because in May 1838 they agreed to take up a new and larger preaching room in Cromford. They were hoping to negotiate the rent down from £15 a year to £10.

Preaching at Middleton was sometimes on and sometimes off. John Spencer had initially hired out a room to the Baptists for £1 and 5 shillings. In January 1839 the Church minutes record that "we provide forms, Bible, hymn books for Middleton without delay." But by December 3rd they are "to see the landlady of the Preaching Room at Middleton and ascertain whether she will take it off our hands at Christmas next, as great unpleasantness has been experienced by its being connected with a Public House."

The decision to relinquish preaching at Middleton was no doubt influenced by the fact that a far more promising opportunity had arisen at Kirk Ireton. Here the Independents had decided to relinquish their chapel, and had handed it over (was money exchanged?) to the Baptists. In April 1841 there is reference to the Sunday School at Ireton.

Mr Underwood concluded his ministry at Wirksworth in the Summer of 1841. He had received a call to Praed street, Paddington. The previous year he had contemplated a call to a Church in Sheffield but had been prevailed upon by the Wirksworth Church to remain with them. The membership at Shottle-Wirksworth at the time of his departure was 206.

Two brief ministries followed: Mr Kerry (1842-45); and Mr Nightingale (1846-48). They were succeeded by Mr Stanion (1848-1854), Mr Yates (1854-63), and Mr Baxendale (1866-1869). Membership of the Church remained about the same, falling within a range of between 169 and 210 members. The Church resumed its preaching at Middleton, and there is reference to other preaching stations at Brayfield and Bolehill (1844). They continued with a preaching room at Cromford. The 1851 Religious Census calls the Meeting Room "Marts Club Room" and records that on 30th March 1851 there were 30 people present at the afternoon service and 30 at the evening service. In August 1853 they were given notice to vacate the room, so that by December they agreed to pay "Sister Roose of Cromford £1 per annum for the use of her house as a preaching room, on condition that she find coal and candles." The house was no longer available to them from 1858, by which time "our place at Cromford is given up for a while as we have no place to preach." (July 1858). Curiously, there is no further mention of the cause at Kirk Ireton.

The main issue for the Bonsall Church was the liquidation of its chapel debt. In January 1839 the Shottle-Wirksworth Church Meeting was requesting the Bonsall friends to make every effort to reduce the debt incurred in building their chapel. The same topic was brought up several times during 1841. On 1st January 1850 the Church Meeting encouraged the Bonsall friends "in every possible way" to reduce their chapel debt. A further £50 was paid off in May 1857. Special Chapel Debt services were held in October 1857. And in September 1859 Mr Yates, the Minister, recorded that a further £70 had been promised towards the outstanding £120 of chapel debt. He then added, "Praise God from whom all blessings flow."

The figures for the Bonsall Chapel at the 1851 Religious Census (30th March) were compiled by John Worthy who recorded that on the day in question there were 125 children in Sunday School (against an average of 131), and that there were 50 and 57 people respectively at the afternoon and evening congregations, against an average of 50.

138

The 1858 report to the Association noted that: "Congregations at Wirksworth and Shottle are good. At Bonsall and Cromford we do not perceptibly advance."

While extensive preaching and, to a lesser extent, building was going on in the branch churches and preaching stations, the main Church in Wirksworth was struggling on with a very unsatisfactory building. The building used from 1818 onwards is described vividly in Jenny Few's History of Wirksworth Baptist Church, 'Living Stones' (1986):

"Underneath was a stable; the approach was very objectionable: an uncovered flight of steps led to the room; a subterraneous passage to the school (when it was made) and a grocer's shop prevented it being seen."

There is no indication of size, but apparently there was a gallery as well as the main body of the Church. During Mr Stanion's ministry the Church bought a plot of land on North End for £140 to use as a Burial ground, but no plans were drawn up to improve or rebuild the Wirksworth Chapel until the Baptists at Shottle gained a new building.

The friends at Shottle had hitherto met in a barn owned by the Duke of Devonshire. Services must have been interesting: "The Baptists were upstairs and the cows downstairs, so that sometime the lowing of oxen could be heard during services."[1] The cows were not included in the 1851 Religious Census but amazingly 60 children attended Sunday School there in the morning of 30th March 1851, and the afternoon service saw 115 people crammed into the barn with another Sunday School with 60 children. When the Duke intimated his intention of demolishing the barn (1877) he was pressed by the Baptists to make available a new site, which he did, along with a donation of £50 towards the cost of the new chapel. Foundation stones were laid on the afternoon of May 12th 1882, and the chapel was opened in September by John Clifford. The Shottle Chapel cost £300, and acted as something of a spur to the Wirksworth friends to put in place plans to renovate their own premises.

These plans were held up by not only the cost of a new chapel but by the fact that their present site, which they wished to retain could not be enlarged until the grocer's shop and house at the front of the chapel had been obtained, and at that stage the owner had no intention of selling.

1. From the 1918 'Centenary booklet of the History of the Baptist Church at Wirksworth and Shottle.'

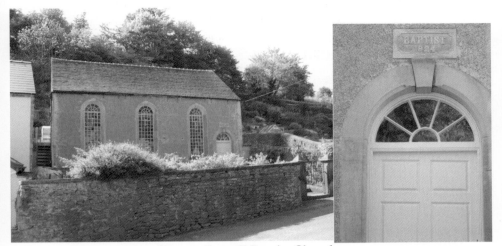

Former Bonsall Baptist Chapel

Former Shottle Baptist Chapel

CHAPTER 12

ASHBOURNE, SACHEVEREL STREET, LITTLEOVER AND WILLINGTON

As a direct result of the fervent preaching and missionary zeal of Brook Street Baptist Church, Derby several congregations sprang up in various locations. Preaching stations were plentiful in outlying villages and small towns. Just a few of these became better established and took on the status of a branch Church of Brook Street. The one exception to this pattern is the story of Sacheverel Street which came about as a split rather than a plant from the mother Church.

Ashbourne

"On Lord's Day, January 25th 1824, Mr Pike opened a large room for public worship at Ashbourn, a small town, 13 miles distant from Derby. He preached three times on the occasion; in the morning from Luke 2: 10 – "Behold I bring you good tidings of great joy." In the afternoon – "Go ye into all the world and preach the Gospel to every creature." And in the evening – "Will ye also be his disciples?"

This is the clearest account of the commencement of the Baptist cause in Ashbourne which is found in the 'Memoir and Remains of Rev J.G.Pike' edited by two of his sons in 1855. The account goes on to say that the congregations on that occasion were good. Mr Sutton preached the next Sunday, and Mr Hudson, later to be a missionary to Jamaica, the Sunday after that.

"A commodious chapel was erected towards which the late Mr John Dunnicliffe of Clifton, a member of the Countess of Huntingdon's Connexion generously contributed £100.... For several years my father devoted much time and labour to the establishment of the infant cause; but, at length, owing to various disastrous circumstances it was given up and the chapel sold."

142

Brook Street's report to the Association for 1824 refers to the fact that "since last Association we have opened a place of worship at Ashbourne."

In July 1825 Pike wrote to Rev Amos Sutton: "Last Lord's Day fortnight we had the first baptism at Ashbourn. The baptism was administered near Clifton. Seven were baptised (for we have been cautious) and afterwards formed into a Church. It was a solemn day. A great crowd assembled near the water side, and though rather noisy at times, offered no serious insult to us. I stood in the gig and preached."

The history of Ashbourne Baptist Church is best traced through its entries in the Association's annual returns. Ashbourne first made an appearance in 1827 when it was listed as having 12 members. The following year the report says: "The cause of Christ among us is suffering for want of a resident minister." By 1830 membership was up to 31 and there is a rather helpful paragraph about the new cause:

"We have had 19 added to our numbers since last year. We attribute this to the labours of our minister, brother Fogg, who settled among us in August 1829." His open air work was especially good. They mention that the debt on their Meeting House is a problem, and that they preach in three villages.

By 1831 membership stood at 58. They had Sabbath Schools in Ashbourne and Clifton. Brother Fogg had, however, indicated his intention of leaving

Membership fell back to 38 in 1833, and to 29 in 1835. They had no minister as such, but were grateful for the ministerial assistance of Mr Finn from Leicester. Through his work numbers were once again picking up.

J.H. Wood lists W. Fogg as minister of the Church from 1829 – 1831; and W. Finn as minister 1834 -36. What the disastrous circumstances were that the Pike family mentioned is impossible to discern, but in 1839 Ashbourne Baptist Church makes its last appearance in the Association reports with a membership figure of 29.

The final stages of the Church's life can be observed through the minutes of Brook Street Church. On December 18th 1840 at a Deacons Meeting it was agreed that "we ascertain what suitable supply can be obtained for Ashbourn, and what the expenses of such a supply would be." Brook Street, it appeared, had resumed responsibility for the Ashbourne work and it had ceased to function as an independent cause.

The General Baptist Repository for 1841 carries a major article entitled: "Re-Opening of the Baptist Chapel, Ashbourn."

"The above named place was closed at the latter end of 1837 principally through want pf pecuniary assistance. At that time the number of members was 19, and the congregations seldom less than about 40, and often much beyond that number, though they were often disappointed in ministerial supplies.

After regular preaching was given up, the members and others met for prayer on the Lord's Day, and the Rev J. Sutcliffe of Rocester frequently preached to them in the afternoon.

The Chapel was afterwards let for a literary and scientific institution; and for upwards of a year it was occupied by the Establishment for preaching in while the Church underwent repairs.

At length circumstances began to draw attention towards this place; and it was finally agreed it should be re-opened. It is now rented to the above institution for the Lord's Day and one night in the week.

On Lord's Day February 21st Rev J.G.Pike of Derby preached two excellent and appropriate sermons in the morning .... Congregations have been good since, and we do not enter a doubt, but that the Lord will arise and bless this part of his vineyard."

On May 31st 1841 (at the time when Brook Street were in the midst of important negotiations over the purchase of the St Mary's Gate property) the Church Meeting spent a considerable amount of time discussing the Ashbourne situation. It was formally agreed that Ashbourne be received as a branch of Brook Street. And at the end of the minute book is an extended set of notes. It explains that Brook Street now had entire management of the Ashbourne Church although the latter were responsible for their own funds. Ashbourne were to have their own membership roll which was to be seen as a branch of

Brook Street. And "that brother John Harrison be deacon for the Ashbourne branch." A list is then provided of the eight people who were to join Brook Street's membership roll, as the Ashbourne branch:

Wm Hage	Anne Brown
Anne Hage	Mary Ann Atkin
John Mansfield	John Ford
Anne Mansfield	Mary Booth

More candidates for the Ashbourne branch were received into the Brook Street membership in July, September and November 1841.

What happened in the next few years is unrecorded. But the final piece of the jigsaw can be found in the 1851 Religious Census. Under the entries for Ashbourne is one for the Church of England, St Mary's Chapel. "Licensed 1845 for the accommodation of the poor, purchased from the Baptists, cost £300."

Sacheveral Street

In 1827, twelve members of Brook Street Chapel withdrew from the fellowship and began to meet in a room at the back of a shop in Osmaston Road near "The Spot". There is little evidence available as to the cause of this separation. B.A.M. Alger suggests that the separation arose out of a "misunderstanding". Nevertheless, by 1830 this small band had formed itself into a General Baptist Church with fifteen members. They had already purchased some land on Sacheverel Street, and on 29th July 1831 a building was opened for public worship. The total cost of the building was £1000, and in Glover's 'History of the County of Derby' it was described as "a handsome brick building". A burial ground was provided at the rear of the building.

The Church developed very quickly. Sacheverel Street is first mentioned in the Association reports for 1832 when it is listed as having 20 members. The following year, however, membership had risen to 56, and by 1834 there were 82 members.

'The Church's first minister was Samuel Ayrton. He is first mentioned in the Church's minutes in December 1832, although he wasn't ordained until the 15th October 1834. By any accounts his ministry was hugely successful. By the time he left Sacheverel Street (to become a school master) the membership of the Church stood at 204. During the year 1840 the Church had seen 27 baptisms.

One of the features of those early years at Sacheverel Street was the missionary zeal of the Church. Although preaching at Littleover was recorded as early as 1812 and was very much part of Brook Street's outreach work, for some reason that work appears to have been transferred to Sacheverel Street when the split took place. The Sacheverel Street minutes are full of references to the cause at Littleover:

"That we have quarterly collections at Littleover." Nov.25th 1834

"Encourage and allow our friends to start a Sunday School at Littleover." October 1836

"Gossip meetings and experience meetings to be held in Littleover." May 1839

J.H. Wood, in his 1847 'History' puts Littleover down as a branch of Sacheverel Street, but also links it to St Mary's Gate. His way of explaining this confusing relationship is that, "The Meeting House at Littleover is used by the Sacheverel Street Church, but belongs to this society." (St Mary's Gate). In other words St Mary's Gate owned the building but allowed the management of the Church to rest with the Sacheverel Street fellowship.

The same appears to have happened with two other causes (Chellaston and Mickleover) that began life at Brook Street but which then seemed to be taken over by Sacheverel Street.

"Mr Richardson of Chellaston to let us know when a suitable place for divine worship in Chellaston becomes available." December 30th 1833

The Melbourne Church had already been involved in preaching in this district and were content to share the responsibility with Derby.

"That we adopt Mickleover as a preaching station." August 8th 1837

"That we resign Mickleover as a preaching station and take to Chellaston, the hope of usefulness being greater." September 17th 1838

The Preaching room at Chellaston was opened jointly by Mr Ayrton of Sacheverel Street and Mr Yates of Melbourne Baptist Church.

Following the conclusion of Mr Ayrton's hugely successful ministry the Church called a student, Mr Amos Smith, on a twelve months trial. His appointment was confirmed in September 1843. His ministry started extremely well. The membership of Sacheverel Street rose from 204 in 1842 to 230 in 1843 and then to 249 in 1844. But then a disastrous episode took place which rocked the Church to its foundation.

On February 18th 1845 the Church had to decide whether to allow Amos Smith to proceed through to ordination. A vote was taken. There were 127 in favour and 104 against. In the light of this unfavourable and clearly divided vote, Mr Smith sent in his resignation on 1st March. In writing to the deacons he referred to "the present divided state of the Church" and to the ill feeling towards him "by yourselves and your adherents." And although the hand writing of the letter is hard to decipher it appears that one cause of the difference between the minister and the deacons was over the long standing issue of the chapel debts, and the unwillingness of the minister and his friends to take personal responsibility for those debts.

The upshot of this disagreement was that the minister and 114 members resigned from the Church at Sacheverel Street and formed themselves into a separate congregation. And needing somewhere to meet they sought and gained permission from St Mary's Gate to meet in the old Brook Street Chapel.

Amos Smith stayed at the new Brook Street cause (which was received into the Association in 1845) for two years during which time the membership figure remained about the same. Mr J. Lewitt came for one year, but his sudden departure and the loss of several members after this caused a marked slump in the membership. So that when George Needham assumed the pastorate of the Brook Street congregation in 1848 there were only 66 members. The work picked up for a while. In 1850 there were 21 baptisms, and membership reached 126. But following Mr Needham's departure and the brief stay of E. Davies the Brook Street Church finally bit the bullet.

The 1854 Report to the Association makes it clear that St Mary's Gate wanted to sell their old chapel on Brook Street, and they gave the congregation meeting in that chapel an option to purchase the property. They were no doubt sorely tempted by the prospect, but eventually decided that they did not have the wherewithal to maintain the premises. For two months they rented rooms in Chapel Street, but effectively their decision had already been made when they declined to purchase the old chapel. On 7th June 1854 the 40 members who were left decided to close the Church and join with other General Baptist Churches around the town.

Sacheverel Street itself similarly went through a very difficult patch following the defection of the 114 members in 1845. To begin with they faced the challenge head on and called a new minister, Mr Stanion. But immediately he was faced with the same problems as his predecessor, namely the management of substantial Church debts. In 1847 he was compelled to travel round on an infamous begging case to raise £250 which urgently needed to be found. Membership rose from 145 at the time of the split to 186 in 1847, but by the following year it was becoming abundantly clear that the Church's finances were in a desperate state, and Mr Stanion resigned.

For the next three years Sacheverel Street limped along. Membership fell to 119 by 1850, and the Church were only rescued by a timely intervention from St Mary's Gate, and their assistant minister, Rev W.R.Stevenson. He chaired meetings, took services, and generally carried a huge amount of the workload for Sacheverel Street. On

February 14th 1850 a letter was sent to St Mary's Gate thanking them for their help during the past 15 months:

"That the most grateful acknowledgement of the Church be tendered to the St Mary's Gate Church and its beloved ministers for the generous, able and invaluable services they have tendered us in the supply of our pulpit during the last 15 months."

They were especially grateful for the fact that during the period of the St Mary's Gate involvement they had been able to repay a lot of their debt. The letter was signed by Mr Winfield.

Things did improve. In 1852 they were able to call another minister, Rev W.Underwood, and during his ministry (1852 - 1855) and that of his successors, S.C.Sargant (1856 - 1857); and W.Jones (1858 - 1867) membership of the Church once more increased.

1855	-	178 members
1857	-	197 members
1860	-	212 members
1861	-	231 members

In fact the Church's membership had grown sufficiently that they began to contemplate a new Church building. Even though they still owed £250 of debt in 1858, a committee was drawn up to consider a new chapel. Instrumental in these plans was Mr Robert Pegg who managed to obtain promises of £1,700 towards such a project. Rev William Jones succeeded in getting more promises from laymen in the town, and with over £2,000 already in hand Mr Pegg met with an architect, Mr Hines, at Scarborough to sketch out the design of an impressive new edifice. The design was based on an early Christian Church in Rome.

Land for the new Church on Osmaston Road, and for the manse on the other side of Charnwood Street was purchased from Mr W.T.Cox of Spondon Hall (High Sheriff of the County and Mayor of Derby). Mr Cox laid the foundation stone on February 18th 1861. The Osmaston Road Baptist Chapel was opened for worship on 3rd April 1862. The preacher at the Morning Service was the Hon. and Rev Baptist W.

Noel.   The total offerings at the opening services and meetings exceeded £600.

Littleover

The earliest reference to Baptists in Littleover is in the Brook Street minutes for 1811 which refers to members in the country divisions, of whom there were 13 associated with the village of Littleover. The census material for 1811 indicated that the population of the village was 352.

According to the St Mary's Gate manual for 1880, "About the year 1815, the Rev J.G.Pike was invited to hold a Sabbath afternoon service in the house of Mr George Cheshire." The meeting was sufficiently successful for a request for weekly services to take place in Mr Cheshire's house. These meetings carried on for several years despite strong opposition from the local squire who applied great pressure on Mr Cheshire to remove the preachers.

George Cheshire had, however, already been hosting meetings at his house prior to the invitation mentioned above. On 5th February 1813 a formal application to the Bishop of Lichfield and Coventry was made registering George Cheshire's house as a place for religious worship. Other signatures on the application were John Pike (Minister), Robert Green, Joseph Walker and Thomas Scattergood. A second house, belonging to Joseph Bullock, was registered on 6th February 1817, and in the June 'a certain barn in the possession of Thomas Radford' was licensed, the application being supported by John Pike, W. Wilkins, G. Wilkins and E. Perry, all from Brook Street Chapel.

Clearly, the small congregation at Littleover was growing, and in 1820 it was decided to construct a chapel on the junction of what is now Park Lane and Park Drive. George Measures unearthed a certificate of registration for this building dated June 6th 1821. J.G. Pike was again one of the signatories. The Brook Street minutes make reference to 'The Trustees of Littleover Chapel' (December 10th 1821), while the Quarter sessions in 1829 provided a list of Protestant Dissenting

Meeting Houses. For Littleover it stated that the Baptists had one place of worship and the sect consisted of six families.

Not everything went smoothly. As early as 1819 the Brook Street minutes refer to "Littleover in disorder." On April 11th 1831 the minutes record that, "Brother Holmes and Bolsover to enquire whether it would be advisable to commence public worship again at Littleover." The implication being that worship had been suspended for a period.

In March 1837 George Cheshire died while walking to Church. He was 67 years old. His removal would have been a heavy blow for this small community of believers.

Between 1834 and 1848 oversight of the Littleover congregation seems to have been assumed by the Sacheverel Street Church. J.H.Wood has Littleover down as a branch of Sacheverel Street in his 1847 History. The Brook Steet/St Mary's Gate minutes carry no mention of Littleover between the 1830s - 1860s after which time once again it appears as one of its branches.

In the 1851 Religious Census Littleover was recorded as having a Baptist Chapel erected in 1820 and capable of seating 100 people. The returns for Littleover indicated that 33 adults and 56 Sunday scholars attended Divine Service (in the morning or afternoon), and 43 adults in the evening. The average attendance over the previous twelve months was stated as 40 adults and 53 scholars. This was at a time when the population of the village had grown to 551.

In January 1866 the St Mary's Gate Annual Meeting reports recorded Littleover with an attendance of 28 morning and afternoon; Chellaston with attendances of between 60 and 70; and Willington with 20 members and an evening congregation of approximately 40.

Willington

The Brook Street Church first began preaching in Willington in 1826. A Sunday School banner, still in the possession of Willington Baptist Church, indicates that a Sunday School was established in 1831. The

151

first recorded candidate for baptism from Willington was Sarah Brown who was accepted for baptism on 15th September 1829. The Brook Street minutes record several other Willington candidates in 1833 and 1834. There was a special request from Willington that the 1834 baptisms could take place in Willington rather than at Brook Street Chapel, and there is a wonderful description of this baptismal service (June 8th 1834) in William Wilkins Diary:

"Baptism at Willington when Robert Gascoyne, Lot Royal and John Kent were baptised in the River Trent. Mr Pike preached from 1Cor.1 v.30,31, Matt.X1 32,33 – 140 partook of the Lord's Supper in a rick yard – the day being very fine. 210 persons went from Derby in a boat to the baptism."

In 1834 preaching appears to have commenced at Repton. In April 1836 there is reference to the "candidates at Repton," and in June 1836 to "Repton and Willington candidates". An issue of Church discipline cropped up in April 1836 regarding Samuel Eyre who had come into membership from Willington in December 1833. He was scolded for disorderly indulging in speaking against other members and getting unauthorised preachers.

The cause at Repton appears to have been short lived. A Brook Street minute (August 14th 1839) records:

"The brethren who have supplied Willington and Repton express a determination to pursue their labours no more. Under these circumstances the Church do not consider it advisable to attempt to continue preaching at Repton, and will cheerfully resign Willington to the Burton friends who it is understood are willing to adopt it."

A minute in November 1839 indicates that they had changed their mind, and that Brook Street would not give up the cause at Willington. But there is no further mention of Repton.

There is little reference to Willington during the 1840's. A brief snapshot of the life of this Baptist cause is provided by the 1851 Religious Census. Willington came in the Burton on Trent

Registration District and the Repton Sub District. They were the only Baptist cause in this Sub District, no Baptist places of worship being recorded in Mickleover, Findern or Repton. On 30th March 1851 there was no Morning or Afternoon Service at Willington, but the Evening Service saw a congregation (including Sunday School scholars) of 60. The building they were meeting in had 70 free seats.

The earliest meeting places for the Willington Baptists were private dwellings: firstly, that of Stephen and Thomas Chambers on Wharf Lane (now Bargate Lane); and subsequently that of Henry Morris, one of two blacksmiths in the village. An official preaching licence was issued by the Bishop of Lichfield and Coventry for the Chambers' house on 31st May 1830, and for Henry Morris' dwelling on 26th January 1833. Thereafter, as the congregation grew larger, they were obliged to move out of these private houses and into hired rooms. They must have occupied these rooms by the time Brook Street moved into St Mary's Gate, because Willington were offered some of their old furniture. They were certainly in the hired rooms by the time of the 1851 Religious Census.

In 1858 ten men contracted with Samuel Pegg, a local shoemaker, to purchase a plot of his land on Twyford Road. They paid £16 and 8 shillings for the land. By Good Friday 1858 a Stone Laying Ceremony was taking place, and on July 11th the Willington Chapel was officially opened. The building contract had been awarded to Edward Dusautoy, a member at St Mary's Gate. The bricks were produced and provided by Charles Dyche, also a member of St Mary's Gate. The final cost of the chapel was £220.

The first Memorandum book of Willington General Baptist dates from 1858 and it provides an account of the Opening ceremonies:

"The Rail Company kindly allowed our friends to take the double journey for one fare, so that there was a large number of people from Derby. A prayer meeting was held in the morning at about half past eight. At 10 0'Clock the Public Services began when Rev J.B. Pike [from Bourne] preached a pleasing sermon from the words, 'I was glad when they said unto me, let us go unto the House of the Lord.'"

Pike preached again in the evening ('Ye are the salt of the earth'); Rev J.Stevenson of Derby having preached in the afternoon.

"This day was one of the happiest ever spent in Willington. From first to last all was agreeable and pleasant .... Our Chapel is said to be a model chapel – it is said to be sufficient – if it had been grander it would have been too grand."

According to an article in the 'Derby and Chesterfield Reporter' for 23rd July 1858, the new chapel, which seated 120 people, was far too small to deal with all the numbers assembled on that occasion, and the services were conducted in a tent outside.

On 26th June 1859 the Church held Anniversary services. Again, the Rail Company offered return tickets from Derby at single fare. This time not as many people from Derby came which caused some disappointment for the Willington folk.

On January 31st 1859 Mary Chambers and Simon Bull were baptised at Willington in the new baptistery. William Gregory, who, along with James Walklate, was one of the principal lay preachers at Willington, conducted the baptism and preached. "The power of the Holy Spirit was with us and we had much holy joy." Gregory and Walklate were both deacons at St Mary's Gate.

The front of the Willington Memorandum gives the names of the members at Willington in 1858 (still a branch of St Mary's Gate). There were 17 altogether commencing with Thomas and Sarah Chambers and including other members of their family, plus members of the Bull family and the Cantrills. Growth at Willington was slow, steady and never spectacular. At the Annual Meeting for 1881 there is a list of the 26 Willington members of St Mary's Gate Church.

The Sacheverel Street Schools, 1931

From the 1971 Osmaston Road 'Rebuilding Story' brochure
Source: Mary Dainty

Osmaston Road Baptist Church

Willington Baptist Chapel
Source: Andrew Eley

The home of George Cheshire,
Shoemaker (1770 – 1834)
Park Lane, Littleover
First Licensed Meeting Place of
Baptists in Littleover

The original Littleover Baptist Chapel
On the corner of Park Lane and Park Drive

CHAPTER 13

ALFRETON AND RIPLEY

The origin of Alfreton Baptist Church was unlike that of any other Baptist Church in Derbyshire. Several members of Stoney Street, Nottingham moved to live in Alfreton. There was no General Baptist Church in the vicinity, although there was the Particular Baptist Church not far away in Swanwick. As a result the friends from Stoney Street applied to Sutton in Ashfield for ministerial aid which was granted. Preaching commenced in the open air during the summer of 1831, and brother Burrows, pastor of the Sutton in Ashfield Church, agreed to supply them. A room was licensed for divine worship, and brother Burrows decided to move to Alfreton. Preaching was extended to Ripley where a few other General Baptists lived, and a room was opened in Ripley by William Pickering of Stoney Street on January 13th 1833[1].

There being no mother Church in the vicinity, it was decided to form this small group as a Church in its own right. Consequently on February 18th 1833 Alfreton Baptist Church was formed with eight founder members. Of those eight, five were from Sutton in Ashfield (including Joseph Burrows and his wife, Mary); two were from Stoney Street, Nottingham, and one was from Quorndon. Brother Austin from Mansfield officially inaugurated the new Church extending the right hand of fellowship to the eight members. Joseph Burrows was chosen for the pastoral office, while brethren Ward of Ripley and Parsons of Alfreton were appointed to the deacon's office.

It was agreed to hold Church Meetings every month at Ripley and Alfreton alternately. An indication of the even split of the Alfreton-Ripley Church can be gauged by the fact that of the first 44 members to join the Church, 17 were from Alfreton and 20 were from Ripley. There were early attempts to buy land in both communities. In September 1835 a fund was established to build a chapel. In then end it was Alfreton that achieved the goal first. In 1836 (the year that the Church first appears in the Association records: with 20 members) Mr

Burrows persuaded Mr Hazlewood to sell him land and a house in Alfreton. The cost was £210. Brother Burrows was sent off on a begging excursion "to solicit the aid of our sister churches in the erection of our chapel." (July 1837). Finally, on 27th February 1838 the Baptist Chapel at Alfreton was completed. The Report to the Association that year recorded the Alfreton – Ripley Church having a membership of 30, and that the Alfreton Chapel was "regularly filled with serious and attentive worshippers." In addition to the cost of the land, the chapel itself cost £219 and there were £130 of additional costs. The total cost of the scheme was £560, and in order to meet that cost a mortgage of £250 was taken out through a Mr Silverwood. Debt repayment was to feature heavily in the life of this new Church.

1838 proved to be a difficult year for Mr Burrows. In June the Church requested him to relinquish his pastoral office due to difficulties in his 'temporal circumstances'. This presumably meant that he was having difficulty paying his creditors. In the August the Church Meeting was threatening him with expulsion if he continued to absent himself from worship. Eventually, by January 1839 he appears to be back at the helm, and the February Church Meeting declared itself satisfied with the way he was conducting his temporal affairs.

The Association Report for 1840 noted that the congregations at Ripley over the previous year had improved and were encouraging. In 1841 plans were put in place to actively look out for land on which to build a chapel at Ripley. It wasn't until 1845, however, that land was finally purchased for a place of worship and a Sunday School. The cost was £180, of which £146 was raised at a Tea Meeting. The building contract was handed to Mr Tomlinson of Belper at a cost of £418 and 10 shillings. In 1846 the Ripley Baptist Chapel was completed, along with its burial ground, which in subsequent years involved the Church in endless debates about who could and could not be buried there, and how much to charge.

Even in the midst of these celebrations there were problems. The first one concerned the pastorate. On January 11th 1847 a Special Church Meeting was called (18 members present) at which brother Burrows tendered his resignation following his decision to move to

Wolverhampton. His decision was received by the Church "with the deepest regret and sorrow." The Church held a special tea for him and his wife and gave them a purse of £10. For thirteen years he had pastored the twin Church, and had seen steady if not spectacular growth. At the time of his departure there were 54 members at Alfreton – Ripley.

But the second problem facing the Church at this time was the difficulties associated with the Alfreton branch. The 1844 Report to the Association mentioned that, "present circumstances and prospects are discouraging." Reference was also made to a "lack of union and co-operation" which hindered the advancement of the work. By 1848 they reported to the Association that, "Our Alfreton branch continues in a very languishing state." The following year it was in "a very low state." And in 1850 the Association was informed that they had "discontinued preaching at Alfreton and closed doors."

There was never any thought of re-launching the work, and all subsequent discussion was on whether to sell the property to the Primitive Methodists or to rent it to them. No mention was made in the 1851 Religious Census of either a General Baptist Church or a Primitive Methodist Church in Alfreton. There was a Particular Baptist Chapel listed for Alfreton which must have been the cause at Riddings. The General Baptist Chapel at Ripley is mentioned. It conceded that the figures for 10th March were distorted because it was the Sunday School Anniversary (418 adults and children at the afternoon service and 450 adults and children at the evening service). More helpfully, it provided an average attendance figure which was for 90 adults and 150 children in the morning services, and a general evening congregation of 180.

Almost immediately following Mr Burrows' departure the Church invited Mr Bilson of Thorpe Le Stoken, Essex, to take the pastoral charge of the Church. It was an appointment which didn't really work. In July 1849 Mr Bilson was censured by the Church Meeting for making indiscreet and unfair remarks about Church Members. Association visitors (Rev J.Goadby and Mr Staddon) were appointed to investigate the allegations which resulted in Mr Bilson handing in his resignation.

A much happier appointment was made in July 1850 when Mr W.Gray of Leicester College was invited, initially for six months. He was ordained on 30th June 1851 and remained until 1858. During his period of office the Ripley Baptist Church began significantly to grow. Membership which had stood at 54 when Mr Burrows left grew to 95 by the time Mr Gray departed. It continued to grow under his successor, George Needham. In 1856 the Ripley Baptists looked into the possibility of constructing additional galleries to cope with the extra numbers attending worship. In the event they were advised by an architect against this venture. Instead during 1857 they significantly enlarged the chapel, had a new baptistery installed, and erected new school rooms. Five tenders for the work were received and that of Mr Roe was accepted (£289.10.10). To pay for this they borrowed £250 at 5% interest from the Oddfellows Lodge, Alfreton. For seven weeks they met in the Unitarian Chapel until the new rooms were opened on 13th July 1857. By 1864 the Church's loan with the Oddfellows Society had grown to £400 at which point they decided to pay the loan off by taking out a new one with Mr John Bradshaw of Leicester who only charged 4% interest.

Mr Gray's activities were not restricted to Ripley. For several years he provided pastoral oversight and preaching at Crich Baptist Church. It was an arrangement that seemed to be mutually beneficial.

One amusing incident took place in November 1857. The Chapel clock had disappeared. (When it went missing isn't said). The clock subsequently turned up (November 1857) in a Pawnbrokers shop, the shop owner having given £1 to the person who brought it in. On discovering the clock was stolen, the pawnbroker allowed the Church to redeem the item for 10 shillings!

One interesting feature of the Ripley Baptist Church minute book is that it usually gives the number of members attending each Church Meeting. Generally, attendance was poor. In the eight Church Meetings between March and November 1854 the attendance at each respective meeting was 8, 17, 11, 10, 15, 11, 15 and 12. This gives an average attendance of just over 12. In 1855 the eight Church Meetings between February and December had an average attendance of just 8.5. The one exception each year, when attendance was quite good, was the annual meeting which also included a Tea. In January 1853 and January 1854 there were 38 members at this Tea Meeting. Church Meeting attendance improved markedly under George Needham's pastorate (1859 - 1868). In the eight ordinary Church Meetings of 1860 average attendance was 22.5.

One possible reason for the low turn out at Church Meetings was because on all financial matters in the Church it appeared that only men were allowed to vote. One suspects, as a result of this, very few women members bothered to attend Church Meetings.

A measure of the health of Ripley Baptist Church at this time can be gauged from the very upbeat report sent up to the Association in 1860:

"Our congregations are excellent and continue to increase. Our Sabbath school is in such a flourishing state that we shall be compelled to make increased accommodation during the summer. We have had an increase of 140 scholars this year. Our two adult classes now contain about 80 young people."

It was observed in the 1858 Report to the Association that they had seen 19 baptisms that year. Of the candidates 16 of them had been from the Sunday School.

The growing Church once again had to look for extra capacity. In February 1862 a committee was formed to see how the chapel could be enlarged. In March it was decided that "until we have more room in our chapel we have our baptisms in the morning instead of the evening." In April they agreed to press ahead with the erection of new galleries. 150 collecting cards were to be produced and put into the hands of the congregation.

On Christmas Day 1862 the Church Meeting requested brothers Bembridge and Argile to find the best way of borrowing £120 for the erection of galleries. By the end of 1863 the galleries were in place. Money raised at the Anniversary Services that year was put towards the gallery fund rather than the alleviation of chapel debt.

Reference has been made in several chapters about the practice of holding Church Meetings on Christmas Day (as some measure of protest at the worldly festivities that generally marked the occasion). At Ripley we are given a full picture of the pattern of their Christmas Day arrangements. In 1861 a Church Meeting was held at 3.00pm, followed by a Tea Meeting at 4.00pm, more food at 5.00pm, "and an experience meeting afterwards to which we invite candidates and enquirers." There were 26 members present at the Church Meeting that Christmas Day. The following year they held the Church Meeting at 2.00pm and the experience meeting at 6.00pm. On Christmas Day 1863 they held a prayer meeting at 10.00am as well as the Church Meeting at 2.00pm and the experience meeting at 6.00pm.

Church growth continued. This involved more building plans (for an extension to the school rooms and a small vestry for the minister), although it isn't clear that these plans were activated. It also involved some embryonic Church planting initiatives.

"That we endeavour to establish a General Baptist interest at Codnor, and that it be a branch of this Church." (Dec.31st 1860)

"That brethren Needham and Bembridge make enquiry respecting a preaching room at Codnor." (Jan. 28th 1861)

"It appears very desirable that we endeavour to establish a branch interest at Marehay.... request brethren Bembridge and Sandars to find a preaching place and Sabbath school." (Jan.26th 1863)

By the 1860s George Needham must have been an old man. These were days long before pension provision allowed anyone to retire. You worked until you dropped. In June 1863 Mr Needham was given a month's rest. In the August he was relieved of ministerial duties for six months. On December 26th 1864 the Church Meeting agreed to increase his salary to £100 "and request him to become a full member

of the National Society for Aged and Infirm ministers, Birmingham."
When Mr Needham did eventually resign (September 1868) the
Church recognised that they had no alternative but to accept it.

1. According to a 1933 Centenary bazaar booklet kindly leant to me by
   Miss Freda Searson the key figure in the formation of the Ripley
   Baptist Church was Mr Thomas Ward who settled in Ripley in 1829.
   A committed Baptist, Mr Ward was convinced that there was
   sufficient scope for a Baptist cause in Ripley. The original meeting
   room (presumably opened by William Pickering) was in a loft over a
   stable in Malthouse Yard.

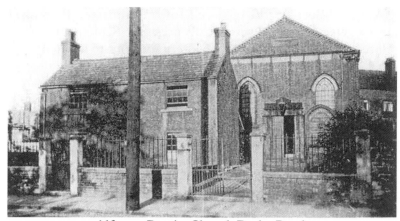

Alfreton Baptist Chapel, Derby Road.
The Chapel was taken over by the Primitive Methodists, and subsequently
became the site of the Watchorn Memorial Methodist Church.

Ripley Baptist Church
Source: Des Greenwood

CHAPTER 14

BURTON ON TRENT[1]

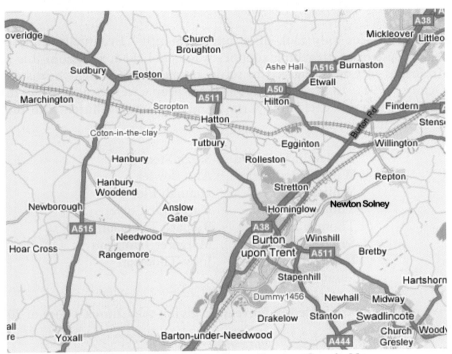

21st Century Map of the Area. Source: Google Maps

The Particular Baptists

"In the year 1780, by the all-wise providence of God, Richard and John Thomson, natives of Lancashire, and members of the Church at Accrington, removed to Burton."[2]

The Thomsons were Calvinistic in doctrine, and were unable to find any Church in their vicinity that suited their taste. They occasionally visited Melbourne Baptist Church and even went as far as Derby. Eventually they received encouragement from Mr Mills, the minister of Shepshed Baptist Church, some 18 miles away, who agreed to come and preach for them. Richard Thomson purchased a property at the bottom of New Street part of which was licensed for Public Worship on January 14th 1790, and on January 26th public worship was conducted for the first time by Mr Mills of Shepshed.

At first services only took place once a month. Eventually a more regular system of preaching supplies was established, and from this a Mr Briggs of Codnor agreed to settle among them as their minister. (October 1791). In September 1792 twelve people were baptised, and in the October it was decided to form themselves into a Church with the following founder members:

Benjamin Millward	Sarah Stenson
William Redfearn	Ann Bowler
William Pearce	Hannah Fletcher
Thomas Bowler	Katherine Colyer
Thomas Thomson	Richard Thomson
Samuel Dickenson	Margaret Thomson
Hannah Bridgnorth	John Thomson
Susannah Thomson	

Five new members joined in November giving the Church a core of 20 members.

One of the problems of the fledgling Church was its inability to retain and attract suitable ministers. With such a small membership-base the salary they were able to offer was often derisory. Mr Briggs left after two years. A succession of probationary appointments was concluded by one party or the other after six months. In the first 77 years of its existence the Particular Baptist Church in Burton was served by 18 ministers who stayed on average 2.7 years!

A good deal of information about the Particular Baptists in Burton can be gleaned from the very helpful Northamptonshire (Particular) Baptist Association minutes and reports.

Burton on Trent is first referred to in the Association records in 1792 at the Nottingham meeting at which William Carey preached his famous, 'enlarge the place of your tents' sermon. The minutes record that on the Thursday morning of the Association gathering, "Brother Briggs of Burton on Trent" concluded the public meeting in prayer.

It is not until the following year (1793) that Burton is listed with the other churches of the Northamptonshire Association which were in receipt of the annual Circular Letter. It continues to appear in the subsequent years. The 1800 list, however, does not include Burton on Trent, and a foot note explains that the Church has in fact dissolved.

The 1802 Circular Letter reports that Burton on Trent "is now revived and again admitted to fellowship with us." And its name appears on the list of churches once again. There was clearly then a break in the continuity of the Particulars meeting in Burton.

The 1803 minutes make reference to "Brother Fletcher of Burton on Trent." Fletcher had been a key figure in reviving the cause after it had imploded through backbiting and mutual recrimination. He was to serve the Church in two spells: from 1802 – 1808, and again from 1815 until his death in 1820. Fletcher was the longest serving minister throughout the Church's first 80 years, and he was in every way the most significant. It was during his first period as minister that the Church constructed its first building which became known as Salem Chapel.

The original Indenture for the land on Station Street (or Cat Street as it was originally called) was signed in March 1803. The agreement was between Richard Thompson[3] who owned the land, and the Trustees for the Church, William Christian, John Palmer, William Nicholls, Benjamin Churchill, James Newell, Thomas Fletcher, William Jacques, John Simpson, John Houseman Barker, William Douglas, Thomas Thompson, Thomas Bentley and John Bates. The sale was for £35.

The Salem Chapel which was subsequently built on Richard Thompson's land was a most impressive edifice. The following year

(1804) a Sunday School was founded, and ten Testaments and forty spelling books were purchased to instruct boys and girls.

Membership at the Church remained quite modest. The Northamptonshire records only begin to list membership figures from 1813 at which point Burton had 43 members. It had fallen to 37 in 1814, a year in which no pastor is identified with the Church. In 1821 the recorded membership was 42, and a new pastor is identified with the Burton Church, Mr Jones.

Burton withdrew from the Northamptonshire Association in 1834, shortly afterwards joining the newly formed Nottinghamshire and Derbyshire (Particular) Baptist Association. Records indicate that in 1838 Burton had a membership of 51. Their minister was Mr Owen who had left by 1840. It was in 1840 that the Church Meeting agreed to open the Communion Table to "pious Paedo Baptists." Subsequent statistical information can be gleaned from the Notts. and Derbys. Reports:

Year	Membership	Minister
1843	58	Morris
1844	65	Morris
1845	67	---------
1847	51*	---------
1848	57	Pulsford
1849	59	Pulsford
1851	63	Pulsford
1852	60	----------
1853	66	Aitchison
1854	70	Aitchison
1855	69	-----------
1856	61	Davies
1857	58	----------
1858	67	Jenkins
1859	92**	Pitt
1860	103***	Pitt
1861	111	Pitt
1862	118	Pitt

* 10 excluded, 3 withdrawn, 6 dismissed, and 3 dead
** 15 baptisms
*** 22 baptisms

Alexander Pitt's ministry at Salem, Burton, was clearly highly significant. As well as this substantial growth in membership, the Church also oversaw the construction of a new chapel for their branch Church at Walton on Trent. On June 10th 1859 Charles Haddon Spurgeon visited them for meetings. A tent was put up on the premises of Messrs Bass and Co. and some 4,000 people heard the famous London preacher. A tea was held in the malt room of the brewery.

On December 31st 1860 Salem Chapel was severely damaged by fire. This disastrous event certainly didn't impede the progress of the Church which continued uninterrupted. Fund raising and rebuilding commenced almost immediately, and the chapel was re-opened in October 1861 with additional land having been purchased at the rear of the site. The preacher on Sunday October 20th was Rev James Ackworth, Principal of Rawdon College.

The General Baptists

The General Baptists in Burton emerged from the tiny village of Cauldwell. Joseph Norton had been responsible for starting a work in Cauldwell back in the eighteenth Century. In 1785, with 40 members, Cauldwell separated from Melbourne and formed themselves into a separate Church. They had 82 members in 1816.

In 1814 the Cauldwell friends licensed a room for holding services in Burton on Trent. The room was at Bond End. Mr Moss officiated for a while. Burton continued as a branch of Cauldwell until 1822 at which point the Burton friends went independent.

William Norton was minister at Cauldwell from 1827 until his death in 1853. He served both the Cauldwell Church and also the Baptist cause at Overseal. On his death the friends at Cauldwell and Overseal sought union with Burton on Trent and from that point onwards they appear in the Association returns as branches of the General Baptists in Burton.

The first minute book for the General Baptist Church in Burton provides details of the early beginnings of their cause.

"On Lord's day January 30th 1825 a small General Baptist Church was formed at Burton on Trent by Mr Orton of Hugglescote and Mr Pike of Derby consisting of 11 members whose names are as follows:

Thomas Norton	Sophia Ball
Elizabeth Norton	Sarah Nutt
George Kinstone	Mary Spare
Ann Kinstone	Mary (??)
Thomas Lovett	Martha Lovett
Ann Norton (later Ann Shaw)	

Thomas Norton and George Kinstone were elected deacons in April 1825.

Sarah Nutt died in November 1847. Thomas Norton died in 1862. But Elizabeth Norton was still heading the membership roll as late as 1873.

The Burton Church first appears in the records of the New Connexion in 1825 when it had 15 members. The following year membership was recorded as 28, and by 1827 it had grown to 33. The entry in the New Connexion reports for 1827 stated that Burton had preaching at three places. One of these was Barton under Needwood.

One of the very earliest entries in the Burton minutes states that Joseph Sanders (or Landers) of Barton under Needwood had been given notice to quit his house at Midsummer "in consequence of allowing us to preach in it." There was a house available to him but it cost more than he could afford. The Church was asked whether they would consider paying £4 towards the rent on the understanding that preaching could take place there. They decided that they would pay the rent for twelve months.

170

The Church Meeting in October 1826 learned that the cause at Barton would no longer receive Home Mission support. The Church at Burton, therefore, decided that they would persist with supplying preaching on Sunday evenings at the station until Lady Day next "with the assistance of brother William Norton who has agreed to go once a month."

The Burton Church continued to supply Barton under Needwood throughout 1827, and in July 1828 their patience was rewarded when news was received that a chapel had become available in Barton which they agreed to lease for seven years. Brother Pike was to open the chapel on September 28th 1828.

The third place of worship referred to (other than Burton itself and Barton under Needwood) was most likely at Yoxall. But a decision was reached in October 1828 to give up the place of worship there. It was, however, a feature of the General Baptists in Burton that they were highly committed to establishing congregations elsewhere. In December 1829 there are references to prayer meetings at Stretton. Preaching at Stapenhill was suspended. In October 1839 there was an application from friends at Newall for a meeting to be held in that place.

The cause at Stretton seemed to last quite some time. In April 1838 it was decided to conduct preaching at Stretton on Sabbath mornings. In September 1840 the Stretton Room was to be fitted up for worship. It was opened on the first Sunday in November. In November 1841 there was reference to the Stretton Anniversary and the Sunday School at Stretton.

Newton Solney was another focus for General Baptist activity. In July 1839 it was agreed to commence preaching at Newton "provided an opening presents itself." In May 1840 the Burton Church agreed to take a room at Newton and to pay half the rent for the friends there. In their report to the Association that year they reported that "Our congregations at Burton and Stretton are good," and that, "We have just opened a place for divine worship at Newton Solney." The report to the Association for the previous year (1839) stated that as well as

171

good congregations at Burton, "at Sutton also our attendance is very good, but we want a more suitable place for worship."

Sadly, virtually all these fledgling causes initiated by the Burton Church failed, and disappeared from the record books. In February 1831 it was reluctantly agreed to give up the Chapel at Barton under Needwood. The cause was becoming a drain on finances, and the Burton Church no longer had even one member living there. A cause at Repton seemed to have promised well, but in April 1845 the Burton Church had to recommend to the Repton friends that they give up the Room and dispose of the furniture. When Mr Peggs came from Ilkeston to be the minister at Burton (March 1846), he agreed to visit the branches at Walton, Stretton and Horninglow. Stretton was still being supplied two years later, after which mention of it seems to disappear.

A cause at Walton on Trent did survive, but from the mid century onwards this was identified with the Particular Baptists in Burton, and appears as a branch Church of Station Street right into the twentieth century.

The one major Church planting success story for the General Baptists in Burton was the cause at Swadlincote. (See Chapter 21).

It is impossible to speculate on the reason for the failure of these various preaching initiatives. Economic factors may have played a part. In its report to the Association in 1842, the Church records:

"The past year has been one of considerable depression in Burton through the entire stoppage of the cotton factories. Our Church and School have both suffered from it; whole families who used to worship with us being obliged to leave the town."

The loss of one or two key people would certainly have affected the viability of some of these fledgling causes.

Whether a cause or effect of the failure of the preaching stations, from the 1840s onwards the Burton Church began to concentrate its energies on the work in the town itself. This was reflected in a growing conviction about establishing a more substantial place of worship for the General Baptists in Burton.

The membership of the Church had grown slowly.

Year	Membership	Year	Membership
1829	64	1843	100
1830	78	1844	102
1837	47	1845	102
1838	63	1846	101
1839	71	1847	99
1840	80	1848	100
1841	91	1849	108
1842	96	1850	96

As early as 1829 the Church was recognising the limitations of its current building given the growing numbers. In its report to the Association that year it maintained that, "Our Meeting House is crowded with hearers, and we believe it will soon be too small for us." In the 1843 report to the Association the same complaint was being made: "We still feel the want of a better Chapel." A committee composed of the male members of the Church was formed in August 1842 to consider "the proposed new Chapel." But delays continued.

One of the reasons for the delays was indebtedness. The 1852 report to the Association again expressed the need for a larger place of worship in a central location, but admitted that they still carried a debt on the present building. But progress was being made.

In May 1852 the Church Meeting heard that £30 had been paid off the existing chapel debt that year. In January 1853 land was applied for on which to build a chapel. A committee looking into building a new chapel was set up, and in the August the Church began to consider selling the existing (old) chapel.

On December 12th 1853 the Church Meeting heard that plans had been designed by Mr Booker of Nottingham (later to draw up the plans for the monstrosity at Ilkeston!) which would provide them with a new building capable of seating 450 people. The cost of the new chapel was estimated at £650 in June 1854. A tender was accepted in August; foundation stones were laid in September 1854; and on 18th September 1855 the new chapel on Union Street was opened. In December 1858 it was reported that the £81 surplus from the sale of the old chapel (after the outstanding debt on the old chapel had been cleared) would be used to pay off some of the debt on the new chapel. The new building was known as Zion Chapel.

Unlike several of the Derbyshire (and Staffordshire) Churches, the General Baptists of Burton had a good track record with its ministers. As early as 1828 they were reporting to the Association that with the presence of a regular minister they would "speedily have an increase of members." Mr Naylor appears to have been their first minister in 1830. Thereafter they had a succession of steady and fruitful ministries.

J.Staddon	1840-1844
J.Peggs	1846-1849
R.Kenney	1850-1867

Richard Kenney in particular had the most extraordinary ministry at Burton. He had previously served the Church at Wirksworth between 1842 and 1845 during which time the Church there had grown steadily. He arrived at Burton in February 1850 having completed a period as minister at Fleet and Holbeach. During his tenure of office at Burton the Swadlincote Church came into being; the new chapel at Union Street was completed; and the membership virtually doubled.

Year	Membership	Year	Membership
1850	96	1857	151
1851	98	1858	161
1852	95	1859	160
1853	91	1860	162
1854	133	1861	162
1855	143		
1856	149		

He retired from the ministry at Burton due to the precarious state of his health. A Farewell Tea Meeting was held for him on Monday 2nd December which he was sadly unable to attend. He presided over an extremely orderly transfer to his successor. Richard Kenney preached his farewell sermon on the morning of November 10th 1867. His successor, Mr Tetley commenced his ministry on the evening of the 10th November!

Burton's report to the Association for June 1868 paid glowing tribute to Mr Kenney, noting that thirteen of the Sunday School scholars had joined the Church in the previous three months, and making the all too apparent observation that Mr Kenney's ministry with them over 18 years had been "abundantly blessed."

Richard Kenney retired to Cheshire where he continued to exercise ministry in the Baptist cause at Wheelock Heath. He died on February 6th 1879 aged 75 years.

In June 1871 Church Membership stood at 189, of which 174 members belonged to the main Church on Union Street, with 15 members belonging to Overseal and Cauldwell.

1. Chapter 1 which explored the earliest Baptist congregations in the county made reference to the 1654 loyal address to the Lord Protector of England from representatives including those "of the Church of Christ at Derby and Burton on Trent." Although no official records of a Baptist cause in Burton exist for that period, the annals of British history do mention one Edward Wightman (1566 – 1612) who was born at Burton on Trent; ran a successful mercer's business in the town; and according to some reports was a minister of the Baptist Church in Burton. Wightman's claim to fame was that following a petition to King James 1 expounding his beliefs he was tried, found guilty of heresy and sentenced to death. Part of the charges against him was his claim "that the baptising of infants is an abominable custom." Wightman was the last person in England to be judicially burned alive. He was tied to the stake, set on fire, and perished at Lichfield on April 11th 1612.

2. Although the records and minute books of Salem Baptist Church are no longer available, a typed record which draws extensively on the early books was put together probably by Rev W.H.Haden minister of the Church between 1933 and 1939. This particular quote is apparently from the first minute book of the Church. I am grateful to Keith Malin for making these sources available.
3. Rev Haden's version insists on spelling 'Thomson' without a 'p'. The copy of the Land Indenture, however, spells Richard Thompson, and all subsequent members of the Thompson family with a 'p'. They are undoubtedly the same people.

Salem Baptist Chapel, Station Street, Burton
Source: Keith Malin

Zion Baptist Chapel, Burton, built 1855 which stood just to the right of the
later building. From 'more post cards of Burton on Trent and district' 1984
Source: Margaret Wombwell

177

CHAPTER 15

AGARD STREET PARTICULAR BAPTIST CHAPEL

Source: Derek Palmer

There have been two attempts to document the history of Agard Street Chapel in the last 30 years. J.M.Shipley put together a very capable school project in the 1970s and a second, anonymous account was put together in 1988. Both studies draw upon a much earlier work produced in 1896, "The Centenary Manual with Historical Review of Trinity Baptist Church, Green Hill, Derby." This latter work was put together by the then pastor of the Church, Rev W.F.Harris. The Historical Review was initially presented on the evening of 21st January 1896 by Rev Harris as part of the centenary celebrations of the Church. It is a very careful and thorough piece of research. It acknowledges the shortage of old records covering the early years of the Church but inspite of that puts together a very compelling story. Although the date of formation of Agard Street Chapel is 1795 according to the nineteenth century Baptist Handbooks, in point of fact the Derby Mercury for 1794 contained a notice for June 5th which stated that: "The Baptist Meeting House recently erected on Nuns' Green, will be opened on Thursday 12th inst. by the Rev Richard Hopper of Nottingham and the Rev Samuel Pearce of Birmingham." Rev Harris managed to trace the date of the Church back before 1794. By trawling through the minutes of the Northamptonshire Association, which at that time included Derby, he discovered that at the Annual Meetings in Northampton in June 1793, "the sum of three guineas was voted to encourage supplies for the new interest at Derby." In fact we can probably go back even further than that. In a bundle of old documents found in the safe of Trinity Baptist Church, Green Lane is a 'Schedule of Deeds and Documents relating to property belonging to the Trustees of Agard Street Chapel and Schools, Derby." The first entry in this schedule is for the 16th & 17th November, 1792: "Conveyance by lease and Release from the Commissioners under the Derby Paving Act to Mr Archer Ward."

Archer Ward lived at Mill Hill House in Derby. The old chapel at one time possessed several memorial plaques, one of which was inscribed with the words: "Sacred to the memory of Archer Ward esq., of Mill Hill House, Derby, who died July 22[nd]1800 aged 56 years." Archer Ward's widow, Ann, subsequently married Mr Thomas Swinburne. They both continued to serve as benefactors of the Church, Mrs Swinburne furnishing the chapel with its first organ in 1827 at a cost of £170.

The congregation clearly prospered because by 1828 the original chapel had been expanded to double its original size and new school rooms had been added. Evidence for this exists in another valuable document uncovered in the safe at Trinity Baptist Church. Simply entitled, "Derby Case" the slim volume contains a list of the contributors to the expansion of the chapel during the ministry of Rev C.E. Birt. Mr Swinburne heads the list of contributors with a donation of £50 followed by one of £20 from Mr Bridgett. There was a sum of £22 and 12 shillings collected at Nottingham and a sum of £43 "collected at the reopening of the place after the enlargement was completed." The book also contains the names of 51 contributors who raised money

179

amounting to £55.15.6 "At Birmingham." So clearly Association support was bearing dividends for the Agard Street cause. The front cover of the "Derby Case" book also contains a small amount of useful historical information:

"The Baptist Church at Derby was formed by a few individuals from the Church at Nottingham about 20 years since, when through the kindness and liberality of a worthy member (long since deceased) a piece of ground was purchased and a place of worship erected thereon at his own individual expense. The interest has never been in that state to call for enlargement until the arrival of the Rev Caleb Evans Birt under whose ministry it has pleased the Great Head of the Church to cause a revival of religion and a considerable increase of members and congregation, so that an enlargement of their place of worship has become necessary – the estimated expense of which amounts to upwards of £500."

According to Rev Harris' Centenary History "the first Pastor of the Church appears to have been the Rev William Smith, who came from Enfield to Derby, and whose name is inscribed on the Communion Cup given to the Church in 1806, and also on the Trust Deeds." In fact, William Smith may not have been the first minister.

Unearthed from the safe at Trinity Baptist Chapel, is a document entitled "Register of (non-parochial) births." In 1837 a national system of registering births came into existence. Prior to 1837, however, the registration of births was carried out either by the parish Church or by a non-parochial Church. Agard Street has a complete register of these births from the commencement of the Church until 1837. The first of these recorded in the book is "William, the son of George and Henrietta Blore(?) of the parish of St Peter, Derby," who was born 8th May 1793. The name is publicly attested on the same date as the child was born, and the person completing the entry is "Benjamin Dickinson, Dissenting Minister."

The Register clearly shows that the cause at Agard Street was active by 1793 even if the chapel itself wasn't completed until the following year, and apparently Benjamin Dickinson was the first pastor of the Church.

He completed the first 11 entries in the book covering the years 1793 – 1796 on each occasion signing himself, "Dissenting Minister". James Newall signed entry numbers 12 – 15 and number 19, but Benjamin Dickinson continued to sign numbers 16, 17 and 18 which cover the year 1797 and at least one entry for the year 1798:

"Benjamin, the son of Benjamin and Sarah Dickinson, of the parish of St. Alkmund, Derby, was born the 27th January 1798 and his name publickly attested by me, Benjamin Dickinson, Dissenting Minister."

No further entries are recorded from Mr Dickinson which would suggest that he served as minister at Agard Street from 1793 – 1798. James Newell signed all subsequent birth registrations (23 of them) covering the years 1799 – 1803. On one occasion (entry 26) he signed himself, "Dissenting Minister" and on another as "Minister", but on all other occasions he merely added his name without title. William Holmes signed the occasional registration in 1798 after Mr Dickinson's departure. He signed a couple more in 1804 and 1805 after which all entries (25 of them) for the period 1805 – 1812 are signed by "W.Smith, pastor". Mr Newall signed another birth in 1813 and Mr Holmes signed two more in 1813 and 1815. Between 1815 and 1827 there were 64 births registered, signed by the pastor C.E. Birt. Between 1827 (August) and June 1837 when the book closed the births were recorded by Pastor William Hawkins.

Clearly then the register of non parochial births throws new light on that period for which there is little documentary evidence. There was a Particular Baptist cause present in the town by May 1793 and the first Dissenting Minister was Benjamin Dickinson. Whether Mr Newall himself served as minister at Agard Street or whether he was a minister from out of town or even a deacon of the Church is less clear. But by the time William Smith arrived in 1805 there had already been 12 years of ministry taking place at the Church.

According to the Centenary History, Caleb Evans Birt, the son of the minister at Cannon Street Church, Birmingham, was ordained as Pastor at Agard Street on 25th June 1825. The non-parochial register

181

reveals he was present in the Church for two years prior to his ordination. Membership records indicate that in 1817 there were 47 members at Agard Street. Mr Birt's ministry blossomed. In 1819 Messrs Holmes and Bridgett, deacons of the Agard Street Church, wrote to the Association meeting at Dunstable a very upbeat record of how things were going:

"When we compare our present with our former state and circumstances, we are ready to say, what hath God wrought!! Through rich mercy we are favoured with the constant ministry of the Word and Ordinances, and we trust, that they have had their desired effect, as some have been awakened and have given themselves up to the Lord, and walk with us in the fellowship of the Gospel – Our congregation continues very pleasing and encouraging. We hope the Lord has some gracious work still to carry on among us."

The building extension work was carried out in the 1820s and by the time Mr Birt left to take up a new position at Portsea[1] in 1827 the membership stood at 64. Mr Birt's successor built on this good work. William Hawkins served as pastor for 14 years. The Centenary History tells us that he was a graduate of the University of Edinburgh, a learned man and one who was very interested in helping to train and equip people for the Baptist ministry. He started "A School of the Prophets" in his own home as a means to prepare candidates prior to their ministerial training at Stepney College. Several young men went through Rev Hawkins' school many of whom played significant roles in the denomination during the rest of the century including the future Dr Brock of Bloomsbury. In addition to this work Hawkins was also appointed the first Secretary of the newly formed Baptist Association for the counties of Nottingham and Derby in 1835, a post which he held with some distinction.

Hawkins' achievements at Agard Street were impressive. By the time he left the Church in 1841 the Church Membership had risen to 148. In addition there was a Sunday School with 140 scholars and 28 Teachers. Hawkins moved to Clifton in Bristol where he died in March 1853 aged 62.

Another document from the Trinity safe reveals the interest and enthusiasm generated by the Baptist Missionary Society at this time. The document is a set of Annual Accounts and Reports for the Derby Missionary Association and covers the period 1827 - 1838. The first public meeting was held in the Agard Street Chapel on Monday evening 24th September 1827 with Mr Bridgett, of Agard Street, in the Chair. Mr Bridgett subsequently became Treasurer to the Derby Group. The first resolution was moved by Rev J. Jarman and seconded by Rev William Yates of Calcutta:

"That this meeting, sensible of the value of co-operation in all Christian efforts and regarding the Baptist Missionary Society as eminently worthy of confidence and support, resolves to unite with the churches in Nottinghamshire, Derbyshire, Sheffield and Burton upon Trent in aid of that institution."

A second resolution, moved by Rev C. Stowell of Swanwick and seconded by Mr Felkin of Nottingham, set out the rules of the new 'Association' which included an annual collection for the BMS in each Church as well as a report on proceedings of the previous year.

Annual Meetings involved the delivery of sermons which on Sunday 21st September 1834 were given by Rev C.E.Birt of Portsea. The public meeting the following night was chaired by Rev J.G.Pike of Brook Street General Baptist Chapel.

A further letter from this period is of some interest. The Annual Meeting of the Teachers took place in the Schoolroom, Agard Street, on 9th January 1837. Mr Hawkins was in the chair and there were 24 teachers present. What should have been an uneventful occasion turned out to be very difficult. The Treasurer, Mr Flower, was scolded by the meeting for paying bills from the School account amounting to £1 and 3 shillings which should have come from the Building Fund Account. He was ordered to "debit himself with the sums so paid" until such time as he could recoup the money from the trustees of the Building Fund. The meeting issued Mr Flower with a humiliating list of rules to ensure that he didn't err in this way again. Ironically the same meeting issued a vote of thanks to Mr Flower for his services as

Treasurer, and he was "requested to continue that office during the ensuing years!"

Following the departure of Rev Hawkins and a twelve month pastorate by Rev John Ford of Dublin, the Rev W.F.Poile of Keppel Street, London became minister at Agard Street from 1842 – 1846. According to the Centenary History "owing to some unhappy differences arising between him and a section of the congregation, he left with about 63 other members and worshipped in a chapel that had been vacated by the New Jerusalem Community." This break away group eventually began to fizzle out with 33 of its former members returning to their old Church which was now enjoying a new prosperity under Rev A. Perrey (1846 – 1854). By the time Rev Perrey departed, the membership was back up to 114.

There then followed a series of short ministries which reflected and contributed towards a very difficult time in the Church. With the departure of Rev Joseph Wild in 1869 the Church had only 36 members and clearly could not afford paid ministry. The Centenary History records what happened next:

"For the next ten years the Church struggled on without a pastor, gradually dwindling in numbers, largely owing to the decline of the neighbourhood, but partly due to dissensions among its members, until in 1872 it had but 14 members, and its yearly income was but £6 13s 5d while its expenditure was £13 1s 2d. The Association Report for that year says of it: 'The cause is getting weaker and weaker. A deputation has been sent to meet the friends, but owing to the low condition of things it was nearly impossible to give any practical council.'"

1. While minister at Portsea, Caleb Evans Birt was elected President of the Baptist Union in 1836. He died in December 1854

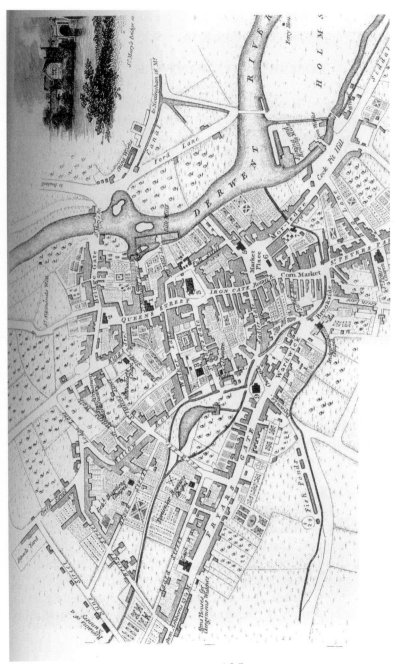

Section of E. W. Brayley's 1781 – 4 map of Derby as amended in 1806:
Agard Street Particular Baptist Chapel is centre left: Brooke Street General Baptist Chapel is just above.
Source: J. Brian Radford and Derby Local Studies library

185

CHAPTER 16

LOSCOE AND SWANWICK

The Baptist Church on High Street, Loscoe has a foundation stone set over the front porch with the date 1722 and the initials F.T. If this was the date for the foundation of the Baptist Chapel it would be significantly earlier than any other Baptist activity in the county outside of the Peak District. In fact looks can be deceiving.

Following the Restoration of Charles the Second in 1660 there were rapid and systematic moves to roll back the ecclesiastical innovations of the Commonwealth period, and to restore the Anglican structures once more. During the Commonwealth period Presbyterianism had formally been adopted as the state Church. Implementation of the Presbyterian structures varied throughout the country, but in Derbyshire there were considerable strides made towards a full blown Presbyterian system of government with Wirksworth in particular having a very comprehensive structure.

The return of the Anglican Church again in 1660 created something of a dilemma for many of the clergy who had firmly espoused the Presbyterian cause. Some found it possible to set aside vows and covenants they had so recently made. But many found it impossible to make this convenient adjustment. The result became known as The Great Ejection.

Nationally 1,156[1]clergy were removed from their livings. In Derbyshire the number was 39. At first many of these conscientious pastors tried to stay in the same communities they had worked in to provide pastoral support for their congregations. But the draconian Clarendon Code included one piece of legislation deliberately designed to thwart such endeavours. The Five Mile Act banned any ejected minister from living within a five mile radius of their previous parish. This was to prove extremely distressing for many of these devoted men.

John Hieron had been the Rector of Breadsall. He was firm in his Presbyterian convictions having been sponsored for the post by Sir John Gell in 1644, himself of a Presbyterian (albeit worldly) persuasion. On being ejected from his parish he spent some time in Little Eaton, but the Five Mile Act compelled him to find a new home, and through the auspices of the squire of Kilburn, Mr Hunter, he was provided with a home in Loscoe.

The Conventicle Act prevented any large gatherings of non-conformist worship, and Hieron did what many of his contemporaries were forced to do, namely hold meetings in private homes. Not until August 1672 was John Hieron officially registered as a dissenting preacher by which time he had established a significant group of followers. Hieron died on 6th July 1682 and was buried in Heanor Parish Church yard. In the national Presbyterian records John Hieron is officially the first minister of the Presbyterian Church in Loscoe.

Other ministers were to follow. Josiah Rogerson served from about 1705 – 1717. John Platts served until 1735. Daniel Lowe served from 1735 -1744, while Judah Jagger was there from 1759 – 1783. In 1722 the Presbyterians built their first chapel in the village. Francis Tantum, the Loscoe Clockmaker, appears to have been responsible for the construction. It is his initials that appear alongside the date on the foundation stone. The stone was originally at the rear of the building and was overlooked by Tantum's house which was just above the chapel.

What exactly happened next is still not entirely clear. C. Gordon Bolam in his study of Presbyterianism[2] suggests that the Presbyterian congregation in Loscoe had declined. This may have been due to the fact that Judah Jagger, their minister, was Unitarian in sympathy, an outlook not shared by the whole congregation. Such a move within eighteenth century Presbyterianism was certainly not unusual. Mansfield Presbyterian Church moved that way in the first half of the century and was called Mansfield Unitarian Church by 1791. Fred Harrison follows Bolam in stating that a wave of evangelical fervour was responsible for shifting the Loscoe Presbyterians in the opposite direction and securing them for the Baptist cause by 1783.

Bolam provides more evidence for his claim. The Trust deed of 2nd May 1836 recites that "about the year 1782 Francis Mather and others became possessed of the chapel premises." He further identifies the ring leader of the Baptist party as William Fletcher who he describes as a "revivalist".

However, what little Baptist evidence that is available doesn't provide support for the idea of a struggle for the soul of the Loscoe Presbyterian Church. Rippon's Baptist Annual Register for 1794 provides a correction to an earlier entry made in the Register that had suggested there were two Baptist Churches, one at Codnor and one at Loscoe. The correction is provided by brother Hopper of Nottingham who insists:

"There is no Baptist Church at Codnor. Formerly our people met there in a house, before they borrowed the meeting at Loscoe of the Presbyterians who are all dwindled away."

Rippon's original confusion was quite understandable. By 1786 the Baptists had applied for admission into the Northamptonshire Particular Baptist Association. But from 1786 when they first appear in the Circular Letters their name is down as Codnor. The 1787 minutes record that at one of the day-time sessions, "Brother Fletcher of Codnor concluded in prayer". And even at the famous Nottingham Association meeting in 1792 which contained William Carey's great missionary sermon and saw the launch of the Baptist Missionary Society, "Bro. Fletcher of Codnor" was again in the thick of the praying. It wasn't until the Shepshed meetings in 1794 that the Circular Letter was issued to Loscoe. An asterix alongside the name Loscoe refers to the simple footnote: "This Church formerly met at Codnor."

We have, therefore, two slightly differing accounts of the transition of the Presbyterian Church in Loscoe to that of a Particular Baptist Church. One account looks to the internal struggles within Presbyterianism for an explanation. (The revivalist Fletcher possibly acting as a catalyst for the move into the Baptist camp). The other account looks to a Baptist cause beginning in Codnor in the 1780s which eventually became sufficiently strong to move into the old Presbyterian building once the Presbyterian congregation had abandoned the place.

One final piece of illumination can be found in the 'Heanor Sunday School Union Magazine' for July 1890 which does begin to make sense of this conflicting evidence. Dealing with the history of the Loscoe Baptists it confirms that the Baptist cause was established in the village in 1783 and that prior to the Baptists meeting in the building it had been a Unitarian cause. The Unitarians, however, met with little success "and there being a few Baptists in the neighbourhood, arrangements were made for each party to hold services on alternate Sundays. This went on for some time, the Baptist services becoming very popular whilst the Unitarians met with little success. Ultimately it was mutually agreed that the Baptists should take possession of the Chapel."

C.G.Bolam records that the legal transfer of the building to the Baptists took place in 1783 when two Baptist nominees were added to the existing private (Presbyterian) trustees. But it still doesn't quite explain why the Baptist cause in that part of the county was still being called Codnor in Association minutes right up until 1794.

William Fletcher was ordained at Loscoe on September 29th 1784. According to notes written into the front of the Swanwick Baptist Church Minute book, the ordination followed "many months trial of the gifts of our brother Wm Fletcher." He was unanimously recognised as someone "whose labours have been much owned by the Lord for our edification and for the conversion of sinners." Taking part in the ordination was Mr Shaw of (....ingham), Mr Jones of Lincoln, and Mr Hopper of Nottingham. The notes regarding the call and ordination of Mr Fletcher were signed by Francis Skerritt, Peter Grundy, Susannah Fletcher, Samuel Skerritt, Elizabeth Barnes and Francis Mather.

The Loscoe Baptist Church Pastor was clearly a man of great energy, determination and vision. Both J.W. Bunting in his history of Swanwick Baptist Church (1931) and David Tarlton in his 1948 study of Loscoe Baptist Church quote the same story.

"At length, one bright evening in May 1794, at the close of a Sabbath Day's work at Loscoe, the Spirit of God directed [Fletcher's] steps to Swanwick. He knocked at the Mill House door and asked for a pulpit." Being informed [not surprisingly!] that there wasn't a pulpit in the house he requested a kitchen chair upon which he delivered a sermon to those who would gather round him on the text, "Arise, call upon thy God". The sermon had such an impact on some of those present that six people wanted to know more and subsequently became baptised members of Loscoe Baptist Church.

During that summer open air services were held at Swanwick. From the autumn they hired a barn by the Cross Keys Public House. But there was growing demand for a chapel to be built at Swanwick.

"Accordingly, on land which had recently become the property of the Pastor, there was erected in 1796 a humble and unprententious meeting house." It was the first place of Christian worship to be built in the village of Swanwick.

In 1804 it was decided that the Swanwick Church should become separate from Loscoe. Between 30 – 40 members of the Loscoe Church formally (and amicably it would seem) constituted themselves as the Swanwick Baptist Church. A minute book for Swanwick Baptist Church was obtained which starts from 1804. The book is still available (and in the possession of Mr John Staniland). It has suffered greatly over the years from water damage and the edges of the pages are eaten away so that it isn't possible to ascertain the names of the founder members beyond the first 29. But head of the list is William Fletcher (Pastor) followed by the six names who previously had witnessed Mr Fletcher's ordination.

The Minutes of the Northamptonshire Particular Baptist Association for 1805 record that:

"The ministers and messengers deliberated on the case of our friends at Loscoe and Swanwick, and resolved that the latter Church, as well as the former, be acknowledged as in connexion with this Association."

Although Mr Fletcher had formally joined the new Swanwick Baptist Church he would appear to have retained pastoral oversight of Loscoe as well. The Northamptonshire Circular Letters and Association records only list the names of ministers from 1814. But in that year William Fletcher is recorded as minister of both churches. From 1815 to 1821 Loscoe have a Mr Swaine as their minister.

As a valuable insight into the respective strength of the Particular Baptist Churches in the county at this period, the Northamptonshire records provide the following Church Membership information:

	1814	1817	1819	1821
Burton	37	41	42	42
Loscoe	41	58	65	56
Swanwick	76	85	105	106
Derby (Agard St.)		47	79	94

Quite clearly the new plant at Swanwick was outstripping the mother Church. While Loscoe made steady progress over this period, Swanwick had a membership almost twice that of Loscoe.

In 1810 Swanwick began a Sunday School. In 1823 they erected a gallery in the chapel at a cost of £80. In 1826 Rev Charles Stovel of Stepney College became co-pastor with Mr Fletcher. The Church continued to grow so that in 1827 the whole chapel was enlarged to accommodate some 600 people. The project cost £511.

The Swanwick Church, however, continued the same missionary spirit it had shown throughout Mr Fletcher's tenure of office. Persistent work in Riddings was rewarded, and in 1813 a chapel was built in the village. It cost £261 to build and two years later it had to be enlarged again at a further cost of £127. Fletcher was joined by William Shawcroft, a native of Riddings. Shawcroft had been converted through the ministry of Abraham Booth and had joined the George Street Baptist Church, Nottingham before returning to Riddings in 1806. Concerned about the spiritual welfare of his village which even by this stage had no public place of worship, Shawcroft established a Sunday School in Riddings several years before the chapel was built.

Shawcroft was honoured for his work of bringing Christian presence into the village, and a memorial to him still stands in St James' Churchyard.

Money was becoming a challenge for the churches. But the Swanwick team were becoming quite skilled and persuasive in raising the requisite sums. According to the 'Church Book' of Swanwick Baptist Church, Mr Shawcroft raised £42 from meetings held in Nottingham. Rev Fletcher collected a further £28, and £15 was raised at the opening of the Riddings chapel.

William Shawcroft died in 1831. William Fletcher died the same year. His death announcement appeared in the Baptist Magazine for that year:

"On Friday, January 14, the Rev William Fletcher of Swanwick, in Derbyshire, departed this life in the 86th year of his age. His labours in the Lord's vineyard have been continued through the unusual period of 60 years. Nearly 15 of which were spent in forming and cherishing the Church at Loscoe. The last 35 years he was pastor of the Christian society at Swanwick, which had been gathered by his occasional labours. Many souls were given to his ministry."

A memorial plaque to the ministry of William Fletcher can be found in the Swanwick Baptist Church expressing deep appreciation for his long ministry. A careful study of the plaque reveals an original text which indicated that the mortal remains of William Fletcher were interred beneath the walls of the present building.

Charles Stovel carried on at Swanwick until 1833 when he moved to London. In 1872 he became president of the Baptist union.

The Swanwick Church Book then introduces another highly eventful chapter:

"In the Spring of 1834 it pleased the great head of the Church to send among us our present, highly esteemed pastor, Mr Pottenger, for which we devise now to record our grateful acknowledgement [.....] We are also enjoying a greater state of spiritual prosperity than at any former period."

Thomas Pottenger was from Aberdeen. Bunting, in his history of the Church, said that Pottenger suffered in the early years from (unfavourable) comparisons with his illustrious predecessor. Nevertheless, he weathered the storm, and during his seven years as pastor the Church blossomed. Financially he was something of a genius. The Swanwick – Riddings Church still had outstanding debts on their buildings despite earlier efforts. Pottenger collected £40 from Nottingham, £12 from Leicester, and £10 from Arnsby towards the liquidation of the chapel debts in 1839. Thomas Baker of Reading gave a further £100, Mr Evans of Allestree Hall gave £25 and Mr B. Haslam collected £20 in Belper. In four years the Church cleared a debt of £540

The numerical growth of the Church matched its financial success. In 1834 the Derbyshire, Staffordshire and Nottinghamshire churches withdrew from the Northamptonshire Baptist Association to form their own Notts. and Derbys. Particular Baptist Association. Records from their minutes again point to the measurable growth in the membership of the Swanwick & Riddings Church.

	1837	1838	1839	1840
Burton		51	51	46
Derby	129	135	139	148
Loscoe	40	52	52	58
Swanwick & Riddings	94	102	111	148

The informative Association returns indicate the number of baptisms in each Church. The Swanwick & Riddings Church had 12 baptisms in 1838; 13 baptisms in 1839; and 40 baptisms in 1840. Consequently, it must have been a bitter blow when Mr Pottenger left the Church. He enjoyed subsequent ministries in Bradford and Newcastle, and was for a period a tutor at Rawdon Baptist College.

In 1842 Rev Isaac Davies became pastor of the Swanwick & Riddings Church. The phenomenal growth of the twin Church continued. Membership stood at 162 in 1843 (22 baptisms that year), rose to 180 in

193

1845 (15 baptisms) and peaked at 191 members in 1847 (18 baptisms and 450 scholars).

On 13th June 1847 Mr Davies wrote to the Church at Swanwick explaining his intention of going full time at Riddings now the latter had decided to become a Church in its own right. This must have come as something of a blow to Swanwick, but they describe the separation as carried out with "entire cordiality and good will," believing it to be "conducive to the well being of the Church in the locality."(25th June). The goodwill extended so far as to allow Riddings folk to be buried in the Swanwick burial ground, and even to allow Mr Davies to carry out the burials!

In truth, the Swanwick Church never recovered from the separation. Riddings faired better. Mr Davies stayed three years. In 1848 Riddings had 103 members (Swanwick had 76). In 1849 Riddings had 119 members (21 baptisms that year). In 1850 they had 121 members (10 baptisms that year). But following Mr Davies' departure membership stagnated at both Swanwick and Riddings, and never approached the combined membership total of 1845 & 1847.

This had clear financial implications for both churches. With a smaller membership there was less money available to pay for ministry. In 1853 the Swanwick Church wrote to Riddings (copy of the letter extant in the Church Book) proposing a way round the financial difficulties that had prevented them looking for a pastor:

"We call to your remembrance former days when we composed one Church and enjoyed times of refreshing from the presence of the Lord. Since our separation we have been unhappy and now we wish to be re-united in the bounds of mutual love and confidence."

A Special Church Meeting at Swanwick on 11th July 1853 was delighted to receive news that Riddings acquiesced in their suggestion. They would stay as two churches but share the same minister. But before plans had even had a chance to get under way Riddings reneged on the deal and proceeded to call their own minister. "The union was dissolved." (October 1853).

194

Unable to afford a minister of their own Swanwick were forced back onto an old alliance with Loscoe. On November 28th the two churches invited Mr W.J.Stuart to the joint pastorate on a salary of £50 per annum. The Swanwick Church were so desperate for Mr Stuart to accept the invitation that a separate letter from the members was issued to the prospective minister: "We believe your visit a few weeks ago was in answer to our prayers; that you are the man God has sent, and the minister we approve." Rev Stuart accepted the invitation and began his ministry at Swanwick and Loscoe on 4th January 1854.

The arrangement lasted for three years. But the next 16 years were to prove something of a wilderness for all three churches.

Loscoe began the period well. In 1848 they had undertaken a major extension and improvement to their old buildings. New windows were put in place, an extended gallery and a new frontage. Its membership grew under Rev Stuart (77 in 1854; 103 in 1858). A Day School was built on Furnace Lane in 1858, and the following year they hosted a public meeting at which Charles Haddon Spurgeon was the preacher. White's Directory provides a useful snapshot of Loscoe at this period (1857):

"Loscoe: a small village which forms the south extremity of the parish, about 1 mile from Codnor, contains 90 houses and 451 inhabitants, of whom 233 were males, and 218 females. The Butterley Company have a colliery here, from which hard and soft coal of good quality is obtained. The Baptists have a chapel, erected in 1848, at a cost of £476 raised by subscription. It is a good brick building and will seat about 400 persons. The old chapel having become too small and much dilapidated, the present one was erected on the site; the Rev W.J.Stuart is the pastor."

From that point on, however, things began to slide. Membership at Loscoe faltered under Rev Hicking (1859 – 1862), and by 1873 had dropped to 55.

Riddings' membership fell, rose and fell again. In 1873 when W. Crick was their minister they had 95 members. Swanwick meanwhile just couldn't get a minister. They were without ministerial support for several years from 1858, and in their report to the Notts, Derbys and Lincs Association in 1873 they rejoiced that thanks to the Association's endeavours they had a minister (Rev T. Hayden) after 12 years without a pastor. Swanwick's membership was 44 in 1854, grew slightly under Rev Stuart and then plunged to 36 in 1859 and 27 in 1860. Little wonder they couldn't get a minister. In 1873 the membership had risen to 45.

For Riddings in 1873 their concern was to liquidate the debts still owed on the chapel building. They wanted and needed more space for the Sunday School but couldn't proceed until the outstanding debts were cleared.

For Swanwick the concern was survival. Their problems were in part due to the establishment of other Christian churches in the village. St Andrews Church of England, the Primitive Methodists and the Free Church Methodists all set up during the 1850s and 1860s. A little later they had severe competition from the Christadelphians. But despite their difficulties Swanwick still tried to establish the Christian cause in other communities. As early as 1840 a minute in the Church Book mentioned brethren Hill, Haslam and Davies inspecting a piece of land at Oakerthorpe with a view to building a chapel. It wasn't until 1864, however, that Amber Row, South Wingfield was established with a small group from Swanwick. By 1873 South Wingfield had just 15 members and were looking to Swanwick for ministerial assistance.

One interesting footnote: the main volume of Notts and Derbys Particular Baptist Association minutes covers the period 1838 – 1863. In 1838 there were 14 churches in the two counties with a combined membership of 1122. By 1863 there were 17 churches with a combined membership of 1127. In 25 years there was no growth at all among the Particular Baptist churches of Nottinghamshire and Derbyshire.

1. The figure of 1,156 Dissenting clergy was provided by the Compton Returns. Fred Harrison, who supplied these figures in his M Phil thesis, believes them to be a significant underestimate.

2. 'Presbyterianism in Derbyshire, Leicestershire and Nottinghamshire 1640-1780' - C. Gordon Bolam: unpublished University of Nottingham thesis 1957

William Fletcher ca.1746 - 1831

Swanwick Baptist Church   Loscoe Baptist Church

William Shawcroft (1847 – 1831)
Source: Judith Smith

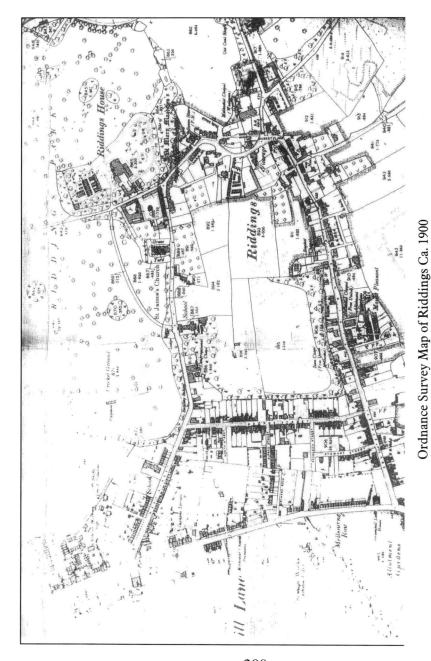

Ordnance Survey Map of Riddings Ca. 1900

Baptist Chapel is bottom centre on what is now the corner of High Street and Bradshaw Avenue. Note the plethora of other Chapels scattered throughout the village.

CHAPTER 17

THE 1851 RELIGIOUS CENSUS

On Sunday 30th March 1851 every person attending a place of worship in England and Wales was counted. The Census was organised by Horace Mann. The findings, when published in 1853, provided a tremendous shock to the Established Church. They demonstrated that large numbers of the population attended no place of worship at all, and that of those who did attend, slightly more frequented Non-conformist chapels than their own Anglican Church. Horace Mann's revelations were to provide a spur to Church of England extension work in the latter part of the century.

Although there was talk of repeating the exercise, in fact the Religious Census was never carried out again. As such it represents a unique insight into the numerical strength of the churches in mid century.

At the time of the Census, and subsequently, commentators have questioned the veracity of some of the information provided. There was a suspicion that Non-Conformists may have inflated figures to exaggerate their actual strength. One of the features of the Derbyshire Returns, however, is honest acknowledgement where figures on that particular Sunday were at variance from the norm. The use of average figures by some of the churches is an attempt to provide a more accurate picture than can be gleaned from one random Sunday's attendances.

These figures for the Derbyshire Baptist Churches have been culled from the excellent study: "The Derbyshire Returns to the 1851 Religious Census" (1995) edited by Margery Tranter in collaboration with David A Barton and Paul S Ell. That study can be viewed in the Local Studies Library in County Hall, Matlock. It covers all the churches in the county. I have simply isolated the Baptist information.

One further word of explanation should be provided. The questionnaire asked those submitting information to list the number of sittings (or places) in that particular building. 'Free' sittings refer to those seats/pews in the building that were not permanently rented out to families from the Church, and which could be occupied by anyone. The 'other' sittings refer to rented pews. The churches only gradually moved over to a system of weekly offerings from the 1860s. Prior to that, and well after that in some churches, 'pew rents' were the principal source of Church income. A family would pay their rent perhaps each quarter. It guaranteed them the same place in Church each week. Pew rents often varied in price; those more prominent pews with better vantage of the pulpit would attract a higher price and were usually in the possession of leading families within the Church. The consternation often expressed in Church minutes about people not taking up their places in Church stemmed from the annoyance caused by people having to stand throughout services while perfectly good pews lay empty. Once a family had rented a pew then no-one else had the right to occupy that place.

BURTON ON TRENT REGISTRATION DISTRICT
Repton sub district

Willington Baptist Church: There was no morning or afternoon service. The evening congregation was composed of adults and children amounting to 60 in total. There were 70 free seats in the building.

Gresley sub district

Walton on Trent General Baptist Meeting House: The building accommodated 40 people. The general congregation at the afternoon meeting was 27. (This would have been the only meeting of the day). The average attendance was 30. The information was submitted by James Pulsford[1], Minister, New Street, Burton on Trent.

Caldwell[2] General Baptist Chapel: erected 1778. The building had 160 sittings. The attendance in the morning was 60; at the afternoon service it was 80. William Norton, Minister, submitted the returns.

BASFORD REGISTRATION DISTRICT

Greasley sub district

Loscoe Particular Baptist Chapel: erected, before 1810

Sittings: free	400
Afternoon general congregation	200
Evening general congregation	250

Remarks: no regular minister; having supplies; Signed by Thomas Hickling, Deacon, Loscoe.

Ilkeston sub district

Langley Mill, General Baptist New Connexion: erected October 1839

Sittings: free	129,	other 21
Afternoon congregation		54
Afternoon Sunday School		89
Total		143
Evening congregation		75

Remarks: this place of worship and the school connected with it are out of debt and are in the hands of trustees appointed by the society. There is no gallery in it, but it is in contemplation to erect one: Signed by Wm Stanhope, Deacon, Langley near Heanor.

Heanor General Baptist Chapel: erected 1849

Sittings: free	200,	other 35
Afternoon congregation		51
Afternoon Sunday School		53
Evening congregation		67
Total		171

Signed: Thomas Cresswell, local preacher, Shipley, Derbyshire.

Ilkeston General Baptist Chapel, South Street: erected before 1800.

Sittings: free	104;	other,	196
Morning congregation			91
Morning Sunday School			107
Total			198

Afternoon Sunday School	122
Evening congregation	204

Signed: Caleb Springthorpe, Minister, Lawn Cottage, Ilkeston.

ASHBY DE LA ZOUCH REGISTRATION DISTRICT
Hartshorn sub district*

*The Derbyshire Returns actually include SEVEN Baptist churches under the Hartshorn sub district. I have only included the THREE which are touched upon in this study and which traditionally have been seen as part of the Derbyshire Baptists. The four churches not included are Measham, Netherseal, and two chapels in Appleby.

Overseal General Baptist Chapel: erected 1840

Sittings: free	244;	other	3
Morning congregation			20-24
Morning Sunday School			24
Evening congregation			75

Average attendance in the morning congregation was 20, and in the Sunday School about 24. Average evening congregation was 40. Signed, William Norton, Minister Cauldwell.

Hartshorne General Baptist Chapel: erected 1845

Sittings: free	84;	other	16
Afternoon congregation			45
Afternoon Sunday School			19
Total			64

Average general congregation = 45

Remarks: The society at Hartshorne is a branch of the General Baptist Church at Melbourne. Signed, John Henry Wood, Deacon, Melbourne.

Ticknall General Baptist Church: erected 1795, enlarged/rebuilt 1817

Sittings: free	240,	others 14
Morning congregation		0
Morning Sunday School		49
Afternoon congregation		117
Evening congregation		250

Remarks: This chapel is occupied once a fortnight by the Wesleyan Reformers, there being present that evening about 250 persons. Signed, John Brooks, Deacon, tailor, Ticknall.

SHARDLOW REGISTRATION DISTRICT
Melbourne sub district

Melbourne General Baptist Chapel: erected 1750; rebuilt and enlarged 1832.

Sittings: free	150	other 420
Morning congregation		200
Morning Sunday School		250
Total		450

(Note: the congregation was below average on 30th March on account of a special occasion)

Evening congregation	350

The average Morning congregation was usually about 250, and the average Morning Sunday School was about 290, giving an average Morning total of about 540 children and adults. The average evening congregation was about 480.

Remarks: Between 60-100 of the smaller Sunday School children attend a separate service in the school room on Sabbath Mornings instead of coming into chapel. These are included in the Morning total. Signed: Thomas Gill, regular Minister, Melbourne.

Weston on Trent: General Baptist Chapel, erected 1845

Sittings: free	90	other 16
Afternoon congregation		20
Evening congregation		50

Signed, Matthew Newbold, manager, Weston on Trent

Shardlow sub district

Wilne General Baptist Chapel[3]: erected 1830

Sittings: free	80	other 70
Evening congregation		70

Remarks: The service is held in this chapel every Sabbath evening, and every Tuesday evening. Signed, Thomas Gilbert, manager, Shardlow.

Chellaston★ General Baptist Chapel: erected 1832

Sittings: free	70
Afternoon congregation	16
Evening congregation	30

The average afternoon congregation was about 20, while the average evening congregation was about 35.
Signed, John Stevens, chapel steward, farmer, Chellaston

★The population of Chellaston is given as 499

Littleover General Baptist Chapel: erected 1820

Sittings: free	100
Afternoon congregation	33

206

Afternoon Sunday School	56
Total	89

Evening congregation	43

The average afternoon congregation was about 40 with some 53 children in the Sunday School, giving an average total of about 93. Signed, Joseph Hadfield, local preacher, 94 Park Street, Derby.

Stapleford sub district

Sawley* General Baptist Chapel: erected 1800.

Sittings: free	145	other 160
Afternoon congregation		130
Afternoon Sunday School		68
Total		198

Evening congregation	120

Signed, William Bennett, Deacon, Sawley

* The population of Sawley with Wilsthorpe is given as 1001

DERBY REGISTRATION DISTRICT
St Alkmund sub district

Baptist, Duffield Road[4] – "as it was not erected for our denomination I cannot ascertain when it was built."

Sittings: free	50	other 250
Morning congregation		87
Morning Sunday School		59
Total		146

Evening congregation	132
Evening Sunday School	27
Total	159

The total average attendance for the morning children and adults was given as 190, while the average evening congregation for all age groups was 200.

Remarks: Ours is an infant cause commenced in a new part of town. Signed, John James Owen, 2 North Parade, Derby.

General Baptist Chapel, Brook Street*: erected 1802

> *This is the group that split away from Sacheverel Street and which gained permission from St Mary's Gate to occupy the old Brook Street Chapel.

Sittings: free	581	other 119
Morning congregation		94
Morning Sunday School		60
Total		154
Afternoon Sunday School		53
Evening Congregation		270

The average Morning congregation and Sunday School was 185. The Afternoon Sunday School normally received about 90 children, while they normally expected about 190 people on Sunday evening.

The report was signed by George Needham, Minister, 32 Sacheverel Street, Derby.

All Saints sub district

Baptist, St Mary's Gate: erected 1750, built as a gentleman's mansion, converted into a chapel 1842.

Sittings: free	322	other 878
Morning congregation		308
Morning Sunday School		116
Total		424

Afternoon congregation	157
Afternoon Sunday School	58
Total	215

Evening congregation	711

Signed, John G. Pike, Minister, Derby

St Peter's sub district

Particular Baptist, Agard Street: erected before 1800

Sittings	500
Morning congregation	160
Morning Sunday School	60
Total	220

Afternoon congregation	40 [at a Sunday School Prayer meeting]
Afternoon Sunday School	71
Total	111

Evening congregation	192

The average afternoon total was given as 180 while the average evening congregation was given as 300. The entry was signed by Abraham Perrey, M.A, Minister, 2 Kingston Terrace, Derby.

General Baptist, Sacheverel Street: erected 1830

Sittings: free	70	other	480
Morning congregation			160
Morning Sunday School			150

Evening congregation	240

Signed, John Winfield, Deacon, 47 Sacheverel Street, Derby

Milford General Baptist Chapel: erected 1849

Sittings: free	150
Afternoon congregation	90
Evening congregation	80

Signed, William Parkinson, Deacon, Milford

Duffield General Baptist Chapel: erected 1830

Sittings: free	100	other	170
Morning congregation			62
Morning Sunday School			57
Total	109 [should be 119!]		

Afternoon Sunday School	67
Evening congregation	95

Signed, Samuel Jennels, Deacon, R.W station, Duffield

Windley★ Baptist Chapel: erected 1847

Sittings: free	100
Morning Sunday School	17
Afternoon congregation	50
Evening congregation	25

Signed, George Houlgate, manager, Hazelwood.

★The population of Windley was given as 219.

Horsley sub district

Kilburn General Baptist Chapel: erected 1832

Sittings: free	65	other	36
Morning congregation			43
Evening congregation			60

Remarks: no regular minister.   Signed, Thomas Bennett, Deacon, Kilburn, Derbyshire.

Smalley General Baptist Chapel: erected 1788

Sittings: free – 168; let – 132; standing –	50
Morning congregation	80
Morning Sunday School	51
Total	131
Evening congregation	160

The entries were made by Edward Roe, Deacon, who explained that the Church alternated between a morning and an afternoon service, but they always had an evening service. On 30th March it happened to be a Morning Service.   Mr Roe estimated that an average afternoon attendance was about 200 people, including a Sunday School of 50. On special occasions the Church had seen between 400 – 450 people present.

Belper sub district

Belper Baptist , Bridge Street: erected, cannot tell

Sittings: free	250	other	100
Afternoon congregation			50
Evening congregation			60

Remarks: no regular minister at this place.
Signed, Abraham Booth, member, Crown Court, Bridge Street, Belper.

Ripley sub district

Ripley, General Baptist of New Connexion: erected 1846

Sittings: free	100	other	120
Afternoon congregation			248
Afternoon Sunday School			170

Total		418
Evening congregation		300
Evening Sunday School		150
Total		450

The entries were made by William Gray, the Ripley Minister. He pointed out that this was an exceptional Sunday since it was the Sunday School Anniversary, and, therefore, numbers were inflated. On an average Sunday afternoon there would be about 90 in the general congregation, and in the evening about 180.

Crich General Baptist Ebenezer Chapel: erected 1839

Sittings: free	152	other 48
Morning Sunday School		90
Afternoon congregation		50
Afternoon Sunday School		84
Total		134
Evening congregation		130

Signed, Thomas Mills, Elder, Crich, nr. Alfreton

Alfreton sub district

Swanwick Particular Baptist Chapel: erected before 1800

Sittings: free – 200; other – 300;
standing – strangers, poor etc

Attendance not taken; averages only supplied

Morning congregation	150
Morning Sunday School	180
Evening congregation	300
Evening Sunday School	220

Remarks: Service for the Sunday School at Ripley lessened the attendance at our chapel yesterday [hence the absence of actual figures and the supply of averages instead.]
Signed, Richard Miller, Minister, Swanwick, nr. Alfreton

Alfreton [Riddings] Particular Baptist Chapel: erected 1813

Sittings: free	204	other 136
Morning congregation		150
Morning Sunday School		107
Total		257
Afternoon Sunday School		107
Evening congregation		360
Evening Sunday School		40
Total		400

Remarks: 122 members in Church fellowship
Signed, John P Barnett, Minister
Jno. Knight, Deacon, Riddings, Alfreton

Wirksworth sub district

Wirksworth General Baptist Chapel: erected 1818

Sittings: free	260	other 140
Morning congregation		70
Morning Sunday School		100
Total		170
Afternoon congregation		50
Afternoon Sunday School		120
Total		170
Evening congregation		180

Signed, Richard Stanion, Baptist Minister, Wirksworth

Shottle General Baptist Chapel: erected – upper room exclusively used.

Sittings: all free
Morning Sunday School	60
Afternoon congregation	115
Afternoon Sunday School	60

Signed, Joseph Malin, Deacon, Lamb House, Shottle.

ASHBOURNE REGISTRATION DISTRICT
Brassington sub district

Bonsall* General Baptist Chapel, Yeoman Street: erected 1824

Sittings: free	250	other 50
Morning Sunday School		125
Afternoon congregation		50
Evening congregation		57

Signed, John Worthy, Deacon, Yeoman Street, Bonsall

*Bonsall's population is supplied; 1,449

CHESTERFIELD REGISTRATION DISTRICT
Ashover sub district

Amber Row[5] Particular Baptist: school room erected about year 1812

Sittings: free	80
Morning Sunday School	69
Afternoon congregation	10
Afternoon Sunday School	71
Total	81
Evening congregation	42

Signed, John Lomas, manager, Swanwick, nr Alfreton

Chesterfield sub district

Chesterfield, South Street, General Baptist: room now used as a chapel

Sittings: free	70
Morning Sunday School	24
Afternoon congregation	20
Afternoon Sunday School	25
Total	45

Evening congregation	35

Signed, Ed. Bombroffe, steward, Packers Row, Chesterfield.

Dronfield sub district

Dronfield Baptist Meeting House

Sittings: free	76	other 24
Morning congregation		25
Morning Sunday School		64
Total		89

Afternoon congregation	14
Afternoon Sunday School	85
Total	99
Evening congregation	82

Signed, Edwin Lowe, Dronfield

BAKEWELL REGISTRATION DISTRICT
Bakewell sub district

Bakewell, Ashford Lane General Baptist Chapel: erected: supposed about 1770.

Not used, but standing void and no services performed there. Sittings: 100
Remarks: The Chapel has been closed about 4 years.
Signed, George Birley, one of the persuasion, Ashford, nr. Bakewell.

Cromford General Baptist: Meeting room or Marts Club room – erected before 1800. Not exclusively used.

Sittings: all free,	standing 100 persons
Afternoon congregation	30
Evening congregation	30

There is no Sunday School

Remarks: The Room has of late been occupied in Mornings by the Reform Wesleyan Methodist denomination and the attendance has been about 50 on an average.
Signed, Samuel Bown, assistant Deacon, Market Place, Cromford.

HAYFIELD REGISTRATION DISTRICT
Glossop sub district

Charlesworth Particular Baptist Chapel: erected 1835

Sittings: free	72	other	176
Morning Congregation			100
Morning Sunday School			54
Afternoon congregation			200

Remarks; we, the Particular Baptists at Charlesworth, had a Room for Religious Worship from 1825 - 35 when the Chapel was built.
Signed, George Beard, Minister, Charlesworth, nr Glossop.

CHAPEL EN LE FRITH REGISTRATION DISTRICT
Chapel en le Frith sub district

Chapel en le Frith, Bowden Edge★, Barmore Clough General Baptist: preaching room erected 1841

Sittings; free	150
Afternoon congregation	27

Afternoon Sunday School   15
Total   42
Signed, Isaac Hallam, officiating Minister, Sittinglowe, nr Chapel en le Frith.

*The population of Bowden Edge is given as 977

1. James Pulsford was the minister at the Particular Baptist Church in Burton. The General Baptists commenced the work at Walton, but the Particular Baptists maintained the work there throughout the nineteenth century.
2. Sometimes spelled 'Cauldwell'.
3. I have found no other reference to a Baptist Chapel at Wilne
4. I have found no othere reference to a Baptist cause on Duffield Road
5. This is South Wingfield Baptist Church

11. All Baptists

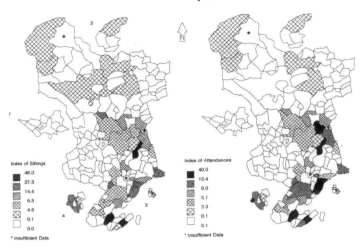

12. General Baptists

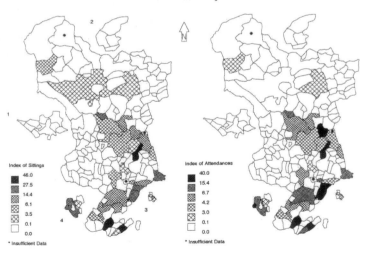

Source: The Derbyshire Returns to the 1851 Religious Census, edited by Margery Tranter in collaboration with David A Barton and Paul S Ell

218

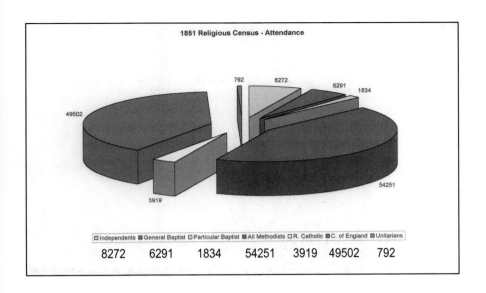

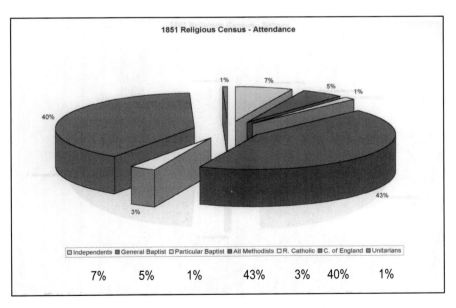

Source: Margaret Wombwell: Local Studies Library, Matlock

PART TWO

1860'S – FIRST WORLD WAR

CHAPTER 18

CHESTERFIELD

The present Baptist Church in Chesterfield traces its beginnings back to the year 1861 and a meeting room in the Market Hall. In fact there was Baptist witness in the town for over a century before that.

The first recorded Baptist preacher in Chesterfield was Rev Abraham Booth from Kirby Woodhouse. Ford's 'History of Chesterfield' has him down as one of the early ministers who supplied a group of Independents in the town. While the 'History of Friar Lane Baptist Church, Nottingham' (by Godfrey and Ward) describes Booth's book, 'The reign of Grace' as 'Sermons first preached in Sutton in Ashfield and some of them afterwards at Nottingham and Chesterfield, where he occasionally laboured with great acceptance." His preaching in Chesterfield can be dated as falling between 1765, the year he finished as Minister of Kirby Woodhouse, and 1769 the year he was ordained as minister of Little Prescott Street, London.

It may have been coincidental, but Abraham Booth underwent a significant theological transformation during the 1860s that shifted him from being a convinced General Baptist, immersed in the life of the Barton Group (witness to Francis Smith's marriage), to becoming an out and out Particular Baptist as evidenced by his mature writings and his ministry in London. When a Baptist congregation was established in Chesterfield it was of Particular Baptist persuasion. In reality this probably owes more to the energies of the Particular Baptists of Sheffield than the theological legacy of Abraham Booth 50 years before.

Ford's 'History of Chesterfield' gives the date of the formation of a Particular Baptist Church in Chesterfield as 1817, although a reference in T.P. Wood's Almanack states. "The Baptists were meeting in Silk Mill Yard in 1805." The initiative seems to have come from Sheffield, and in particular from the Townhead Street Particular Baptist Church which itself was formed in 1804. Mr John Jones served as Minister of the Townhead Street Church, and it was a Mr John Jones who, according to Ford, gave the opening address at the formation of the Chesterfield Church on August 3rd 1817. "In the evening," continues Ford, "two persons were baptised by Mr Morton in a river adjoining the town, and were added to the Church."

This same Mr Morton subsequently handed pastoral charge of the Church to Rev David Jones, formerly of Brentford. The Church grew under his care, and their Meeting House had to be enlarged, re-opening for Public Worship on November 7th 1821. Ford, however, indicates that difficulties in financing the ministry led to the eventual closure of the Church in the 1820s. The precise date of this closure is uncertain. Rev G. Hall's 'History of Chesterfield' (1823) still refers to the Baptists having a meeting place in Silk Mill Yard. Rev D. Jones of Chesterfield was present at the opening of the Congregational Church on Soresby Street in May 1823. While an 1829 Directory of the County of Derbyshire still lists the name: Jones, David – Baptist Minister of Chesterfield.

What is clear, however, is that the Particular Baptists had ceased to meet by the end of the 1820s.

The next initiative came from the General Baptists in Derbyshire. J.H. Wood's condensed History of the General Baptists (1847) describes the formation of the Church:

"A few members of General Baptist Churches in neighbouring counties came to reside in Chesterfield; these were collected together and assisted by the North Derbyshire Home Mission. A room was hired and fitted up for worship in which preaching has been maintained by ministers connected with the Home Mission Society."

The North Derbyshire Conference minutes trace the detailed development of the General Baptist cause in Chesterfield during this period.

It was at the Conference at Ripley on August 1st 1842 that a suggestion was made about starting up a Baptist cause in Chesterfield. Brother

223

Ingham was to visit the town and explore the feasibility of such a venture.

A letter was sent to Mr James Smith in Chesterfield explaining the Conference's feelings. It transpired that Smith had already made contact with several Baptists in the town with a view to their forming a Church. The happy coincidence of this letter contributed to the general sense of providential guidance, and things moved at a pace. On September 10th 1842 a large room for Divine Worship was opened. Richard Ingham preached to the newly assembled gathering (before his visit to Yorkshire and untimely death). Rev Burrows from Alfreton preached in October and Rev Kenney of Wirksworth preached in November.

Mr Kenney was very interested in the work at Chesterfield and had already arranged (October 11th) for his congregations at Wirksworth, Shottle, Bonsall and Cromford to take up collections for the new cause. Once the cause was formally adopted as a Home Mission station (1843) then all of the North Derbyshire churches were asked to contribute to the work at Chesterfield.

The North Derbyshire Conference on December 26th (Belper) reported that Messrs Kenney and Peggs should go to Chesterfield on February 12th to form the friends in that town into a Church. Chesterfield Baptist Church made its first entry in the New Connexion's records for the year 1843 when it is listed as having 13 members.

On Christmas Day 1843 the Derbyshire Conference at Belper presented £10 to the Chesterfield Church for the fitting out of the chapel and for the provision of a pulpit and forms.

Although favourable progress was reported, it was pointed out in the Report to the Association (1844) that many of the members lived a long way from Chesterfield. They also explained to the Derbyshire Conference (August 5th 1844) that, "If we had a resident minister it would be much better for our spiritual improvement and the good of the cause." Conference's next meeting (Christmas Day 1844) mentioned that Mr Goodliffe had been asked to spend the next two

Lord's Days at Chesterfield with a view to taking on the work. Mr Goodliffe duly settled in the town, and Conference agreed (March 1845) to raise £15 towards his stipend. They made the same commitment the following year, and at the same time (April 1846) were earnestly requesting Mr Goodliffe to continue.

Sadly this did not happen, so that (no doubt with a heavy heart) the North Derbyshire Conference on Christmas Day 1846 reluctantly decided to discontinue Chesterfield as a Home Mission cause. Individual churches were still at liberty to support the friends in Chesterfield if they wished to do so. The final entry for Chesterfield in the New Connexion statistics is for 1846 when it is recorded as having 19 members.

The decision to discontinue Home Mission support did not mean that the Church should fold. But without financial support from the county the likelihood of the cause surviving was drastically reduced.

A lifeline was thrown to the struggling cause from Sheffield. In the General Baptist Repository for 1849 is an article entitled: "Chesterfield: Recommencement of the General Baptist interest." The article explains that friends from Chesterfield had applied to the Church at Eldon Street, Sheffield for help. The Rev T. Horsfield from Eldon Street had preached for them and had gathered the remnant of the Chesterfield Baptist Church together and formed it as a branch of Eldon Street. A baptismal service was conducted by the Sheffield Minister on August 12th 1849 who subsequently administered the Lord's Supper to about 20 people, "all Baptists".

The Repository recorded, later in the year, that "On Lord's Day, November 11th a commodious room in Holywell Cross, capable of accommodating 100 persons, was opened for Divine Worship by Rev T. Horsfield. The congregations were large and attentive."

The Chesterfield Baptist cause is listed in the 1851 Religious Census. Entries were submitted by Mr Ed. Bombroffe, steward, Packers Row, Chesterfield. They were meeting in a room now used as a Chapel. There were 24 children in Morning Sunday School; 45 adults and children meeting in the afternoon; and 35 in the evening congregation. But the end was near.

The Derbyshire Conference (August 1851) declined to accede to Eldon Street's request for help at Chesterfield. And in April 1852 the Conference even declined to buy the furniture from the Baptist Chapel, which had clearly been forced to close. After ten years, the General Baptist experiment in Chesterfield had ended.

By 1861, however, the Baptists were back, and this time permanently. The Derbyshire Times for October 5th 1861 reports: "We understand that the Baptist friends have taken the Market Hall and intend opening a large room for public worship in the course of a week or two, but they now meet and worship in the Magistrate's Room."

The 'Baptist Recorder' goes on to say: "In October last Mr Larom of Sheffield preached the first sermons … and formed a Church of 22 members. The friends there now contemplate the erection of a place of worship. The town is an improving place and now has 12.000 inhabitants."

Mr Larom had been Minister of Townhead Street Particular Baptist Church since 1821. Prior to that he had helped establish a Sunday School in that Church in 1814. In 1846 he had been instrumental in establishing the Baptist cause in Dronfield.

Larom's involvement here in Chesterfield points again to the indebtedness of Chesterfield Baptists to their Sheffield neighbours. If the General Baptists in Eldon Street had supported the Chesterfield cause in the 1840s and 1850s, it was the Particular Baptists at Townhead Street that were to help them now.

Rev T.A.Taylor, who compiled a thorough and exhaustive study of the Baptists in Chesterfield (1961), is fairly confident that of the 22 members who formed this Baptist Church in 1861, a remnant was left from the General Baptist cause in the 1850s. This is more than likely. He is equally confident that another group making up this new Church were defectors from the Congregational Church on Soresby Street. Of the list of withdrawals from Soresby Street in 1861, three names appear as Trustees of the Baptist Church in 1863 (Walter Pike, Thomas Mason, and Henry Morton); while Ellen Pike, Elizabeth Ratcliffe Pike, and Elizabeth Pike, whose names also appear on the list of defectors from the Congregational Church, reappear on the Baptist Church Membership Roll that was produced in 1873. Emma Pike, who left the Congregational Church in 1862, was also a Baptist Church member by 1873.

A Stone Laying Ceremony was held for a Baptist Chapel on Durrant Green (Brewery Street) on 29th July 1862. The building was to accommodate 350 people and cost £960 to build. Rev Larom addressed the assembled gathering on that occasion. The building was opened for worship on 20th January 1863. The Trust Deed compiled that year recognised the Church as a Particular or Calvinistic Baptist Church, but it also accommodated both the General Baptist and Congregational roots of the new Church by establishing it as an Open Communion fellowship.

Progress at this newly formed Baptist Church was rapid. By 1871 Chesterfield Baptist Church already had a membership of 101. In 1874 this had increased to 117, and by 1877 membership stood at 130. The ministry of Rev W.F.Harris proved to be especially efficient and successful. Called to the Church from Metropolitan College in August 1879, Harris came with a very warm commendation from Charles Haddon Spurgeon. The Annual General Meeting in February 1881 reported a net increase in the membership of 23 in the year. (They also had a wonderfully printed Statement of Accounts for the year ending 1880!) The following year's AGM reported an increase of 16 members, but with 16 deletions the membership remained at 138. There was reference to a mission at Spital and one at Langford Street or Sanford Street. The Church Treasurer said that the finances were in such good shape that they could afford to give Mr Harris an increase of £5 a year.

The AGM in January 1883 recorded a membership of 140. Mr Savory presented a short account of the work at Spital. It was also agreed to take over the pastoral oversight of Stonebroom for 12 months. By the time Mr Harris left in 1884 (to take on the pastorate of Trinity Baptist

Church, Derby) the membership at Chesterfield had reached 148. The Baptist Handbook for that year lists Chesterfield having branch churches at Spital and also at Stonebroom (20 members). The work at Spital seems to have faded away by the 1890s, but Stonebroom grew steadily reaching a membership of 91 by 1906.

Chesterfield took on some responsibility for a cause at New Whittington. Rev Mesquitta, who served as minister from 1886 to 1898, had some involvement with that cause in his early days. New Whittington was never officially a branch of Chesterfield. In 1906 it had its own membership of 31.

Financial strains in the Church after Rev Harris' departure were in part the result of defections. Some of the pioneers of the 1861 cause left Chesterfield during the 1880s, including Arthur George Early, who returned to Soresby Street Congregational Church. In 1900 Chesterfield had a membership of 111. By 1906 it had increased to 129, but never quite recaptured the strength of those days in the early and middle 1880s.

Rev. Abraham Booth 1734 -1806
Formative member of the New Connexion and Minister at Kirby Woodhouse
Pioneer Baptist preacher in Chesterfield
Subsequently, Minister of Prescott Street Particular Baptist Church, London
Source: The Angus Library, Regent's Park College, Oxford

Brewery Street Chapel

Cross Street Chapel
The home of Chesterfield
Baptists from 1928

CHAPTER 19

CLAY CROSS AND SOUTH WINGFIELD

Baptist witness in Clay Cross did not begin until about the year 1862. On September 14th that year a few Christians, who held distinctive views on baptism, began to hold services in the house of Mr Eli Slater, 127 Cellar Row. Their first preacher was Mr J. Purdew who preached two sermons on that occasion. The group continued to hold cottage meetings until January 1863 when they felt sufficiently strong to hire a room above the Furnace Inn, Market Street. The rent was £5 per year. This 'temporary chapel' was opened for public worship on January 4th 1863 by Mr T. Small of Dronfield. Two weeks later, on 18th January, the congregation was formally constituted as a Church. Deacons and office-holders were appointed. The five people who appear to have been instrumental in establishing this Baptist cause, and who took on early responsibility, were William Slater, Henry Bowan Wells, William Foster, William Hilton Machin, and James Booth. Two men whose names became prominent subsequent to the founding of the Church were Eli Slater and James Bailey.

For reasons that are not clear, this Church from the outset leaned towards Sheffield and Dronfield, and took on a Particular Baptist character. Its name appears in the Particular Baptist Notts, Derbys and Lincs Association with a formation date of 1863. Mr George Slack from Derby appears to have provided both financial and preaching assistance in the very early days.

The small congregation carried large ambitions, and by 1865 they were already making plans for a building of their own. They approached Mr Charles Binns of the Clay Cross Company to secure for them a plot of land upon which they could build a chapel. Within two years, impressed by the endeavours of this small band, Mr Binns was able to acquire a piece of land for them on Market Street. In 1867 plans were drawn up by Mr W. Bramham for a chapel, tenders were invited, and in August Mr E. Bradley of Clay Cross was invited to undertake the construction.

On Thursday September 5th 1867 a stone laying ceremony took place, opened by Rev Charles Larom of Sheffield. Charles Binns of the Clay Cross Company was presented with a silver trowel to mark the occasion. The Company was clearly very supportive of all the churches in the town. Mr Binns observed in his speech that this was the ninth chapel to be erected in the town (population 5,000), and the Clay Cross Company was a friend "of all the different denominations in the place." He even went so far as to say that should the Baptists require more land at a later date then they only had to ask!

The new chapel, with a seating capacity of 250, was opened on Sunday February 9th 1868. The 'Derbyshire Courier' for the 15th February carried an account of the Chapel Opening: "The Baptist friends at Dronfield evinced their sympathy with the cause, a bus load being present from that place." Mr Thomas Smelt of Dronfield spoke at the Tea. "He believed they would succeed, and he hoped that this beautiful chapel would be the birthplace of many souls."

In the 1873 Notts, Derbys and Lincs (Particular) Baptist Association records, Clay Cross is noted to have 34 members, seven more than the previous year. They certainly appeared to be a very busy Church. Their report to the Association for that year refers to an early morning prayer meeting; a singing class; Band of Hope; Young Men's Mutual Improvement Society; and a Tract Society. "The Church here is in a healthy state and enjoys tokens of God's presence and help." The debt on the chapel had been reduced by £155 since its opening in 1868. They hoped shortly to be able to sustain a pastor.

In June 1874 the Church wrote to C.H.Spurgeon requesting students from his College to supply their pulpit for a month. On September 2nd an invitation was extended to Mr W. Williams from Spurgeon's College to serve as their pastor. The invitation was accepted.

Mr Williams had a most impressive three years at the Church. On arrival there were 39 Church Members and 253 children in the Sunday School. In 1876 the Church Membership had risen to 83, and in 1877 there were 108 members. Clay Cross found themselves unable to retain

231

the services of this able young man, and he moved to a London Church that same year.

According to an early twentieth century account of the Clay Cross Baptists, the Church, flushed with success, decided to purchase larger buildings. New Sunday School and Lecture Hall buildings were constructed at a considerable expense. The debt resulting from these overly ambitious projects crippled the Church until it was necessary to sell them off to the Clay Cross Council who eventually used them as the Town Hall and Council Chamber.

A succession of very short ministries followed:

>Rev Joseph Watnough 1880
>Rev I.A.Ward   1881-1884
>Rev F.Samuels   1885-1888
>Mr Baker   1888-1890

The Church declined. Membership fell from 112 in 1878 to 48 in 1890. Between 1893 and 1895 a Mr Bage had involvement with Clay Cross through a mission he conducted. The venture bore little fruit and by the end of that period Clay Cross turned to Dronfield Baptist Church again for pastoral oversight. Rev C.J.Rendell from Dronfield conducted week night services and once a month on a Sunday. An attempt was made to join forces with Stonebroom Baptist Church for joint ministry, but when this approach failed Clay Cross decided to step out in faith and invite a minister of their own. Rev W.R.Ponton was invited on April 7th 1898. The Church at that time had a membership of 37.

By 1903 a respectable 71 members were recorded as belonging to Clay Cross Baptist Church. In 1905 the membership was 99, and in 1903 there were 103 members at Clay Cross listed on the official Association records. There were 212 scholars as well.

New Trustees were appointed in 1900. The list provides a useful insight into the social structure of Clay Cross Baptist Church at that time. The nine new Trustees were: William Foster (retired grocer);

Joseph Wheeler (engine winder); George Silkstone (colliery deputy); William Henry Priest (turner); Joseph Wood (railway goods yard manager); Henry Lee (coke burner); William Henry Longmate (butcher); Frederick Harrison (labourer); George Harrison (coal miner).

The historical note produced by Rev Ponton towards the close of his ministry at Clay Cross refers to a "depression in trade and the consequent removal of some of our best workers." Growth was checked, and by the start of the First World War Church Membership had fallen back to 67.

Birches Lane, South Wingfield

"The Baptist interest at Amber Row originated about the year 1845 in the self denying labours of Joseph Burton, Swanwick. To him the cause is mainly indebted for its commencement and its success during his connection with it. In the year 1849 he left the land of his birth, went to South Australia, and died there in 1859."[1]

The Swanwick Baptist Church history notes that 18 of its members separated from Swanwick in 1862 to form a separate Church at South Wingfield. South Wingfield's own history puts this date as 1863. The Notts, Derbys and Lincs (Particular) Baptist Association received South Wingfield into the Association in 1864.

During 1864 land was purchased from Mr James Godber on Birches Lane, South Wingfield. Ten Trustees were appointed, and three Church Officers: Joseph Henshaw (Deacon); Lancelot Beastall (Deacon); and James Godber (Secretary). Throughout 1865 plans were drawn up for a Church building. The contract was awarded to Mr Ray of Selston (July 1865); building work started that same month; and it was completed in November that same year. The Opening Services were held on December 17th by Rev Thomas Lomas of Leicester.

The South Wingfield congregation moved from their original home on Amber Row to their new premises on Birches Lane.

The Church Membership Roll at Birches Lane reveals one or two interesting pieces of information. The first member of the new Church was John Smith of Toad Hole, Furnace. In December 1869 Smith was appointed Senior Deacon and Church Secretary, and played a crucial role in the development of the cause. As an indication of the geographical spread of the Church Membership at Birches Lane, the Roll informs us that of the first 28 members of the Church:

> 7 lived at Toad Hole, Furnace
> 4 lived at Wessington
> 8 lived at Oakerthorpe
> 2 lived in Amber Row
> 2 lived in Birches lane
> 4 lived in South Wingfield
> 1 lived in Brackenfield.

In 1867 James Godber built the Chapel House adjacent to the new Church building for £50. Tap water was installed in 1903.

In May 1874 the burying ground was completed. This was a substantial area of land to the rear of the building. Throughout 1875 the Church debated the rules and terms for burials. Hannah Argyle was the first burial in the ground (May 18th 1875). She was thirteen years old. The subsequent chronological list of burials provides a sobering indication of the spectre of mortality that hung over Victorian England. The ages of those interred in the burial ground were:

10 months	1 year
11 months	2 years, 7 months
1 year	7 years
39 years	1 week
6 months	8 months
2 years, 8 months	16 years
3 months	9 months
1 week	8 months
14 weeks	2 years
6 weeks	1 year, 9 months
1 year, 11 months	6 years
1 year, 9 months	

In 1878 a Sunday School was formed, and two new classrooms or vestries were constructed.

The Church's first minister was appointed in 1878. Mr J. Wood had written to Charles Haddon Spurgeon for the recommendation of a minister. Spurgeon wrote back (in a letter still treasured by the Church) suggesting the name of Rev E.P.Barrett from Hereford as a suitable person. Spurgeon, however, went one better than a mere recommendation. In his letter of 29th April 1878 he promised a donation of £25 if the Church chose Mr Barrett and gave him a salary of £120 per annum. The Association would provide £30 so that the Church at Birches Lane would only have to find £65. Not surprisingly, the Church gratefully accepted the offer. Mr Spurgeon suggested that he may repeat the offer for the second year, but NOT after that.

E. P. Barrett commenced his ministry at Birches Lane, South Wingfield in June 1878. At the Annual Tea Meeting prior to Mr Barrett's arrival the Church reported that they had 147 scholars on roll; 12 teachers; and during the year 12 from the adult classes had been baptised and joined the Church.

Alas, Mr Barrett's ministry was very short-lived. Recognition Services took place in September 1878. By the following September it was already clear that the money to pay the minister was just not available. Even in partnership with the Baptist causes at Stonebroom and Shirland they could not raise the necessary money. On September 16th 1879 a Church Meeting was held at which members from Stonebroom and Shirland were present. The pastor read out his letter of resignation, and brother Evans of Shirland, and Halladine of Birches Lane, proposed and seconded that his resignation be accepted. Mr Barrett concluded his ministry on 3rd December 1879.

One of the features of the South Wingfield Church was that its membership never really grew, and consequently it frequently joined together with other churches to become viable for ministerial oversight. At the outset of the cause in the 1840s the people at South Wingfield had been members of Swanwick Baptist Church. When they became separate it was quite natural for them to carry on with the

Particular Baptist linkages. In the Baptist Handbook for 1871, Birches Lane has its own entry and records 15 members. This had increased to 17 members by 1874. In 1877 and 1878 Birches Lane appeared as a branch of Swanwick Baptist Church with 17 members. In 1879 it again had an entry to itself in the Handbook, but this time with Stonebroom and Shirland as its branches. The combined membership figure was 36. The Stonebroom Chapel was recorded as seating 250 people. The Shirland Meeting House seated 40. In 1884 Birches Lane appeared in the Handbook as a branch of Trinity Baptist Church, Derby. Recorded Membership was 21. Not until 1897 was Birches Lane again receiving a separate entry (26 members). And its membership was to remain virtually the same until the First World War.

Shirland, under its nominal leader William Evans, had never enjoyed the status of branch Church. Relationships with Birches Lane were fractious and ill tempered. When the latter turned to Derby for ministerial oversight, Shirland took the opportunity to shake off its old mantle, and to come under the care of Riddings Baptist Church.

The Stonebroom Church in Alfreton had quite a different story. Between 1884 and 1890 it appeared as a branch of Chesterfield Baptist Church. It had a membership of 28 in 1890. In 1894 it had a separate entry, and was recorded as having a membership of 50. This grew steadily until by 1906 Stonebroom Baptist Church had a membership of 91 with 121 scholars on roll.

Birches Lane was never to enjoy such numerical growth. A minute of Swanwick Baptist Church for January 7th 1886 records that, "The Birches Lane friends are in great need of help." The Church survived, but only through a series of alliances and coalitions.

In 1908 the South Wingfield Church agreed to change the stone on the front gable of the building to read, 'Baptist Church' instead of 'Particular Baptist Church.'

1. Church minute book, 1863.

Clay Cross Baptist Church

Birches Lane,
S. Winfield

The Baptist Church at Stonebroom was on the High Street opposite the old
Mayfield Public House. It occupied the site of the present Rowan Tree House.

CHAPTER 20

JUNCTION, WATSON STREET, AND PEAR TREE, DERBY

Junction Street, Derby

"Years ago, in Parcel Terrace, (known as 'Little Sodom' then),
With its half clothed little children, wretched women, drunken men,
Came a youth with loving piety, fostered by His Master's love,
And his heart ached for the children whom he longed to lead above.
In a cottage, old and dingy, shattered windows, broken floor,
He commenced his little mission, and within that cottage door
Only just five little children (left the gutter), left their play,
And to ROBERT HILLIARD listened on that opening Sabbath Day."[1]

The work at Junction, Derby, is technically another branch of St
Mary's Gate. In reality it sprang from the initiative of five young men
from St Mary's Gate who subsequently normalised proceedings by
having the cause accepted as a branch of that Church.

According to Alger's 'History of the Derby and District Affiliated Free
Churches' (1901), these five young men had met together "for mutual
improvement" for twelve months before Robert Hilliard, one of their
number suggested they should obtain a room in Parcel Terrace in order
to start a mission and a Sunday School. Alger's description of Parcel
Terrace is very vivid, but probably quite accurate. Parcel Terrace was
one long row of houses inhabited principally by the workers from the
neighbouring chemical works, brick kilns, and nail makers' smithies.
"The neighbourhood was notorious for its wickedness ... frequently
the scene of the wildest riot and disorder ... dog and hedgehog
fighting, immorality and every species of wickedness." It carried the
unenviable name of "Little Sodom".

The five young men approached Mr Robert Pegg, a long standing
member at St Mary's Gate who had recently joined Sacheverel Street
and subsequently became Mayor of Derby. They asked to rent one of
his properties on Parcel Terrace. Pegg allowed them to have one of the

empty properties free of charge, and the team set about cleaning, whitewashing and equipping the room. On May 4th 1856 they opened for Sunday School. Five local urchins attended (with no shoes or socks) and the work began. Before long the team needed an adjoining property for the expanding work which Robert Pegg willingly supplied.

Opposition to the cause was fierce, especially from the nail and brick makers.

"Not unfrequently when they came to clean the place on Saturday in preparation for Sunday services, they found the windows broken, or the panels of the entrance door broken with a pick. Sometimes when holding a prayer meeting their persecutors would open the door and throw pieces of burning rag in amongst them, which had been dipped in oil."[2]

Inspite of opposition the work flourished.

"Seldom have teachers had the happiness to see such extensive and real good resulting from their labours, the appearance and character of those under their care undergoing a radical change."[3]

A young woman's class was formed. On September 15th 1858 there were two candidates for baptism (Miss S. Denston and Miss A. Varney). By 1860 thirteen of the young women had joined the Church. A young men's class saw eight of their number join the Church at the same time. On 19th July 1860 they moved out of Parcel Terrace. There were 140 scholars and ten teachers. The following month they moved round the corner into their new chapel on Junction Street.

In June 1860 those connected with Parcel Terrace/Junction Street entered into a covenant with one another, and the first members' meeting of the branch was held on 28th May 1860. Mr John Harrison was elected Chairman and Mr Robert Hilliard was elected Secretary. In 1862 Mr E.C. Ellis took on the role as Secretary, a position he held until 1890. Hilliard became Chairman. By 1863, the Junction branch of St Mary's Gate had a membership of 60.

Growth continued at a remarkable pace. By 1869 the Sabbath School had over 750 scholars and 16 teachers. Plans were drawn up for an enlargement to the Junction Chapel. Mr Ellis offered £26 and 6 shillings to the project. Eventually, a decision was made to completely rebuild the chapel on the same site. A second plot of land was purchased adjoining the existing site, and a new chapel was constructed covering the two plots. There were ten classrooms on the ground floor. The new chapel was opened on Sunday September 3rd 1871. Rev Crassweller, the Minister of St Mary's Gate, preached in the Morning. Thomas Goadby, Minister of Osmaston Road, preached in the afternoon. The total cost of the building was £1,300

One interesting feature of the life of Junction Street Church was the practice of holding their Annual General Meeting on Christmas Day. The meeting was always preceded by a breakfast at 8.00am at which numbers ranging from 36 (1868) to 91 (1882) "sat down to an excellent breakfast." By 1895 numbers attending Christmas Morning breakfast had reached 120.

In 1885, a further enlargement became necessary. The School had so rapidly increased that 900 scholars were in regular attendance. The chapel itself could only seat 400. Additional rooms were added at a cost of £500, and the extension was opened on October 25th 1885. A third plot of land was purchased at the same time for £120, anticipating a possible future expansion.

A list of members of the General Baptist Church, St Mary's Gate, Derby dated Dec.31st 1886 helpfully provides not only the names and addresses of those in membership at the main Chapel in St Mary's Gate, but also those of members at the branch churches of Littleover, Willington and Junction. There were 154 members of the Church belonging to the Junction branch. Robert and Elizabeth Hilliard of Parliament Street dated their attachment to Junction back to 1854. William Chambers of Boyer Street similarly joined the cause in that year. Sarah Gadsby's membership began in 1856, and William Featherstone's in 1859. But 94 of the members had joined the Church since 1880.

With growing numbers there came fierce competition for the various offices and posts the Church needed to fill. Each year, in advance of the AGM, a list of nominees for the various posts was made available to the membership along with a lengthy voting paper. In 1888 the voting paper confronting the membership looked like this:

Weekly offering committee - 3 places; 5 names
Finance Committee - 5 places; 6 names
Conductors to the seats - 2 places; 4 names
Sick visiting committee - 10 places; 13 names
Property committee - 4 places; 8 names
Conductor of singing - 1 place; 2 names
Harmonionist - 1 place; 2 names

In June 1893 Junction Street first considered the idea of calling their own Minister. When it came to the vote, however, there were only 17 in favour of the idea with the same number against and 16 abstentions. In February 1894 the idea was put to the Church meeting again, this time obtaining a majority of 44 (65 in favour; 21 against). Within a few months they were in contact with Rev Philip Hudgell from Waterford, Ireland, and in February 1895 Rev Hudgell became the first minister of the Junction Street cause. The appointment was with the full approval of the St Mary's Gate Church.

The first act of the new ministry was to insist that a baptistery be built at Junction Street. (Previous baptisms must all have taken place at St Mary's Gate). As if to prove the need for the baptistery, Junction Street saw 37 candidates baptised between June and September 1895. By the November the baptistery was built and completely paid for.

The Church, however, was still heavily indebted. They still owed £810 in January 1888, which naturally made them cautious about following brother Murfin's plan in October 1896 for a new chapel. Undaunted, the Church did agree to purchase two houses for £750 in 1897 which they believed would make an excellent site for a future new chapel.

In April 1897, Robert Hilliard formerly proposed the separation of Junction Street from St Mary's Gate. The latter were happy to comply with this request. In July the Rev Mills, from St Mary's Gate, along with other ministers in the town, presided over a ceremony which officially established Junction Street as an independent Church in membership with the Baptist Union. In 1900 Junction had a membership of 254 with a Sunday School of 900 scholars.

Watson Street, Derby

On Tuesday November 21st 1967 the Derby Evening Telegraph carried an article entitled: "Centenary of a Baptist Church."

"A meeting of a few people in a house in Parker Street, Derby, on November 19th 1867 was celebrated at the Baptist Church in Watson Street at the weekend. For the meeting was the start of the Watson Street Church."

Situated in the old West End of Derby, between Ashbourne Road and Kedleston Road, Watson Street and Parker Street were in the middle of a very densely populated part of the town. The Evening Telegraph article went on to say:

"By 1870 the group were negotiating a purchase of land on the site which the Church and School now occupy, and thanks to an initial gift of £100 from Mr Slack the Herbalist, they began to erect buildings which are still in use."

Unusual among the history of the Baptist Churches in Derbyshire, the Watson Street cause did not have a natural mother Church. According to an account in the 1877 Reports to the Association, the Watson Street cause originated with the Derby Baptist Preachers Association. A mission room was opened; preaching commenced and a Sabbath school was opened with just 9 children. The 1877 account went on to explain that in a short while a Church was formed consisting of 14 members. According to a centenary history of Kilburn Baptist Church produced in 1932, Mr George Slack was described as the founder of the Watson Street cause, "assisted by Mr George Dean."

Perhaps because of the heavy population density around the Church, growth at Watson Street was marked and rapid. The Church features for the first time in Association records in 1872 when it is listed as having 49 members, and provides the following information:

"After an existence of four years as a mission Church, we have succeeded in building a comfortable chapel that will seat 300 persons, at a cost of £530. Our debt at present is £350. The congregation is very attentive."

The Church reported having 115 children in the Sabbath school.

Church membership rose steadily:

1873	-	56 members
1874	-	59 members
1877	-	69 members
1878	-	74 members
1879	-	78 members

A day school was started in connection with Watson Street. The Church informed the Association in 1873 that the school was thriving "notwithstanding the active opposition of the State Church authorities in our neighbourhood."

In 1874 they reported to the Association that "Mr William Millington, who has been the Secretary to the Church since its formation, has been received into Chilwell College as a student." In 1876 they reported another year of success. They had 170 scholars; had reduced their chapel debt by £115 (only £100 remaining); and, "We have a clothing club connected with the Sabbath School which is well supported."

So successful was the Watson Street cause that by 1878 plans were underway to enlarge and improve the premises. In 1879 the Church informed the Association:

"Since last Association we have completed the improvement and enlargement of the chapel, together with the erection of vestries and class rooms. This has cost us about £450 towards which we have raised more than £100." In 1882, as numbers continued to grow, the Church constructed another class room at a further cost of £200.

In keeping with the origins of the Church, Watson Street had no stated minister. Most years, in their report to the Association, they expressed their thanks to the Derby and Derbyshire Baptist Preachers Association. They also expressed their thankfulness to old Dr Underwood who for several years took services for them and exercised a degree of pastoral oversight at Watson Street.

By 1890 the Church Membership had risen to 96. In 1897 it reached its peak with 101 members. Thereafter membership plateaued before undergoing a marked decline. By the time of the First World War the Church Membership was recorded as 59, with 117 scholars on roll.

Pear Tree, Derby

"About 1870 cottage prayer meetings were commenced in the Pear Tree district by Mr T.H.Harrison and other Osmaston Road friends."[4]

Pear Tree was, as its name suggests, a quiet rural part of the town which was slowly being developed for housing. The Midland Railway Company provided the catalyst for this house building with its demand for workers at its expanding works in Derby. Between 1872 and 1902 the population of the town increased from 43,091 to 105,785. Much of that increase in population came from the Pear Tree district.

Osmaston Road Baptist Church (or some of its members at least) saw the potential for a Baptist cause in this new housing area. In 1871 Mr John Smith, from Osmaston Road, purchased a small wooden shed, which had been used as a joiner's shop, and placed it at the end of Princes Street. Known locally as 'Noah's Ark' the building seated about 60 people, and from this makeshift accommodation the first missionary work into Pear Tree began. A Sabbath School was started on the same site on October 10th 1871.

In 1872 Mr Thomas Swingler, another Osmaston Road member, donated a parcel of land he owned on Rutland Street as a site for a more permanent chapel. On April 8th 1872 Osmaston Road appointed Trustees for the new Chapel .and Schoolrooms; a Memorial stone was laid by Mr Swingler on 14th June 1873 and, according to Alger's 'History,' the new building was opened in September at a cost of about £1,500.

Work at the Pear Tree branch of Osmaston Road Baptist Church carried on quietly over the next few years. When mention of the branch does occur in the Osmaston Road minutes it is usually to look at the scheme of management of the branch for which, understandably, Pear Tree wished to have more responsibility. The 1885 scheme was revised in 1890, and was to change again in 1893 when Osmaston Road called an assistant minister from Regents Park College, London to take pastoral responsibility for the Pear Tree branch. Rev William Alfred Richards was invited for a twelve months period and stayed for 23 years!

Because Pear Tree was only a branch of Osmaston Road Baptist Church there are no official figures for the membership of the branch until the early twentieth century. The Baptist Handbook for 1895 does mention that Pear Tree had 435 Sunday School scholars, compared to the 786 scholars at Osmaston Road. The only evidence of membership strength for this period is an historical reminiscence from 1914 to mark W.A. Richards' 21 years at the Church. Mr Will Curtis, the Church Secretary, commented that when Mr Richards came to Pear Tree they had a membership of 68. When Pear Tree does feature independently in the Baptist Union Handbook (1903) it is recorded as having a membership of 144. Will Curtis refers to the fact that in 1914 that membership stood at 245.

The growth of the Church reflected the growth of population in the community, and it soon became apparent that the building on Rutland Street (seating capacity 200) was simply not big enough to handle the numbers of children and adults attending.

On June 2nd 1897 the Osmaston Road Church Meeting approved the scheme to purchase a plot of land on the junction of Goodale Street, Portland Street and Pear Tree Road. Fund raising went on apace at both the Osmaston Road end and the Pear Tree branch.

The architect for the new building (which included a 600 seat sanctuary as well as a Lecture Hall) was Mr A.H.Goodall of Nottingham. The builder was Mr John Young, who had supplied the lowest tender, and who also happened to be the Pear Tree Church Secretary! The Stone Laying ceremony took place on 15th November 1902. Four stones were laid, one of them by Mr Alfred Swingler, whose father had given the land and laid the foundation stone for the Rutland Street premises. The event was presided over by Councillor John Smith who had commenced the work at Pear Tree 30 years before. A Public Tea was held after the stone laying ceremony at which Sir Thomas Roe MP took the chair.

In an account of the Stone Laying preserved in the Pear Tree minutes it becomes clear that only the Church itself was being built in November 1902. There was a strip of land between the Church site and Dr Wright's residence which had been identified for a Lecture Hall but at that precise moment in time the Church did not own it. At the Stone Laying Ceremony it transpired that the owner of the strip of land was Alderman T.H.Harrison, one of the founders of the original cause. Mr Harrison presented the Church with the title deeds at the Ceremony thus enabling them to proceed with the Lecture Hall.

The 'Baptist Times and Freeman' for November 21st 1902 carried a detailed account of the Stone Laying ceremony, (along with A.H.Goodall's sketch). It also contained a fairly severe reprimand for the Derby Baptists (who had not contributed to J.H.Shakespeare's 'Twentieth Century Fund'):

"It is to be hoped that this event marks the beginning of a new epoch of aggressive work on the part of the Baptists of Derby, who have not kept pace of late years with the growth of the town, and have much lost ground to recover."

It is hard to imagine the 'Baptist Times' making such a jibe today!

On Wednesday July 1st 1903 the new building was officially opened. Alderman T.H.Harrison unlocked the doors of the building with a silver key. The cost of the whole enterprise was estimated at £4,400 for which various loans were secured and repaid over many years.

While there are no records available which detail the process the Church went through in deciding its building and design requirements, one tell-tale remark was unearthed in a joint minute book of the Osmaston Road and Pear Tree deacons for 1916 in which Osmaston Road explained they would be reducing their financial support to Pear Tree, "The Rev W.A.Richards called to mind the cost of the Lecture Hall was saddled upon the Pear Tree people inspite of our protest." The implication of the minute is that the design of Pear Tree Road Baptist Church was a much grander affair than the Pear Tree people themselves desired. Osmaston Road clearly held the upper hand.

Formal separation of the two churches happened between 1904 and 1908. But financial assistance carried on much longer. Osmaston Road Baptist Church contributed £25 each year towards Mr Richards' stipend until 1916. The East Midlands Baptist Association made additional financial contributions towards stipend costs until 1922. Although Pear Tree had a large membership (235 in 1914) many of its congregation were poor and there were limits to the money the congregation could be expected to raise. This was something accepted and understood by the Association.

Undoubtedly the genius behind the cause at Pear Tree was William Alfred Richards. A young man straight from college when he arrived in 1893, he married Charlotte Louisa Heycock from Osmaston Road in 1901, and went on to establish a very effective ministry. Richards was well travelled. He regularly gave lantern lectures on his tour of Egypt. He was a good administrator, and in 1900 he succeeded W.F.Harris as County Secretary to the Association, receiving the ultimate honour in 1914 when he was elected President of the East Midland Baptist Association.

His address to the Association was delivered in Mansfield at the Annual Meeting that June. It was entitled "The place of the Church in the life of the nation." In the address he acknowledged the primary need of human beings to be changed from within. No social reformer can change men, only the grace of God. But having acknowledged that important point he went on to recognise that powerful social forces were at work that conspire to keep people in degradation and sin. "We (the Church) ought to be the first in the field against all wrong, and especially against those social conditions which hinder the work of evangelisation among the masses." "Slums are the breeding places of vice as well as disease, and they must be swept away." He concluded his address:

"Cannot the Church of Christ take her courage in both hands and go forth again as a pioneer into this new land of Social Reform. Her master, the friend of publicans and sinners is there already."

W.A.Richards concluded his ministry at Pear Tree in 1917 after a period of over 23 years. He and his wife moved to Kirby Muxloe, where again he exercised a very happy and fruitful ministry until his premature death in 1928.

1. Found in a written memorial to Robert Hilliard which is part of a collection of material gathered for the Church's Golden Jubilee in 1978, now in the County Record Office, Matlock.
2. Alger's 1901 'History' page 65
3. Junction Baptist Church's first minute book: Historical summary and introduction.
4. From the Pear Tree Church Membership Roll and the introductory historical survey.

Robert Hilliard   Rev. P. A. Hudgell
Source: County Record Office, Matlock

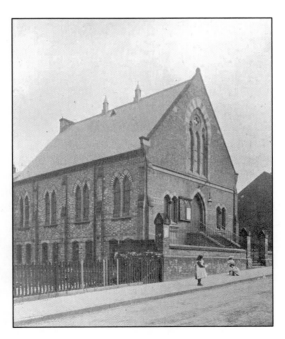

Junction Street Chapel

Rutland Street Chapel, now Padley Development Centre

BAPTIST CHVRCH. Pear Tree Road. Derby. A H Goodall Architect Nottingham

William Alfred Richards

Minister at Pear Tree
1893 – 1917

Secretary to the County Union
1900 – 1909

President of the EMBA
1914 – 1915

Watson Street Chapel, Derby 1940
Source: Derek Palmer

CHAPTER 21

SWADLINCOTE

While there is no evidence of very early Baptist preaching activity in Swadlincote there are one or two references which suggest an early interest and involvement in this small village, south west of Burton on Trent.

In the records of the General Baptist Midland Conference held at Burton on Easter Tuesday 1849 it was resolved that, "brethren Gill, Yates, and Norton be requested to see the writings of the ground belonging to the General Baptist Connexion at Swadlincote, and make their report at the next Conference." When the next Conference came round (at Castle Donington on Whit Tuesday) the perfunctory comment is that "the friends who have management of it see to it as formerly."

Quite clearly then, land had already been obtained for a chapel in the village by 1849 which would probably indicate some level of preaching work before that date. It may be that the work faded.

The earliest reference to any significant engagement at Swadlincote appears ten years later in the minutes of the General Baptist Church at Burton on Trent:

January 3rd 1859 "That brother Cooper endeavour to learn the views of Mr Smith of Swadlincote respecting the introduction of our cause into that village."

In September 1859 a minute of the Burton Church reads: "That we thankfully accept the house offered us at Swadlincote to preach in." And a further minute records, "That we solicit the advice of the next Conference respecting the erection of a new chapel at Swadlincote."

In the records of the Midland Conference held at Archdeacon Lane, Leicester on September 27th 1859 there is a major entry entitled:

252

Concerning building a chapel at Swadlincote

"The Church at Burton on Trent having asked for the advice of the Conference to the propriety of building a chapel at the village of Swadlincote where they have been preaching some time and where there is a plot of ground belonging to the Connexion, it was agreed, that we most affectionately recommend the Church at Burton to build a chapel in that village."

The reference to a plot of ground already belonging to the Connexion must relate back to the early references in 1849.

Having obtained permission to proceed in 1859, the process of carrying out the building work was slow and tortuous in the extreme. In October that year, the Burton Church wrote to the neighbouring Baptist churches in Melbourne and Ashby presumably seeking financial assistance. Letters to these two churches continued throughout the whole of 1860, but when it became clear that no help was to be forthcoming the Burton Church agreed (May 1861) "That the friends at Swadlincote be recommended to erect a chapel and we as a Church agree to assist them to the best of our ability."

Curiously, even after this pledge of financial assistance nothing seemed to happen. On October 8th 1863 the Burton Church Meeting "advises the Trustees of the Swadlincote property to unite their efforts to obtain (.....) to commence building a chapel." It was still three more years before a building was completed. The Burton minutes observe (May 7th 1866) that "We invite Mr Jones of Derby to preach the opening sermons of the chapel at Swadlincote on Wednesday July 25th." On 2nd July the Burton Church Meeting discussed providing preaching supply for the new chapel at Swadlincote.

Little information exists regarding this first chapel at Swadlincote. A Centenary booklet does mention the fact that the first home of the Church was a cottage which stood at the rear of the present building on Hill Street. A newspaper article in the EMBA archive suggests that the first chapel was on the present site and subsequently became incorporated into the School Hall of the second chapel.

253

While the process of building the chapel was slow and protracted, events which followed moved at break neck speed. A first Church Meeting was held on May 14th 1867. At the second Church Meeting (July 14th 1867) they appointed three officers: Henry Cooper, Secretary; George Coulton, Treasurer; William Whetton, Deacon. They also extended a 'cordial and unanimous invitation' to Joseph Cholerton of Ashby to serve as a part time pastor.

Joseph Cholerton was the son of a Derby Baptist family who had entered the ministry and served the churches at Pinchbeck and Sutterton in Lincolnshire before his health broke down. He moved to Ashby in 1864 and set up a business as a draper. He remained an active servant of the Baptist Church in Ashby before becoming linked to Swadlincote.

When, at its third Church Meeting (December 13th 1867), the Church invited Rev J.H.Lummis to become its first full time pastor on a salary of £90 a year, Cholerton's involvement didn't end. In 1871 he transferred his drapery business to Swadlincote, and in 1875 formally transferred his membership from the Ashby Church. Thereafter he was to remain at Swadlincote until his death in 1903. Recording his death on December 15th 1903, an extended minute and tribute in the Swadlincote books observes that "For 30 years he devoted his energies to the wellbeing of this Church .... He filled all its offices from time to time with signal ability and devotion, and deeply endeared himself to all its members as well as to serving the community in every good work."

Rev Lummis commenced his ministry in January 1868, having concluded his time at Hamsterley, Durham. On February 3rd the Burton Church were perturbed to receive a written request of transfer of members from their Church to the Church at Swadlincote. This was somewhat improper since Swadlincote was still part of the Burton Church.

On February 19th a deputation from Swadlincote met with a group from Burton and agreed that 10 names should be transferred to Swad.. These were Henry Cooper, Ann Cooper, John Sheene, Elizabeth

Sheene, John Coulton, Sarah Coulton, George Coulton, Thomas Coulton, Joseph Withnall and William Brotherhood. On 25th February 1868 the Midland Conference, meeting at Baxter Gate, Loughborough, received Swadlincote as an independent Church.

Before they had time to catch their breath, however, a request came (November 1[st]1868) from the Melbourne Baptist Church asking Swadlincote to take Hartshorne as a Preaching station. Hartshorne had been associated with Melbourne for many years. A chapel had been opened in the village on March 19th 1843, but, according to the G.B. Repository, the Gospel had been preached in a friend's house in Hartshorne for 30 years before that. Hartshorne was closer geographically to Swadlincote than it was to Melbourne, and there was an obvious logic to the transfer. On November 24th it was agreed that a deputation be formed to confer with the friends at Hartshorne regarding the practicability of re-opening the chapel there as a preaching station. And on 26th January 1869 the Swadlincote Church Meeting agreed to take responsibility for the preaching at Hartshorne provided Melbourne retained responsibility for the building. Melbourne wrangled over this throughout 1869, but eventually by November 14th this arrangement was agreed, and a Re-Opening Service was planned. Hartshorne thus became an official branch of Swadlincote. For the next 40 years a committee was appointed by the Swadlincote Church to take on the day to day management of Hartshorne, and it reported back at the Annual Meeting every year with financial updates as well. A Sunday School was established at Hartshorne. Occasional candidates for baptism were forthcoming. There were occasional skirmishes with Melbourne regarding repairs to the Hartshorne Chapel. And each year Hartshorne appeared on the statistical returns for the Swadlincote Church. No separate membership figures were issued for Hartshorne until 1900 at which point this village station had a membership of 12. (Today, the chapel no longer exists, but its location was on the left hand side of Ticknall Road coming from the Admiral Rodney Public House)

Hartshorne was not the only village in which Swadlincote conducted preaching. In August 1873 there is reference to cottage prayer meetings in Gresley and Woodville. A little later that year they also began a prayer meeting at Albert Village. By 1874 the prayer meeting at Woodville was discontinued but there was much encouragement at the other venues, especially at Gresley.

Of the first 70 members joining the Church (up to February 1873) 24 were from Swadlincote itself, but 21 were from Gresley. There were 11 members living at Woodville and only 1 in Hartshorne. While there is no apparent reference to Gresley or Church Gresley in the second Swadlincote minute book, it is worth observing that in 1900 Swadlincote is recorded as having both a branch at Hartshorne and at Wilmot Road (Church Gresley). The Wilmot Road membership stood at 35 in 1900, and was at 64 in 1906 at which time they also had 163 Sunday School scholars on the books.

Membership at Swadlincote grew steadily. In 1871 there was a membership of 44. This had grown to 59 in 1874 and to 76 in 1876. The membership plateaued at 87 between 1878 and 1880 before making major leaps forward so that by 1884 the Church had a membership of 146.

This increase in Church Membership reflected the growth of Swadlincote as a town. With the growth of the clay and pottery industries following a national drive for improved sanitation and pipeworks in the 1850s, population flooded into the once rural backwater.

Population of Swadlincote

1831 – 645	1871 – 1343
1841 – 858	1881 – 2214
1851 – 1007	1891 – 2945
1861 – 1076	1901 – 4017

Figures are from the Victoria History of the County of Derby vol.2

Church growth necessitated enlarged premises which in turn generated still further growth. In April 1869 it was agreed to spend £25 in enlarging the premises at the rear of the chapel. This was in part to accommodate growing numbers of Sunday School scholars. But these minor alterations proved quite inadequate to deal with the numbers attending. In 1876 a much more considerable project was undertaken which involved the reconstruction of a new chapel. The Church accepted the tender of Mr Slater (£1,475.14.9) in June 1876, and the new chapel was opened on September 5th 1877.

The increased capacity paved the way for the remarkable growth of the Church during the 1880s. The Report to the Association in May 1894 was extremely upbeat, describing a vigorous and healthy Church:

"The attendance at the Sunday Services, especially at night, indicate a growing interest. One pleasing aspect of the congregation is the presence of a large number of young men and women. The Sunday School is full to overflowing, and a larger building is much needed."

The Report went on to describe the range of activities and organisations sponsored by Hill Street which included a Sunday afternoon adult class, Christian Endeavour, Mothers meeting, and Band of Hope.

The fortunes of ministry at the Church were very mixed. In the main, ministers stayed a very short space of time.

Rev J.H.Lummis	1868 – 1872
Rev J. Greenwood	1873 – 1875
Rev J.J.Irving	1877 – 1880
Rev E. Carrington	1881 – 1883
Rev B. Dicken	1886 – 1889

Mr Carrington was unfortunate, and seemed to become the victim of character assassination on the part of the fledgling Temperance movement in the town.

Mr Greenwood was compelled to leave on health grounds: "The district does not agree with me." Other ministers who were invited to the Church but who subsequently declined the invitation clearly found the industrialised nature of this growing town very unpalatable.

257

George Needham was invited to the pastorate in April 1876 but declined on the grounds of his health, the difficulties of educating his children, and the want of a suitable house to live in.

The biggest difficulty in retaining and attracting a minister was finance. From the outset Swadlincote had been designated a Home Mission Church and received generous support from the denomination. Mr Greenwood's salary of £100 a year was made up of £60 from Swadlincote and £40 from Home Mission. But even with this financial support the Church struggled to pay its way. Mr Lummis resigned following the Church's inability to cover their side of the ministerial costs. In 1888 the Church was obliged to reduce the salary of Mr Dicken from £120 to £100. Unsurprisingly, this triggered his decision to look elsewhere for a Church. And at least one candidate who was invited to the pastorate declined the invitation on the grounds that his current Church was paying him more than Swadlincote was able to offer.

The reason for these financially straitened circumstances was the heavy burden of building debt carried by the Church. Repayments were draining this Church, as so many others, of money that could have been used for consistent ministry. More than once the Church admitted that the absence of a minister would allow them to make significant in-roads into debt repayment.

There is one exception to this pattern. In November 1890 the Church invited Mr Kenneth Bond to the pastorate on a salary of £100. He accepted the invitation and commenced his work early the following year. In January 1892 the Church was so delighted with his work that they proposed to increase his salary to £120. Mr Bond refused. Whilever there was debt outstanding on the chapel he would not take an increase in his salary. Mr Bond became the longest serving minister at Hill Street, Swadlincote, serving the Church for 14 years between 1891 and 1905. On his departure he received a glowing tribute from the Church Secretary, Mr Thorp.

Hill Street, Swadlincote Baptist Church

Baptist Chapel, Wilmot Road

CHAPTER 22

COTMANHAY and LONG EATON

Although a Baptist Church at Cotmanhay did not formally come into existence until the 1880s, there had in fact been Baptist preaching in the district since the eighteenth century.

The minutes of Ilkeston Baptist Church reveal significant interest in this neighbouring village.

April 1796: "began to preach at Cotmanhay on Lord's Day evenings only."

July 15th 1798: "It was agreed for Mr Felkin to preach at Cotmanhay once a fortnight on Sunday evenings."

In October 1799 Mr Felkin laid down his terms for staying at the Ilkeston-Smalley Church. It included preaching at Cotmanhay "as before."

Very early at Ilkeston we find people being baptised and received into membership who came from Cotmanhay.

October 11th 1801: Baptism at Ilkeston: Mr Wetherell, Cotmanhay

May 30th 1802: Baptism at Ilkeston: Samuel and Mary Cook, Cotmanhay

June 19th 1803: Martha Henshaw, Cotmanhay. She died August 20th 1806 aged 62.

Cotmanhay also features in matters of Church discipline as well. Around 1802 Sarah Sysson of Cotmanhay was removed from membership for non-attendance and for "associating with very carnal people."

The Baptist cause in Cotmanhay was still strong in the 1820s. The Ilkeston minutes record that in October 1822 it was agreed that there should be "a collection for the new forms at Cotmanhay." This would clearly indicate that there was a designated room where preaching took place. On July 26th 1823 the Ilkeston Church Meeting agreed to have collections at Cotmanhay "towards the support of the cause of Christ (at Ilkeston)." Since Cotmanhay was receiving pastoral support from Ilkeston it was deemed appropriate that it should also contribute towards the expenses of the mother Church.

The last apparent reference in the Ilkeston minutes relating to Cotmanhay appears on August 23rd 1848: "Agreed that the preaching at Cotmanhay be discontinued for the present." There is no mention of a Baptist preaching station at Cotmanhay in the 1851 Religious Census.

Ilkeston was still connected with the village, and several new members joined the Ilkeston Church from Cotmanhay. A list of the members of the G.B. Church, Ilkeston for 1862 included the name of John Sisson from Cotmanhay. Reuben Limb from Cotmanhay was baptised in August 1863, and Mary Horridge of Cotmanhay was baptised that year as well.

It was not until 1882, however, that a major attempt was made to launch a separate cause in Cotmanhay. The name associated with that particular initiative is that of Mr Enoch Beardsley.

According to traditions handed down in the history of Cotmanhay, Enoch Beardsley was originally a Primitive Methodist. Along with a group of friends (who called themselves, 'Christ's disciples') they came to a conviction, through Bible study, that baptism should be by immersion. They applied to South Street Baptist Church, Ilkeston, and the group were subsequently baptised as believers.

As a result of this action the Primitive Methodists banned them from speaking from the pulpit, and consequently the group withdrew from the Methodists and began holding their own meetings in Prince Street, in the home of a Mrs Slater.

Enoch Beardsley's determination to see a Baptist building in Cotmanhay resulted in him setting off on an old fashioned fund raising campaign. He ran into difficulty, however, in Boston where the police arrested him for begging and compelled him to spend a night in the cells before proof could be obtained from Ilkeston that he was in fact fund raising for a new Church building!

O November 4th 1882 the group managed to purchase a 437 square yard plot of land off Norman Street for approximately £49 and 3 shillings. The original Trustees of the Church were: Enoch Beardsley (general dealer); Ezekiel Booth (joiner); Israel Whitehead (coal miner); John Hallam (coal miner); Thomas Booth (joiner); Samuel Fisher (coal miner); and William Bostock (coal miner).

Enoch Beardsely, the founder of Cotmanhay Baptist Church, died in 1887. He was only 49 years old.

Hardly anything is recorded about the building that was constructed at Cotmanhay. In 1885 the Church officially came under the wing of The Tabernacle Church, Nottingham. It is recorded as a branch of The Tab. (along with Cross Street, Arnold) in 1885 when it had a membership of 25. Cotmanhay had 12 teachers and 120 scholars. The seating capacity of the building is noted as 350. An entry in 1899 (again under The Tabernacle, Nottingham) lists Cotmanhay as having 30 members.

In 1907 Cotmanhay appeared in the Baptist Handbook for the first time as an independent Church. Its membership was recorded as 40 and they had 135 children on roll.

Cotmanhay's own minute books started in 1905. Brother Wain was elected Secretary. Brother Barton was Treasurer, and Brother Whitehead was presiding Elder. The Deacons were Messrs Barton, Beardsley, Beardsmore, Eaton and Wain. There were also two deaconesses, Sisters Henshaw and Bethel. There were 41 names listed on the membership roll for 1905.

At the AGM on December 4th 1905 Brother E. Beardsley was elected as organist. He was to continue to play a hugely prominent role in the Church for the next thirty years, serving as Chairman and as Secretary at one time or another.

Long Eaton

Unsuccessful attempts to start the work at Long Eaton had taken place earlier in the nineteenth century. Concerted efforts began again, however, about 1860. The Sawley minute book for September 19th 1860 reports that, "Three friends be appointed to go to Eaton to make enquiries about the propriety of beginning a cause there – Allen, Wood and Bennett be the persons to go."

According to the Centenary History of Station Street Baptist Church, Long Eaton, there were seven people from Long Eaton who made the journey over to Sawley each week. In December 1860 the Sawley Church looked at the cost implications of starting a work at Eaton. They estimated it would cost £10 a year of which £4 or £5 had already been pledged. The Church, therefore, agreed to "commence the cause and friends Taylor, Wood and Bennett be a committee to confer with the Eaton friends and make arrangements accordingly."

The Sawley minutes for January 30th 1861 record that a room had been engaged at Eaton and was being fitted out for preaching. The Station Street Centenary book says that the room in question was above a carpenter's shop in High Street, public services commencing in the spring with a bank manager named Marshall conducting the first service "in the dimly lit loft".

The Sawley minutes provide evidence of the growing number of people joining the Church from Long Eaton.

Nov. 1861 "Robert and Martha Hooley of Long Eaton received into fellowship of this Church."

Jan. 1862 "Ann Wheeldon of Long Eaton proposed as a candidate for baptism. Catherine Woolley of Long Eaton be received into our fellowship from the Church at Ilkeston."

March 1862 "Lewis Wheeldon of Long Eaton be received into our fellowship from the Church at Barton. Caleb Grove of Long Eaton be received from the Church at Beeston."

In July 1862 the Sawley meeting were delighted to hear of the availability of a public hall in Long Eaton. And in May 1863 a deputation from Sawley was to "confer with Long Eaton friends respecting the propriety of building a chapel and selecting a proper site." By September that year Sawley were in agreement with purchasing a site for building a chapel (identified by the Long Eaton friends) provided the money could be raised. In January 1864 they agreed to build a chapel at Long Eaton.

The Station Street Centenary book notes that the original chapel building in Long Eaton was on the then Tythe Barn Lane. The site was secured or £67. 10s. 0d and the building was erected at a cost of £350.

So buoyant was the Sawley-Long Eaton work that in July 1870 the Sawley minutes record the appointment of a committee "to visit the members in order to ascertain their views and feelings in reference to a separation from Castle Donington, and how much they can do in a pecuniary point of view towards supporting the cause if such a separation be made."

The separation with Castle Donington was made easier following the Sawley Church's decision (May 1870) to install its own internal baptistery rather than relying on the Castle Donington Church's baptistery as before.

The Long Eaton branch went from strength to strength. In December 1870 the Long Eaton friends asked permission to appoint their own deacons. Sawley agreed. Church Meetings were to alternate between Sawley and Long Eaton. On May 5th 1872 fifteen people were baptised and received into fellowship at Long Eaton. And on May 8th 1872 it was agreed to appoint two Church Secretaries, one for Long Eaton and one for Sawley, as well as purchase two separate minute books. The Association Report for June 1872 (in the name of Sawley and Long Eaton) recorded a combined membership of 159. They had seen 23 baptisms that year.

It was with this renewed optimism that Sawley felt able to indicate to Castle Donington their desire to separate given the unwillingness of Dr Underwood to provide Sawley with more than one service a fortnight.

A Special Church Meeting called for September 20th 1874 rejected a revised offer from Castle Donington which would entail Dr Underwood taking three Sunday afternoons a month. Instead the Sawley Church was exploring a joint ministry arrangement with Long Eaton, and for the rest of 1874 and 1875 a plan was drawn up for pulpit supply between the Sawley and Long Eaton churches. A natural break with Castle Donington and a re-alignment with Long Eaton was moving ahead. Then came the bombshell.

May 31st 1876 "We regret the decision to which the Long Eaton friends have come in separating themselves from Sawley as regards supplying the pulpit."

Long Eaton were not content with becoming a fully fledged Church, they now felt strong enough to call their own minister.

According to the Association Report submitted in June 1876 the Long Eaton and Sawley churches combined had a membership of 187. This divided into a membership for Sawley of 99 and for Long Eaton of 88. Long Eaton clearly felt they had the managerial competence and business acumen as well as the financial resources to go it alone.

On September 24th 1876 the Long Eaton Church issued an invitation to Rev C.T.Johnson of Coalville to become the first minister at Station Street Baptist Church, Long Eaton, on the enormous salary of £120 per annum. Not surprisingly, Mr Johnson accepted the offer.

Sawley finally bowed to the inevitable. In a rather sour and bitter note (February 7ᵗʰ 1877) the Sawley minutes record that: "Considering the cause at Eaton was commenced by the Church at Sawley, and the assistance we have rendered it, we cannot regard their wish to separate from us as reasonable. But rather than have contention and strife, we resolve quietly to submit to it."

The Reports to the Association in June 1877 were issued separately by the two churches.

Long Eaton didn't look back. A dedication service was held on May 15ᵗʰ 1877 to mark the coming into being of this newly independent Baptist Church. The Rev Stevenson from Loughborough conducted the service. Within a short while building plans were again being explored.

As the Church continued to grow it was decided that larger premises were needed. The site next to the old chapel was bought for £350 and plans were drawn up for a new Church building. At a cost of £1,570 the new building was opened for public worship on October 20ᵗʰ 1880. The opening services were conducted by Rev Dr John Clifford. Clifford had been born in Sawley, but brought up at Beeston Baptist Church where he was baptised (1851) and subsequently received his call to the Christian ministry.

The defection of the Long Eaton members was a bitter blow for Sawley. They had always been supported in ministry – mainly by Castle Donington, more recently by Long Eaton – and standing alone unaided was a very daunting prospect. Clearly Sawley lacked the monied and business interests of Long Eaton.

Postscript: Sawley Baptist Church

Cut off from both Castle Donington and Long Eaton for ministerial supplies, Sawley received a further crippling blow when, in 1882, John Stenson left the district. Stenson was John Clifford's maternal uncle.[1] He had been the Sawley Church's Day School Master since 1850 but had also been de facto Church Secretary and unofficial minister, carrying out much of the preaching in the chapel. Denied his services the Church turned instead to the strengthening Baptist Union for support, and through its auspices obtained a grant from the Augmentation Fund which enabled them to call a minister of their own. Rev G. Towler (from Audlem) accepted the call to Sawley in the autumn of 1888 on an annual salary of £80. He was to remain at the Church until his retirement in 1894.

1. See: 'Dr John Clifford' by Sir James Marchant (1924) page 10

Cotmanhay Baptist Church, Norman Street

Mr Enoch Beardsley (1837 – 1888)

THE OLD CARPENTER'S SHOP, 1861

THE FIRST CHAPEL, 1864

THE NEW CHAPEL, 1880

Station Street Baptist Church, Long Eaton and earlier meeting places

CHAPTER 23

RIFTS, SPLITS AND DIVISIONS

Burton: the General Baptists

The General Baptists in Burton had seen steady growth in the decade 1864 – 1874. Membership had risen from 174 to 195. Rev J.P.Tetley (not to be confused with Rev W.H.Tetley of Osmaston Road, Derby) took over at Zion Chapel, Burton following Richard Kenney's retirement in 1867. Mr Tetley stayed at the Church until 1873 when he moved to sunnier climes in Taunton.

In July 1875 the Church called to the pastorate Alfred Underwood who had been in membership at Castle Donington. Not long into his pastorate he became unwell, the Church offering him six weeks rest from his pastoral duties in February 1876. His ordination had to be postponed due to ill health. Generally, however, the work seemed to go well. A mission work was started in Uxbridge Street in a Mr Hardy's room. Membership stood at 211 in 1877.

On 25th August 1878, Alfred Underwood sent a letter of resignation. The letter was quite bitter. He referred to those who were implacably opposed to his ministry, and others who were simply cool. He would conclude his time with them in November.

Alfred Underwood, however, did not leave the Church on his own. There were already several members of his family in the Burton Church. Thomas, Emma and Rebekah Underwood had joined Burton from Barnet in 1864. Emily Underwood joined in 1869 and Sarah Underwood was baptised at Burton in 1871. All these left the Church and became founder members of a new cause which became known as Emmanuel Baptist Church, Parker Street, off the Horninglow Road.

There were 21 founder members of Emmanuel Baptist Church, all from Zion, Burton. In addition to members of the Underwood family there were also several members of the Garner family with whom the

Underwoods were clearly related. Arthur Underwood Garner was the first Church Secretary to the new cause who died tragically (aged 23) on July 3rd 1881.

Into this decidedly family network, strode Rev Dr William Underwood, the former Principal of the Midland Baptist College, who transferred his membership to Emmanuel Baptist Church from Castle Donington in May 1880. Dr Underwood (see appendix 5) was a figure of national significance and was to play a major role within a few years in the bringing together of the General and Particular Baptists into the Baptist Union. In 1880 he came to support his son, Alfred, in this new pioneering venture. The two men agreed to exercise a joint pastorate and to offer their services free of charge.

Parker Street Church was formally constituted on November 30th 1879. Alfred Underwood, Richard Massey and Henry Cowley Sweatman had purchased a parcel of ground near the Horninglow Road, in an area devoid of any Church activity. Trustees were appointed, made up mainly of members of the Underwood – Garner family along with Richard Massey and George Plinn. Dr Underwood officiated at the launch of the new cause which had taken place in the schoolroom of Gilmore House, Needwood Street. Eight days previously (November 22nd 1879) memorial stones for the new chapel were laid, and the whole building was opened on Wednesday 17th March 1880. According to the Church's entry in the Association reports, the Church building cost £1,300 of which £500 had already been subscribed, "chiefly by the townspeople."

The 1881 Report to the Association was even more upbeat. Mention was made of their "flourishing Sunday School." Land had been purchased for a Schoolroom next to the new chapel. "Congregations are increasing, and we are making satisfactory progress in membership, proving the high esteem in which our ministers are held, and their devotion to the spiritual interests of the Church." Membership in 1880 had been 25. In 1881 this stood at 31. In 1880 there had been 62 Sunday School scholars. In 1881 there were 120 of them.

The 1882 Report was a little less encouraging. The Church of England and the Wesleyan Methodists had moved into the district and set up rival Sunday Schools which was impacting on numbers attending the Baptists. But 1882 saw the completion of the Baptist Schoolrooms which were officially opened on the 15th and 16th October that year.

The first real blow to the fledgling cause came in 1883 when Alfred Underwood indicated that he would be leaving Burton and taking up a pastorate in Croydon. (This was in a Congregational rather than a Baptist Church). His departure in the April left the aged William Underwood to carry the pastoral office alone. He had signified his willingness to carry this responsibility for a while until alternative arrangements could be made. But no alternative arrangements were made, so in May 1884 Dr Underwood indicated that he too would relinquish pastoral responsibilities that summer. He remained in the Church carrying out several duties (visiting people for membership for example), but the Church were obliged to look elsewhere for ministerial support.

In July 1884 the Church appointed Mr Monti, on a six months contract. They chose not to renew this at Christmas. In May 1885 they invited Mr G.E.Payne to the pastorate, on the dismal salary of £70 a year. His ordination took place on 30th September. Church membership in 1885 was 48, and stood at 50 twelve months later.

In June 1886 the Church once again submitted a very positive appraisal of their situation. They were most grateful for all Mr Payne's efforts. "The spiritual condition of our Church has improved, and the congregations increased. The school is in a flourishing condition." They were contemplating a bazaar to help reduce the chapel debt.

The chapel debt was a problem. In September 1886 they still owed £700. They managed to get the interest charged on that amount reduced from 5% to 4%, and by June 1887 they had reduced their indebtedness by £140. But financial reports from the treasurer indicated that outgoings were outstripping incomings.

There then followed a spate of resignations. Mr Garner resigned as Church Secretary in December 1886. Mr Ireland took over, who himself resigned the following May. On March 15th 1887 Mr Massey handed in his resignation as choirmaster along with the resignation of the whole choir. He also indicated his intention of removing his organ from the Church. A rather down-beat Report to the Association in June 1888 said that Sunday congregations were not so large as they would desire, and that Mr Garner had resigned his office as Church Secretary (again?)

This is the last entry in the minute book of Emmanuel Baptist Church. The Zion minute book for this period does, however, contain further information.

On September 22nd 1888 a letter was addressed to the Pastor and Deacons of New Street Baptist Church, Burton from Thomas Garner and Thomas Underwood:

"Circumstances have arisen which render it necessary for us to dispose of Parker Street chapel. We write to ask if you will take to it and work it as a branch of your cause. We feel it would be a great pity for the chapel to go out of the connexion...."

The Burton Church agreed to this request and on October 24th began to make plans to appoint an assistant minister with responsibility for the work at Parker Street. On February 13th 1889 the New Street Church Meeting was informed that the Sunday School at Parker Street was very encouraging with between 50 – 60 children attending each Sunday morning and between 70 – 80 in the afternoons. By the November, however, the deacons were recommending that the Church dispose of the Parker Street property. The friends at Parker Street should be given first refusal but thereafter it should be placed on the open market.

The 1890 Report to the Association from New Street, Burton summed up the sad affair:

"We are sorry that having last year taken over Parker Street chapel with a liability of over £600 we have been compelled to close it. A little help from Home Mission might have saved the cause."

Money, or the lack of it, clearly lay at the heart of the failure of the Parker Street Church. The Loughborough District and West Leicestershire Union Magazine for 1897 carries an account of the Baptist Churches in Burton. It makes it quite clear that "financial difficulties" were the reasons why it was found necessary to discontinue the effort at Parker Street. It remains a mystery why Home Mission support was never forthcoming for this cause when it was made available to many other causes in less promising situations. The Loughborough Union Magazine went on to say that "the chapel was ultimately disposed of to the Primitive Methodists, who had a chapel a short distance away and needed a larger one." It also added that, "the necessity for a Baptist Chapel was not so great as formerly, the requirements of the neighbourhood being well met by the commodious Tabernacle in Derby Street."

Burton: the Particular Baptists

The General Baptists in Burton were not the only ones to experience friction and fracture. In December 1871 a group of 18 members from Station Street Particular Baptist Church, Burton, signed a joint letter of resignation objecting to the treatment of the minister of Station Street Church, Rev T. Hanson. The Station Street Church had been having financial difficulties, and the Church Officers had effectively given Mr Hanson (minister there for just over two years) notice to leave by 10th October. Inspite of Mr Hanson's best efforts to find a solution he was compelled to leave, and subsequently had to take legal action to secure £10.4.6 owed to him by the Church.

The seceding group held their first service of worship on December 24th 1871 in St George's Hall Assembly Rooms. Rev Hanson assumed the pastorate.

On 31st March 1872 Mr Hanson sent this new group his own letter of resignation. His health was not good and he had been advised on medical grounds to leave Burton. His letter is most touching. He refers to the great regret and pain he had in leaving them; to the great kindness they have shown to him and his wife. "We never expect to meet with truer friends among imperfect mortals." His one consolation in leaving was that the group had decided to stay together.

The following Sunday Mr Hanson formally constituted the group into a Church in their own right. Deacons were appointed: Richard Hill, Edwin Bates, Wm R. Porter; Abraham Blant.

In May 1872 the Church entered into negotiations to purchase a piece of ground on Guild Street on which to build a chapel. A friend offered to lend them the money on two and a half per cent interest. That same month a Farewell Tea was held for Thomas and Martha Hanson. A purse containing £50 was handed over along with gifts for Mrs Hanson, and books for Charlie and Alfred Hanson. The family moved to Bingley in Yorkshire.

The small group meeting in the St George's Hall were clearly not impoverished. The gift to Mr Hanson was equivalent to half a year's stipend. They went on to invite Rev Rodway to take up the pastorate of the Church in May 1872, offering him £80 a year. The following January they increased this to £100. This was with a membership of no more than 20.

Land had been obtained for a chapel, but no building had been constructed. In February 1873 they decided to erect a temporary structure on the site. It was to be a prefabricated building, and to be erected by the congregation themselves. Early attempts at construction proved abortive when one night the tin shed blew down! Eventually, on April 26th 1874 the second hand iron chapel was opened for worship. It was always regarded as a temporary arrangement.

On August 9th 1874 the Church invited Mr John Askew from Spurgeon's College to the pastorate. It was to prove a providential appointment. Rev Askew was to exercise one of the longest and most fruitful ministries in the county. Guild Street Church was to be the only Church he served as pastor.

Ilkeston

There had been a rift at Queen Street, Ilkeston in 1859 when the Church had refused to increase the salary of Rev T.R Stevenson forcing his departure for Burnley. A disenchanted group began to meet in the old South Street premises. It took a whole year before reconciliation was possible.

In October 1879 Ilkeston invited Rev Perriam to the pastorate of the Church. They did not have the money to pay him, but six members agreed to advance the money to the Church. He commenced his ministry in the December with Recognition Services held on Shrove Tuesday 1880.

On November 10th the deacons recommended to the Church that Mr Perriam's appointment should be extended only for twelve months. When the recommendation was put to the Church Meeting on the same day, it was rejected in favour of an open ended invitation to Mr Perriam to stay as their pastor.

Mr Sisson and the deacons saw this as a vote of no confidence. The Church Meeting, however, reaffirmed its confidence in them. Clearly there were strains in the relationships between various sections of the Church.

In September 1851 some 53 members of Queen Street, Ilkeston (including all the deacons) seceded from the Church and obtained permission to meet in the old South Street buildings. They commenced public worship there on September 4th 1881.

The dispute was not over doctrine but mainly over personality and style of management, Mr Perriam being accused of despotism!

The Association appointed a Board of Arbitration (as they had done in 1859) to meet the two groups. This time there appeared to be no prospects of reconciliation, and the recommendation of the Arbitrators was that "for a season" the two parties should meet and worship separately. The season was to last until 1920!

On February 26th 1882 South Street Baptist Church formally came into being at a service conducted by Rev Yates of Newthorpe. Deacons needed to be chosen, and following a ballot of all the male members of South Street, all the old Queen Street deacons were elected, namely Messrs Sisson, Briggs, Hollis, Handworth, Cook, Spencer, and Knighton.

For several months the arrangement between South Street and Queen Street involved them sharing the South Street premises. But following several unfortunate mix ups and misunderstandings the Board of Arbitration recommended that South Street be sold to the seceders, an action that was completed in October 1882. South Street paid over £200 for the old premises (the money was loaned from members within the Church); new trustees for South Street were appointed, and the separation was complete.

Armed with £200 cash the Queen Street Church set about a major renovation and extension to their premises. A new gallery was installed and new schoolrooms constructed. The Church's seating capacity increased from 400 to 500.

Mr Perriam married a young woman in the Church, and in July 1884 he concluded his ministry at Queen Street, taking up the pastorate at Dewsbury in Yorkshire. Queen Street Baptist Church became a hot bed for the Temperance movement in the latter part of the century which did not go down well with some of the other clergy in the town!

The membership at Queen Street inevitably took a nose dive in the years following the South Street secession. In 1890 they only had 76 members, while South Street had a membership of 81. But the minutes of the South Street Church indicate a somewhat fractious group of Christians. They had some difficulty getting the office holders to attend meetings regularly. In the early twentieth century, the fortunes of both causes were reversed. In 1903 membership at Queen Street had grown to 127. At South Street it had fallen back to 51. In 1914 Queen Street had a membership of 173 with a Sunday School of 380. South Street had 144 children on roll, but only 49 Church Members.

Long Eaton

After a steady beginning in the 1860s, the Baptist cause in Long Eaton then went through a period of spectacular growth which saw it obtain its independence from Sawley, and the appointment of its own minister. In 1887, however, the Church faced a major crisis.

Little has been written down about the events which led to the separation of members from Station Street Baptist Church. The only account available today is the brief one found in the front of the first minute book of St. John's Baptist Church, Long Eaton compiled by the Church Secretary at St John's, Mr Adkin:

"This Church was founded as the result of serious differences arising out of matters of Church discipline among the members of the Station Street Baptist Church. In August 1887, 55 members resigned in consequence and for a time held meetings in Mr J. Wardle's room in Conway Street. Having decided to form a separate Church, the old Primitive Methodist building in Chapel Street was rented and for 8 years the members worshipped here as the Chapel Street Baptist Church."

There is no way of discovering the precise nature of this issue of Church discipline. One or two of the older members of the respective Long Eaton Baptist Churches did believe that it pertained to the unequal treatment of richer and poorer members of the Church with regard to matters of Church discipline. It is particularly noteworthy that of the 55 names listed on the members' roll of St John's Baptist Church there are no members of the Hooley family.

In the EMBA Archives in Market Harborough there is a copy of a brief "History of the Long Eaton St John's Baptist Church" given at Long Eaton St John's Baptist Women's League by Mr G.N.Adkin on 19th October 1936. This Mr Adkin (who joined the Church in 1899) stated that:

"In 1887 an unfortunate division of opinion arose among the members of the Station Street Church (mainly on political issues) and in August 1887 some 55 members resigned their membership."

Whether this account is any more accurate than some of the oral explanations is impossible to determine.

The older Mr Adkin's account of the origins of the second General Baptist Church in Long Eaton (in the St John's minute book) explained that the first officers of the new Church were elected on September 9th 1887, and that on Sunday 18th September a Sunday School was formed. In February 1888 Rev Henry Wood, former pastor of the Station Street Baptist Church, took over pastoral responsibility for the new cause.

In March 1890 a building fund was commenced in order to secure a site for new buildings. A site was purchased (October 1892) for £288. The tender of Mr G. Youngman was accepted in April 1895; a stone laying ceremony took place on June 25th 1895; and the buildings of St John's Baptist Church were opened on November 5th that same year.

St John's, Clumber Street, Long Eaton

It is now home to the New Testament Church of God.

Rev Evan Webb of Haverfordwest College was elected pastor of the Church in March 1893. He appears to have concluded his ministry in something of a hurry towards the end of 1900, and under something of a cloud, with certain money unaccounted for in an account he was handling. Inspite of that, the St John's Baptist Church did experience tangible growth. In 1890 they had a membership of 81. By 1900 the St John's Church had a membership of 101, and by 1903 they were already drawing up plans for a new building despite still owing £190 on the existing one. At the outbreak of World War One, Church Membership stood at 111, with 302 children on the Sunday School register.

One interesting piece of information is found in the financial records of St John's Long Eaton. For the year ending December 31st 1899 the weekly offerings totalled £93 8 shillings and 1 penny. The minister's salary for the same year amounted to £90. The Church's annual turnover was £116 7 shillings and 9 pence. Approximately 80% of the Church's total income went to pay the minister.

Station Street Baptist Church recovered well from the devastation of the 1887 split. Although they had no paid ministry for ten years after the debacle, the Church definitely prospered. Church Membership was recorded as 113 before the split (1884). Even after the defection of the 55 members in 1887, the membership at Station Street had climbed back to 115 by 1897. In 1906 the Church recorded a membership of 143, and by the outbreak of the First World War the membership was an impressive 182, with 212 scholars on roll.

Station Street also prospered financially as well. In 1898 Ernest J Hooley, grandson of one of the founders of the Church, donated a house to the Church When (November 1902) Mr James Cottam was called to be their minister the Church offered him a salary of £130 for his first year and £140 for his second year. This was far in excess of anything that St John's were able to pay their minister.

In 1906 Ernest Hooley began to draw up plans for a new Church building and schoolrooms. The tender of Messrs Stevens and Warren (members of the Church) was accepted. It amounted to £2,187. The old premises were demolished, and Foundation Stones for the new building were laid on November 5th 1907, the new chapel and Schoolrooms being opened in the summer of 1908.

By the time of the First World War the two Baptist Churches in Long Eaton had a combined membership of 293. Both were in healthy shape and were exercising significant influence in the town. The split that occurred in 1887 seemed to have acted as a spur to growth and missionary enterprise, and paradoxically appeared to have benefited the Baptist work in Long Eaton.

Melbourne

In November 1900 Melbourne Baptist Church celebrated its 150th Anniversary. Special Services and a Tea were held to mark the occasion. The Church's glory days had long since passed. Its membership had peaked in 1861 (325 members), and from that point onwards had shown relentless and remorseless decline. At the AGM on 26th December 1900 the Church recorded a membership of 170.

The Rev A.H.Coombes had assumed the pastorate of the Church in October 1898. In January 1901 it was decided to withdraw the suggestion of increasing the minister's salary. This was partly because of financial constraints and partly not "to divide the Church on the matter." In January 1902 the minutes of the Officers' Meeting refers to "several grievances that exist among the members which was causing considerable friction." However, it isn't clear whether the grievances were directed at the minister or at the deacons.

A clear tussle went on between the Church leadership and the membership throughout those early months of the year. Demands for a Special Church Meeting from members were turned down by the five-strong diaconate. In March a vote of no-confidence in the deacons was narrowly defeated by 56 votes to 43. On May 22nd the minister, who had been ill with all the stress, took the unusual step of recommending that two vacancies on the diaconate be filled by Joseph Barton and James Coxon. If the Church did not back this suggestion by a two thirds majority then he would resign. The deacons refused to endorse the proposal, and at the subsequent Church Meeting the minister's proposal gained a majority (57 to 43) but failed to gain the necessary two thirds. Mr Coombes resigned.

At the close of the meeting the supporters of the minister gave notice of their intention to hold a meeting on 28th May in the Schoolroom. The upshot of that Wednesday evening meeting was that the group decided to temporarily withdraw their membership from the Church; to have their own services in the Public Hall; and to invite Mr Coombes to minister to them. The seceders' letter accused the deacons of arbitrarily trying to govern the Church.

A deputation from the Association failed to mend the breach. On 31st December 1902 the seceders decided to make their breach permanent, and on New Year's Day Miss Margaret B Earp, Secretary of the Derby Road congregation, wrote to Mr Smith, Church Secretary of Melbourne Baptist Church, informing him of this decision. Mr Smith's reply expressed bafflement and dismay at their decision. He saw no justification in their action. He did not feel that Melbourne warranted having two Baptist Churches (We can't fill one never mind two!) The whole idea of separation "seems to us most absurd." On February 4th 1903 fifty one members tendered their resignations to Melbourne Baptist Church. They were received into the Association as a separate Church (with some misgivings on the part of the EMBA) in 1904.

The Melbourne Church, reduced now to 130 members, picked up where they had left off. A student minister served them throughout 1903. They called Rev J.F.Archer to the pastorate, and agreed to enlarge a house, bequeathed in a legacy, to make it a more suitable Church manse. (They had refused to do this for Mr Coombes). The Derby Road congregation also began to develop a life of its own with its own programme of activities. One interesting feature of the Church (their minute books are preserved in the Melbourne records) is their practice of recording the gender of those attending Church Meetings. On December 27th 1905, for example, the pastor was present along with 7 male and 15 female members. In January 1907 the pastor was present at the Church Meeting along with 4 male and 21 female members. In June 1908 there were 5 male and 24 female members present.

The Derby Road Church was upbeat in its reports to the Association. In 1905 they reported that congregations at Sunday and week night Services had kept up, and School attendance had been maintained. They also reported that finances were in good shape. (They paid Mr

Coombes £120 a year, which some churches with three times the membership struggled to afford.)

The fledgling Baptist cause received a terrible blow in December 1907 when Mr Coombes announced he was leaving, having received a call from Sale Baptist Church, Manchester. The Derby Road Church decided to carry on, and in June 1908 they called Rev Eric Roberts from Glasgow to the pastorate on a salary of £100 a year. Mr Roberts' ministry was appreciated and fruitful so that by 1911 the Church intimated in their report to the Association their hopes to obtain premises of their own. The membership at Melbourne and Ticknall that year was 145; at Derby Road the membership was 60.

The background to the 1912 Report to the Association was the vacancy of the Melbourne pastorate. The Derby Road congregation reported:

"In September we opened negotiations with the other Baptist Church here with a view to reunion, and made a united and earnest endeavour for three months to achieve this end, but the two churches did not succeed in arriving at an arrangement satisfactory to both."

Three years later, the roles were reversed. Melbourne had called Rev Ivor Evans as their minister in 1914. Shortly afterwards Eric Roberts left the Derby Road congregation. In 1917 Derby Road no longer appeared as an entry in the Association list of churches. Melbourne and Ticknall by contrast were recorded with a membership of 210, a net increase of 60 on the previous year. Of those 60 new members, 56 were transfers in.

Fifteen years after the breach took place, Melbourne had a united Baptist Church once again.

CHAPTER 24

MORE BUILDING WORK

Heanor

Following the attempt by two of the Tag Hill Trustees to sell the chapel in 1854, financial and preaching support had been made available to the Church by the North Derbyshire Conference. In 1860 the Smalley Church Meeting received a deputation from Tag Hill requesting a formal separation of the two churches. This was granted, and the following year Heanor Baptist Church was received into the North Derbyshire Conference – with some hesitation. There was general regret expressed at some of the smaller churches in the Connexion fragmenting and weakening themselves in this way.

Independence was premature. In the 1864 Baptist Handbook Tagg Hill still appeared as a branch of Smalley. The mother Church was attributed a membership of 83; Tagg Hill had a membership of 30. In 1867 another meeting with the friends at Smalley agreed that while remaining separate in their responsibilities they should once again be considered as "mutually joined, and act together as one Church in reporting members and progress to Conferences, and in presenting the annual statement to the Association." The subsequent 1868 Report to the Association was in the name of Smalley and Heanor. The Report observed that, "Heanor are making strenuous efforts to pay off the remaining £100 on their chapel debt."

Enormous strides must have been made, because in 1875 Heanor Baptists embarked on an ambitious new building scheme, and the erection of a new chapel. An appeal for funds appeared in the General Baptist Magazine for March 1875:

"Tag Hill, Heanor, Derbyshire: the friends here have long needed more room for their school work and for worship. It is resolved to build a Chapel and Schoolroom at a cost of about £800. The people are mostly poor, but have generously raised the first hundred and intend to have a bazaar on Easter Tuesday. This is village work, and help is greatly needed and deserved. Rev J. Wilshire of Derby [St Mary's Gate] or I. Bircumshaw, Tag Hill, will gratefully receive goods or money towards this object."

Some support must have been forthcoming because the April edition of the Baptist Magazine included an acknowledgement to those who had supported them (and a further appeal to "any in sympathy with the project."). The article said that the Easter Bazaar and a Good Friday Concert had yielded £122 to the building fund.

The New Heanor Baptist Chapel and Schoolrooms were constructed in 1876. Their Report to the Association for 1877 provided brief information on the work. It cost £1350 to build, and they had raised £400 towards this amount. Never one to miss a trick, the Report also mentioned the poverty of the Church Members and ended with a further appeal for financial assistance!

The 1879 Report to the Association provided additional information regarding the financing of the building of the Chapel and Schoolrooms. £700 was borrowed from the Derby Building Society (to be paid back in monthly instalments of £5 12 shillings), and a further £200 was borrowed from the General Baptist Building Fund. In other words the Church borrowed two thirds of the cost of the building work. This was either brave or foolhardy given the impoverishment of its Church Members. The 1879 Report went on to add that servicing the loans was a strain upon our finances "in the present depression of trade."

In 1883 Heanor Baptist Church narrowly escaped another disaster. On the first Sunday in December the chapel caught fire. But for the quick witted attentions of a little girl who lived opposite the chapel and who noticed smoke coming from the buildings, the whole place would have gone up in smoke. As it was, help was summoned, the fire contained, and the damage was limited to £126. A new pulpit seemed to have been the main item needed following the incident.

With heavy financial commitments through servicing their building loans there was little money available to pay for regular ministry. In

1882 the Church rejoiced in the calling of Rev E. Hilton in conjunction with Smalley and Kilburn. By 1884, however, Mr Hilton had decided to concentrate his endeavours on Smalley and Kilburn (to great effect), and withdrew his involvement with Heanor. The Church's Report to the Association that year reflected a sombre mood: "dark clouds are over us."

Membership at Heanor stood at 30 in 1864. By 1874 this had risen to 40, with an additional 170 Sunday School scholars on roll. Thereafter they continued to make steady progress:

1877	-	52 members
1879	-	67 members
1882	-	83 members (and 269 scholars)

Numbers fell back following the departure of Mr Hilton (membership was only 65 in 1890). The new East Midlands Baptist Association encouraged Heanor to consider joining with Langley Mill and Loscoe for ministerial purposes (December 1892). This never materialised. The following year Ripley Baptist Church asked Heanor if they would like a share of their minister. Nothing came of this suggestion. Eventually, Heanor did manage to link with another Church for ministry. In February 1895 Rev G.D.Jeffcoat was recognised as Pastor of Heanor Baptist Church at the same time as he served at Queen Street, Ilkeston. The arrangement lasted for three years.

In 1900 Heanor had a Church membership of 90. It was in that year that they called Rev J.T.Owers as minister, ushering in what has been referred to as the 'Golden Age' of Heanor Baptist Church. In 1909 the Church constructed the Sunday School Hall at the rear of the building at a cost of £1,500. Additional improvements were made to the chapel itself at a cost of £800. These amounts were all cleared during Mr Owers' ministry at Heanor. In 1914 Heanor had a membership of 108 and a Sunday School roll of 292.

Crich

Following the hiatus of revival, and then the dramatic departure of Rev Shakespeare, Crich Baptists eventually settled back into a more stable form of existence. Their report to the Association for 1868 reads:

"Our congregations are tolerably good, and the Gospel is faithfully preached. The attendance at the Lord's Table is generally good, and at times truly refreshing. We have reduced the debt upon our chapel and expended considerable sums in improvements. Our Sabbath school is very encouraging and steadily increasing which leads us to contemplate the necessity for increasing our school accommodation."

Crich had no minister and was not to have one for many years. Church Membership in 1864 stood at 43. Preaching was supplied by the friends from Derby and Ripley for which Crich continually expressed their appreciation.

The Report to the Association for 1871 mentioned that they intended to hold a bazaar to clear off the small debt on the old chapel "with a view to building a new one." By 1876 plans had more or less come to fruition.

"We have not yet got our new chapel property signed over to us: our solicitors have entered the case in chancery. We hope, however, it will ere long come out on the right side. The property and site is a very desirable one for a chapel, as it is in the centre of the village and Market Place. The cost of the purchase is £660 in the first instance, but we fear more will be added by law, which causes us much anxiety as we are poor."

This report to the Association highlights a degree of controversy over the purchase of the Market Place site. One explanation of the controversy is recorded in J.G. Dawes, 'A History of Crich' published in 2003.

"The Baptists opened their first chapel in Crich in 1839 on Roe's Lane, but by 1875 it was in a dilapidated state and they made a bid for the present site on Market Place." [This was Wheeldon House, owned by Ralph Wheeldon Smith. He was experiencing some financial difficulties and had to part with some of his property.] "Smith claimed the Baptists wanted the site, the auctioneer for the cottages was a Baptist, and Smith lost his house before he knew what was happening. To the end of his life he insisted that he had been the victim of sharp practice."

Dawes goes on to say that there was much bad feeling in the village over the incident which was considered a swindle. Many in the village thought that "all the Baptists ought to dangle like tassles at the end of ropes."

The matter once resolved in favour of Crich Baptists the building work commenced. The 1877 Report to the Association recorded that the walls were up to the first floor windows. The 1879 Report recorded that everything was now completed:

"The past year has witnessed the opening of our new, commodious and beautiful chapel, situate in the centre of the Market place. It has cost about £2,400 towards which £900 has been realised. The Opening Services were held last August. The interior of the chapel is very compact and is pronounced the nicest country chapel in the county. It contains a good organ. The congregation is much improved since we left the old chapel. There is a new clock put in the front elevation, which cost £50 ... the funds for the clock were subscribed by the public."

In August 1879, Rev John Clifford, the doyen of English General Baptists, preached at Crich and delivered a lecture. He was to pay them a second visit in July 1881.

The debt on the building remained with them for years. In 1881 they told the Association that their chapel debt stood at £1510. In 1886 they were able to inform the Association that they had managed to pay off £500 of debt in eight years. The Church was never in a position to look for a minister. Each year they expressed their appreciation to the

Derby Baptist Preachers Association and the students from the Baptist College in Nottingham for supplying their pulpit.

When Crich began to think about the building scheme in 1871 they had a membership of 35. This grew to 48 by 1884 and to 63 by 1890. But thereafter membership slipped back to the same levels it had been prior to the new building scheme. In 1906 Crich Baptist Church had a membership of 34 and had 105 Sunday School scholars. By 1914 they had 42 members and 89 scholars.

Trinity Baptist Church, Derby

Agard Street Baptist Church, Derby, was on the verge of extinction, and would undoubtedly have faded away into the annals of history had it not been for a remarkable intervention. In 1876 the Great Northern Railway Company received permission from Derby Borough Council to set up a station and line in competition with their great rival the Midland Railway Company. The GNR proposal required a new bridge to cross the bottom of Friar Gate and the compulsory purchase of properties on Agard Street including the Baptist Chapel. The trustees were paid £3,000 for the site and the old building came down[1].

The congregation of about 30 people entered into a nomadic existence for a number of years, meeting for a while at the Friends Meeting House and then later in a loft on Agard Street. Throughout this period the search went on for a new site for a place of worship.

One of the complications in purchasing a new site was in connection with the Trusteeship of the Church. According to the 'Schedule for Deeds and Documents' a new set of private trustees had been appointed in December 1856. When, towards the end of 1877, purchase of a new site looked imminent the firm of Joseph Bright, Solicitors, of Nottingham wrote to the trustees (7th December) requesting them to attend an urgent meeting at the Bell Hotel, Derby, on 18th December. Many of the replies from the trustees still survive. The replies contain apologies for absence, news of the death of the trustees, and several letters of resignation including one from

C.H.Spurgeon who had no idea he was still charged with that responsibility.

The inability of the Church to gather its trustees together caused difficulties for the legal team. Eventually on December 12ᵗʰ 1877 Mr Robotham, acting for Joseph Bright Solicitors, outlined a plan which he had floated before the Charity Commissioners. It basically entailed the trustees for the School (who were separate from the trustees of the Chapel) using some of the money from the GNR to purchase land for a Sunday School and proceed with the construction of the Schoolrooms. Subsequently, a Scheme was to be drawn up which transferred the Trusteeship of the Chapel to the trustees of the School thus, in effect, amalgamating the two Trust bodies.

According to a note of 5ᵗʰ November 1877 on 'Notts, Derbys, and Lincolnshire Baptist Association' headed paper the original hope had been to purchase a plot of land on Duffield Road which was coming up at auction. "In the event of failing to obtain that property, to negotiate for the purchase of the site next to the School of Art in Green Lane, Derby." The Church did not manage to obtain the Duffield Road site. Instead in 1879 new Schoolrooms were built on the Green Lane site, and the following year a new chapel was constructed next to the Schoolrooms. As if reborn, the Church decided to give itself a new name. Trinity Baptist Church came into existence.

The 20 members of the old Agard Street Baptist Chapel moved into their new premises on Green Lane, Derby in 1880. Rev W. Woods, from Nottingham, had been acting as pastor of the Church at the request of the NDL Baptist Association. In January 1881 he handed over these 20 members to the pastoral care of Rev J.H.Millard who was aided by the Baptist Home Mission and the Notts, Derbys, and Lincolnshire Association. According to the Centenary Manual, Mr Millard died in post in 1883 having increased the membership to 33 and raised £200 to help clear off the outstanding debt on the new chapel.

In January 1884, Rev W.F.Harris arrived as the minister having served at Chesterfield for four and a half years. Mr Harris' ministry was a quite extraordinary one, especially given the lamentable condition in which the Church had found itself during the 1860s and 1870s. Writing in the Centenary Manual (1896) Harris was able to report that in the previous 12 years the Church had "become larger than at any previous period of its history. About 300 have been received into fellowship since, and instead of 33, the membership stands now at 200: there were 88 scholars in the school then, and there are about 400 now." The Church had also successfully raised over £5,000 during those 12 years. Some of this was for ordinary Church purposes; but £800 had been raised for a new organ and gallery, and for renovating the chapel and schoolrooms; a further £880 had been raised for Foreign and Home Missions. The Church had become independent of outside financial help in 1888.

Mr Harris' ministry represents the high water mark of Trinity Baptist Church. It coincided with a period of rapid house building and population expansion in the borough of Derby, and reflected an increase in congregation and membership enjoyed by most of the Baptist Churches in the town. Nevertheless it represents a remarkable turn around from the sad times of only a few years before. According to a copy of the pastor's Report for 1901 there had been a net increase in membership during the year of 7, bringing the total membership figure up to 218. Alas, the progress wasn't to continue.

When the Deacons and Church Meeting Minute Books commence in 1904 we find Rev E.M.Yeomans serving as the Minister. Mr Yeomans had been the assistant Minister at Victoria Road Baptist Church, Leicester. Miscellaneous correspondence in the Trinity Baptist Church archive include letters recommending Mr Yeomans to the Church including one from the Secretary of the Baptist Union of Great Britain and Ireland, Rev J.H.Shakespeare. Mr Yeomans began his ministry in Derby in July 1903. Unfortunately he was not to stay long at the Church. The Church Meeting minutes for November 17th 1905 contain an extremely sad letter of resignation from Mr Yeomans stating that,

"there are elements in the Church and in the diaconate which not only make it useless for me to continue my work among you as a Minister of the Gospel, but which alas make that work impossible........"

Clearly he had not had an easy time at the Church. Numbers had fallen. The 200 members referred to by Rev Harris in the Centenary Manual (1896) had fallen to 138 by 1907. In a bundle of correspondence covering this period there are several notes from Rev W.A.Richards of Pear Tree Road requesting the transfer of members from Trinity who had started worshipping at Pear Tree. Things did improve during the time of Rev W.A Coventry who succeeded Mr Yeomans, with membership rising to 172 in 1912 before falling back again by the time he left in 1916.

Reading the Church Meeting and Deacons Meeting Minutes for this period there is a definite sense of what might have been. As early as 1912 the Derby Education Committee approached the Green Lane Church to enquire whether they could purchase their premises for an extension to the Technical College next door. By 1914 negotiations had become very serious. In September 1914 the Church informed the Town Clerk that they wanted £4,000 for the site. The Town Clerk wrote back in November offering them £3,500. Whatever the outcome of the bargaining, by January 1915 the Church had set up a working group to look for a new site for the Church in view of the anticipated sale.

An indication of the importance and interest generated by these events can be gleaned from the fact that on February 17th 1915 a deputation from the Baptist Union arrived to encourage the Church to pursue the sale and to give serious consideration to purchasing a plot of land on Breedon Hill Road. The deputation consisted of J.H.Shakespeare, Dr Gould and Rev Harris. By April it became clear that the Breedon Hill Road site wasn't viable but Dr Haslam, another national Baptist figure, reported on two further sites, recommending one on Overdale Road and eventually securing willingness of the owner of the land, Mrs Hall of Leeds, to agree to the sale for £800.

The First World War was to bring the curtailment of these plans. In June 1915 the Education Committee informed the Church that due to restrictions on capital expenditure during the War they would have to withdraw their offer for the chapel. The disappointment must have been palpable. Four months later Rev Coventry informed the deacons he intended to look for another Church.

Wirksworth

In February 1879 Rev Caleb Springthorpe arrived at Wirksworth, and, according to the 1918 Centenary booklet, "From the beginning of his ministry his heart was set upon the erection of a new house of prayer for Wirksworth."

The first obstacle to overcome was the purchase of the house and shop in front of the existing Church. This was eventually achieved, but a formal legal notice requiring Mr Palin, the tenant, to quit had to be issued in September 1884.

Finance was always going to be the big problem. Here the Church was particularly fortunate to have the support of the Spencer family, who proved enormously generous benefactors to Wirksworth Baptist Church. Mr Robert Spencer and his wife Mary retired to Wirksworth from Manchester in 1871, and joined the Church. He became a deacon, and when he died in 1882 he left a legacy of £500 to be issued to Wirksworth Baptist Church whenever the Executors of the will determined the Church were ready to build a new chapel. This sum was to be augmented by Mr George Spencer on the condition that building work did not commence until £1,200 was already in hand. Thomas and William Spencer from Manchester also provided practical advice as members of the building committee.

Plans for the new chapel were designed by Mr Wallis Chapman of London. A contract was signed with Messrs Walker & Sons, and on May 28th 1885 Memorial Stones were laid. Two further stones were laid in the vestibule in October by William and John Malin, sons of the late Mr George Malin.

On March 15th 1886 Dr John Clifford conducted the opening service of the new Wirksworth Baptist Church. The total cost of the new buildings, including fittings and furnishings amounted to £3,000.

The completion of the chapel was the crowning glory of Rev Springthorpe's ministry. J.H. Starkey's Centenary Booklet (1918) refers to Springthorpe's "declining years" and suggests that infirmity caused his eventual retirement to Leicester in 1887. The Church minute books, however, suggest that finance was another reason for his resignation. He was refused a pay increase in March 1887, and resigned in the May. The Church, mindful of their heavy chapel debts, decided not to look for a minister. It was not until November 1889 that Mr Noble was invited to the pastorate.

The construction of a wonderful new building usually led to an increase in congregation and membership. That did not happen at Wirksworth. A membership of 112 in 1882 was 102 in 1894. One reason for this drop was the separation of the Bonsall Church.

There had been grumblings between Wirksworth and Bonsall throughout the 1880s. Bonsall complained that the preachers didn't always turn up. Wirksworth complained that Bonsall didn't pay their dues regularly either. There was also a dispute over the deeds to the Bonsall property. On October 13th 1897 the Wirksworth Church Meeting requested the friends at Bonsall, "to withdraw from the Wirksworth Church and form themselves into a separate Church." Mr Noble would no longer exercise any pastoral responsibility for them after 31st December 1897. In March 1898 16 members were transferred from Wirksworth to Bonsall.

By 1914 the membership at Bonsall had risen to 26. At Wirksworth it stood at 116.

Belper

In 1864 Belper Baptist Church had a membership of 19. The North Derbyshire Conference, in the light of that church's numerical weakness, but also its persistently fractious nature, recommended closure. Belper refused. They jumped ship, joined the Midland Conference in the hope of better advice, but found here too an unwillingness to invest in the Church's future. The Church did, however, survive.

In December 1870 they invited Mr Beddowes to become their pastor. True to form, the arrangement proved to be a disaster. In May 1871, Mr Beddowes left the Church with a cluster of other members and for three years set up a rival congregation meeting in the Infant School. The 1874 statistics reveal that the Bridge Street Church, Belper had a membership of 34, while the secessionists in the High Street had 20. No further entry for Mr Beddowes congregation appeared.

From this point onwards the Belper Baptist Church began to turn a corner. The 1877 Report to the Association was totally unlike any that had previously appeared:

"Our Sabbath school is very good, but we are still labouring under very great difficulties for the want of a school room. The ladies have been working very hard at their sewing meetings in order to raise funds for the above object. We have been trying some time to purchase land on either side or at the back of the chapel, but it seems impossible. We are hemmed in all round, and our neat little chapel is being destroyed by holding the school in it. We have come almost to the conclusion, to alter the chapel, making the chapel above and the school room below."

In 1879 the Church reported to the Association that they had great cause to rejoice. The Spirit of God was working in their midst. Their minister was working hard, and his labours were abundantly blessed. There were seven candidates for baptism; congregations were very good and the Sunday School was increasing in numbers.

The 1881 Report was even more upbeat. They had had a wonderful year. Services were well attended. They had just enjoyed the most successful Sunday School Anniversary the Church had ever witnessed. There were more baptisms. "Our fellowship in the service of the Gospel has been a joy and a blessing." Church Membership in 1882 reached a peak of 61.

In 1883 the Church proudly boasted that it had raised £160 in the course of the year towards the cost of the land for the new chapel. The land was on the other side of Bridge Street. There was still a further £200 to find before they officially owned the land. In the 1886 Report to the Association this money had now been found. The site was paid for, and they were expecting to hold a bazaar in the Autumn towards the building fund. It was still to be several years, however, before any building work was to begin.

In the first ever East Midlands Baptist Association Reports (1892), the Rev W.F. Harris, the Derbyshire County Secretary, provided a brief summary of what had been happening in the Derbyshire churches over the previous year. In his summary he reports: "Belper seems about to realise its long cherished dream of a new and handsome chapel, which will be an ornament to the town and a credit to the denomination." Two years later, Rev Harris' report makes the following reference to Belper:

"The new chapel at Belper approaches completion and will probably be opened for public worship in August."

Belper's membership in 1894 had fallen back to just 40. It had grown to 55 by 1897, and to 73 by 1900. By 1914 they had 82 members and 155 Sunday School scholars on roll.

Littleover

We have seen already that there were Baptists in Littleover from at least 1811. Much of that time the cause was associated with St Mary's Gate, Derby, although there would appear to have been connections with Sacheverel Street in the 1830s and 1840s.

A place of worship was constructed in 1820 on the corner of Park Drive. Congregational growth was slow, and it was to take until the 1920s before the Baptists in Littleover felt sufficiently strong to become independent of St Mary's Gate.

The first minute book of Littleover Baptist Church begins in January 1882. Mr William North was the President of the branch Church. On 25th July 1887 it was proposed that a new chapel should be built. It was also proposed and agreed that they needed to move to a more "eligible position." A building committee was formed in October 1887.

Few details have been unearthed about the building process. The Church minute books are very uninformative. At the St Mary's Gate Annual Tea and Public Meeting on January 2nd 1888 it was announced that, "At Littleover the friends were about erecting a new chapel and school room and the project was being approached with considerable enthusiasm and liberality."

The land in question was on a new street (Thornhill Road) which linked Burton Road with Old Hall Road. William North had recently purchased a large plot of land in that area, a part of which he now released to the Baptist Church Trustees. The Church minutes for July 1888 make reference to an impending Opening Service but no details are forthcoming. In March 1889 the new chapel was insured for £400. Bulmer's Directory for 1895 said that the Baptist Chapel, built in 1888, seated 180 people.

Curiously, the new Baptist Chapel had no baptistery. When, in April 1892, 18 people from Littleover were to be baptised, the service had to be conducted as before, at St Mary's Gate. At the Annual Church Meeting in January 1895 the Littleover branch began to consider the additional expense of the construction of a baptistery. It was still to take until July 1898 before it was finally agreed to have a brick baptistery constructed at the cost of £21 and 10 shillings. In November 1898 Rev Abraham Mills, the Minister at St Mary's Gate, performed the first baptismal service at Littleover. Minnie Phillips, Teresa North, Annie Marriott, Alfred Spencer, and Mr T. Phillips were all baptised. In January 1899 the baptistery was found to leak, and the builders had to be brought back in.

Throughout 1899 the Littleover friends looked at the possibility of buying more land for the construction of a schoolroom. William North was willing to release to them another portion of the land he had obtained several years previously. There was discussion about how large a building they could afford to construct. In the end (January 1900) they agreed by 8 votes to 5 to build a larger building, 27 feet by 18 feet.

A Stone Laying ceremony took place on Wednesday July 31st 1901. Opening Services were held in November 1901, but the builder was still being asked to complete the job in the December.

Throughout this entire period, William North served as President of the Littleover branch of St Mary's Gate, and was instrumental in many of the changes that happened at Littleover Baptist Chapel. North was for many years the manager of the branch of the Co-operative society in the village. He lived at number 2 Thornhill Road. In July 1911 the Church celebrated William North's fifty years service as a Baptist Sunday School and chapel worker. He was presented with a large print Teacher's Bible. The inscription inside hoped that "Heaven's smile may rest upon him and with peace and joy sustain him till his welcome home."

William North was re-elected President of the Church in January 1916. He died on August 16th that same year at the age of 79. A wall tablet was erected near where he usually sat in the Church. The inscription included the words: "He was the friend of the children, a wise counsellor, an example of faithfulness and self-sacrifice, and respected by all."

Burton

Following the unfortunate episode with Alfred Underwood, the General Baptists in Burton moved on very quickly. In July 1879 they invited Rev S.S.Allsop to be their minister. He arrived in the October and was to exercise a highly fruitful and significant ministry.

Church Membership stood at 191 on Mr Allsop's arrival. Zion Chapel (built only in 1855) was clearly already bursting at the seams. In the Report to the Association in 1880 the Church record that "the present chapel is too small (all our sittings are let) and we hope soon to see the way clear to erect a larger place of worship." They had already raised £300 for that specific project.

On Tuesday 5th October 1880 the Church held a Tea Meeting on the occasion of Mr Allsop's first Anniversary as minister at Burton. At this meeting Councillor Ellis gave an address, and promised £100 to the building fund. Five similar sums of money were given or pledged (including one from the minister himself) along with a handful of smaller amounts which meant that by the end of the evening they had raised £715. A New Chapel committee was formed to prepare details and to organise fund raising. In the November it was decided to build the new chapel on the site of the old school rooms and some houses that were in the possession of the Church.

In September 1882 Mr Allsop followed his generous donation with a promise of £40 a year to the building fund until the Church was free from debt. By the end of 1882 the Church had £2676 in the building account. They had seen a net increase of 11 members that year.

The New Chapel was opened on Tuesday 18th September 1883. By any standards it was an impressive building, seating 820 people. The two-storey Sunday School building with assembly hall and classrooms was opened the following year. The total cost of the chapel was £5,000, but furnishings and accessories brought that up to nearer £7,000.

In February 1890 Rev Allsop indicated his intention to move on from Burton on health grounds. He left the town in June. Church Membership at this time stood at 224. His successor, Rev James Porteous, was to exercise an even more significant ministry. Membership at the new Church seemed to grow at an incredible rate.

1894	-	256 members
1897	-	274 members
1903	-	319 members
1906	-	329 members
1910	-	352 members (and 314 scholars)

The General Baptist Church at New Street, Burton was one of the three largest churches in the whole county.

The division of the Particular Baptists in Burton in 1871 had led to the formation of the Guild Street Church. In August 1874 the Church invited Mr J. Askew to be their minister. It turned out to be a lifetime's appointment. Church Membership at that time stood at only

25. Within two years the Church was recording a membership of 51, and in 1877 there were 76 members at Guild Street Particular Baptist Chapel. Thereafter membership continued to rise at an amazing rate:

1879	-	96 members
1880	-	126 members
1882	-	135 members

With such phenomenal growth there was little wonder that the Guild Street Church quickly turned its thoughts to a new building.

On September 14th 1881 the Church minutes read: "We have made arrangement for a piece of land in Derby Street for a new chapel. We therefore agree as a Church that the present chapel in Guild Street shall be sold at some future time for a sum of money."

Nothing further happened for some while. On September 28th 1885 the Church Meeting gave the pastor and the deacons permission to press ahead with the scheme for building a new chapel on the Derby Street land. Promises amounting to £144 were made on that evening.

A Stone Laying ceremony was held on July 24th 1886, and in November of that year the Guild Street premises were sold to Mr Henry Lakin for £500. In February 1887 the new Derby Street (Tabernacle) Church was opened. The preacher on that occasion was Charles Spurgeon, son of the famous London preacher.

The new building for the Derby Street Baptists did not bring the same good fortune as it had for the General Baptists in New Street. Membership at the Derby Street Tab rose to 180 in 1890, but thereafter fell back to 133 in 1894, and had only slightly increased to 149 by 1906. Throughout this entire period, John Askew continued his remarkable ministry. In 1899 the Church marked his 25 years as pastor by a special service at which he was presented with a purse containing £100.

In 1910, after 36 years as pastor, during which time he had brought the Church from a tin hut in Guild Street to the Derby Street premises, John Askew died. He was succeeded as pastor by his son.

Very little information is available concerning the Salem Baptist Church on Station Street. In 1872 Rev J.T.Owers arrived as minister having concluded his ministry at Loscoe. Membership of the Station Street Church stood at 94 in 1874 but soon began to grow appreciably. There were 110 members in 1875 and 118 in 1876. By 1879 membership stood at 190, and in 1882 there were 202 on roll. Thereafter membershiop slipped back, and never quite managed those dizzy heights again. Rev Owers moved to Grimsby and after that to Heanor. By 1903, with Rev E. Williams as minister, Station Street had a membership of 144 with 200 Sunday School scholars. They also had a branch Church at Walton on Trent.

St Mary's Gate: Boyer Street

The minutes of the Deacons Meeting held at St Mary's Gate, Derby on October 27th 1877 contain the following item:

"Our Pastor [Rev John William Williams] stated that he had been in the neighbourhood of Boyer Street and thought it was a place where a successful branch cause could be commenced."

The deacons suggested that he ascertain what level of support there was from the membership before proceeding. There must have been sufficient interest because at the Church Meeting on November 19th 1877, "Our pastor stated that a Sunday School had been commenced by some of our friends at a house in Boyer Street under very favourable circumstances."

On September 12th 1878 the deacons met with the male teachers at Boyer Street Mission. It had grown from 46 to 76 children, but there were concerns about their behaviour. It was agreed to appoint a Superintendent from St Mary's Gate to oversee the work. Mr Thomas Burton was chosen, and was assured that the post would not involve him in any personal financial responsibility for the mission.

Things clearly remained unsettled. In March 1879 St Mary's Gate set up an enquiry into the workings and requirements of the Boyer Street Mission. The committee reported back that the Mission continue, but recommending, "The purchase of an eligible piece of land in the neighbourhood for the erection of a building suitable for the work."

In May 1879, the Mission Room they had been hiring was demanded back by the owners, and the Boyer Street Mission Committee and then the St Mary's Gate deacons agreed on taking another room at an annual rent of £27.

St Mary's Gate were undoubtedly committed to the new Mission (especially during Rev Williams tenure of office). The St Mary's Gate Accounts for the year ended 1879 reveal that Mr Williams' salary was £300 (which was an enormous sum of money compared to all his Baptist ministerial colleagues). This was, unsurprisingly, the highest item of expenditure on the annual accounts. The second highest single item of expenditure was £79.18.4 which was the money expended on Boyer Street Mission.

In February 1880 Mr John Wilson was appointed Superintendent of the Boyer Street Mission "to replace our late lamented brother, Thomas Burton." The work had clearly developed beyond simply a Sunday School since the February 1880 meeting that appointed John Wilson also recommended the Boyer Street friends to adopt the Weekly Offering Scheme to meet the expenses of the mission.

On August 1st 1880 Rev Williams baptised nine people at St Mary's Gate, this included:

Joseph Richardson	132 Boyer Street
Elizabeth Richardson	132 Boyer Street
Joseph Webster	9 Boyer Street
Ellen Moltmann	84 Boyer Street
Sarah Hudson	Boyer Street

The Church Meeting that same month decided to defer any decision about increased accommodation for Boyer Street unless a suitable building could be secured.

In February 1881 Rev J.W.Williams tendered his resignation. He regretted he had not been more successful. His attempts to introduce an eldership system into the Church had met with stiff resistence, and one suspects that not everyone shared his enthusiasm for the Boyer Street Mission. (The pastor told the deacons in December 1880 that they had been offered the chance to purchase a piece of land on Boyer Street for a chapel, but no further reference to the matter occurred in the minutes.) Rev Williams returned to his native Wales and to the Baptist Church in Newtown, Montgomeryshire.

Rev Williams' departure left Boyer Street Mission quite exposed and vulnerable. On 23rd May 1881 the Boyer Street friends informed St Mary's Gate of their urgent need for a proper place to meet in, "as what progress they made in the summer was lost in the winter on account of the unsuitableness of the room."

When, in the July, the Boyer Street friends gave St Mary's Gate an ultimatum, the deacons unanimously advised the Church to relinquish the efforts at Boyer Street and recommended the teachers to induce the scholars to attend St Mary's Gate or Junction Street Schools.

The deacons, having called their bluff, found that the Boyer Street friends backed down. They must have soldiered on through another winter. When St Mary's Gate appointed Rev T.R. Stevenson (September 1881) as their minister, one of the very first actions he performed (November 1881) was to visit Boyer Street with two others. In July 1882 it was agreed that the Mission should continue, but one detects little enthusiasm for the work at St Mary's Gate, and in October 1885 the pastor and deacons were again recommending its closure. This decision was subsequently rescinded after receiving information "of a more hopeful character" but in September 1886 the Mission was again in trouble. The teachers could not work in harmony, and as a result John Wilson tendered his resignation as Superintendent. Mr J.J.Doughty was appointed in his place in March 1887

Thomas Stevenson concluded his ministry at St Mary's Gate in July 1888. In November that year a sudden breakthrough happened in the quest for a building for the Boyer Street Mission. A piece of land, on

Boyer Street, had become available for purchase with a 78 feet frontage and 64 feet deep. Mr Eaton was offering the plot at 9 shillings and sixpence a yard. Remarkably the Church Meeting on December 11th 1888 agreed to the purchase price of £260.

The architect of the Boyer Street Mission building was Mr A. Heaton of St James' Street. Mr Alfred Brown was the builder. Mr Dusatoy was the Building Fund Treasurer. At the Stone Laying Ceremony (October 30th 1889) Mr Hudson, representing the Boyer Street congregation, gave a vivid description of the early struggles of the mission and the rough material with which they had originally had to deal. Some of the children, said Mr Hudson, were very turbulent and had threatened frequently to "knock his eyes into one!" Memorial stones were laid by Mr Councillor James Hill, and Thomas Meakin esq. The building was named Baptist Centenary Mission Room and School in recognition of the 100 years since Dan Taylor first preached in Derby on Willow Row.

The building was completed in summer 1890. The total cost of land, buildings and furnishings amounted to £1043.15.11. In July 1890 the debt outstanding on that amount was £697.4.4

St Mary's Gate came good. At their AGM in January 1891 25 people contributed into a special fund for Boyer Street Mission (which yielded £14.9.6). In February St Mary's Gate decided to hold special collections in St Mary's Gate when the first anniversary of the Boyer Street Chapel came round. When, in August 1892, Mr Doughty informed the Church that there was a £12 shortfall on the Boyer Street financial statement St Mary's Gate agreed to pay this amount, and they were to make similar contributions for the next few years.

By 1903 Boyer Street was being recorded as an official branch of St Mary's Gate, alongside Littleover and Willington. Boyer Street was attributed a membership of 11 with a Sunday School of 190. By 1914 the adult membership of Boyer Street was 20 while the Sunday School scholars amounted to 147.

Overseal

The Baptist cause at Overseal seems to have been started from Cauldwell where the Norton family exercised successive and successful ministries. A pair of cottages were rented (on Burton Road, opposite Coronation Street), and the two front bedrooms were turned into one. In 1840 the Cauldwell Church issued its Report to the Association in which it mentioned plans to build a chapel at Overseal. This was completed in 1841.

In 1854 the General Baptist Church in Burton reported to the Association that "In consequence of the death of our esteemed friend, Mr Norton of Cauldwell, the friends there and at Overseal expressed a desire to unite with us." In 1860 the Burton Church issued its Report stating that while the cause at Cauldwell was low, there were good congregations at Overseal. The membership at Overseal and Cauldwell was given as 15 in June 1871. In 1873 membership at Overseal was given as 17.

In 1878 a split occurred between the friends at Overseal and the Burton Church. On February 3rd 1878 William Freeman wrote to Burton on behalf of the Overseal Church:

"Believing permanent peace will not be enjoyed while our union with Burton remain, we agree that our union with Burton shall at once cease to be, and that we do not (any longer) recognise Mr Underwood as our minister."

There is every reason to believe that this split stemmed from a dispute with Alfred Underwood (who himself resigned in the August to set up the Parker Street church). Mr Allsop, who arrived at Burton in 1879, proved to be much more acceptable to the Overseal people, and in May 1884 Mr Allsop was able to inform the Burton Church Meeting that the Overseal friends wished to be received into membership with them again. There were 21 members at Overseal at this time. At the AGM on February 1st 1888 Mr Allsop presented an upbeat report on the cause at Overseal:

"Our Pastor said the cause at Overseal was in an encouraging condition. Congregations are very good – more money has been raised for the foreign mission than ever – and mainly through a sale of work £70 has been paid off their chapel debt."

The following year's AGM (February 13th 1889) had an even more encouraging report. Cauldwell had improving congregations, and they were to thoroughly repair the chapel throughout the summer. Overseal again had very good congregations, but what was particularly gratifying was that 12 or 15 young men wished to join the Church.

Mr Allsop left Burton in 1890 due to the state of his and his wife's health. Overseal, however, continued to provide great encouragement. At the AGM in 1894 it was noted that the Cauldwell Church was improving as a result of the commencement of a Sunday School. Overseal congregations were doing so well that they badly needed a new chapel, and the Burton Church pledged to see what they could do to help them. A building fund was started the following year. In 1896 Overseal reported to the Burton AGM that they had had 9 baptisms that year (from the Christian Endeavour Society). In 1897 they reported to the Burton AGM a membership of 42 with 70 Sunday School scholars.

On 22nd April 1897 the 'Burton Chronicle' carried an extensive piece on the Stone Laying Ceremony at the new Baptist Chapel and Schools at Overseal. The event took place on Easter Monday and was well attended by friends in Burton and much wider afield. Rev James Porteous (New Street, Burton) presided on that occasion, but Rev Allsop (then at Ripley) was also present. Mr J. Cooper, one of the earliest members of the Church, provided details of the construction of the first Overseal Baptist Chapel back in 1841. Mr Samuel Moore, whose family played such a key part in the life of Overseal Baptist Church, layed the first stone (and also made a donation of £100). Further donations were made, and with the collection and money already in hand, the Church had raised £606 by the close of the day towards its estimated target of £1000. The architect was Mr Yardley of Swadlincote.

At the Burton AGM (February 9th) in 1898 Mr James Moore from Overseal presented a report from the Overseal branch. The work was progressing slowly and was due to be completed at Whitsuntide. Later that year Rev W.F.Harris, Derbyshire County Secretary to the new East Midland Baptist Association, presented his summary of the work in the county for that year:

"Perhaps the best piece of work accomplished during the year is the erection of the New Chapel and Schools at Overseal ..... The new chapel is a credit to the villagers themselves, many of whom have gratuitously worked upon it with their own hands, also to the New Street Church, Burton of which it is a branch ..... Any friends who contemplate building a village chapel cannot do better than visit Overseal and adopt it as their model. Its brightness, elegance and adaptation to its purpose are only surpassed by its smallness of cost."

The Church went from strength to strength. On June 3rd 1902 the Rev E.W. Cantrell[2] was invited to become the first minister of Overseal Baptist Church. Membership grew markedly:

1900	-	48 members
1903	-	54 members
1906	-	74 members
1910	-	83 members
1914	-	97 members (and 115 scholars)

The village of Overseal was transformed during the course of the nineteenth century. A quiet rural back water, it experienced major industrialisation from mid century onwards. The clayworks and potteries, along with the Leicester to Burton railway, and the canal, brought employment opportunities and with that a growing labour force. The Baptists of Overseal flourished on the back of this industrial revolution.

Kilburn[3]
The Baptist Church in Kilburn went through a very long gestation period. According to Fred Annable's 1932 Centenary History of the cause, the original Baptists were from Denby village, but being unable

to obtain a place to meet in Denby they were offered land in Kilburn by Mr W. Kerry.

The 1830 Report to the Association from Smalley Baptist Church mentioned that attendance at Denby was good, and also mentioned that open air preaching had been commenced in Kilburn. The 1832 Report from Smalley records: "We have built a Chapel at Kilbourn which was opened on 10th June by J.G.Pike of Derby." The Report went on to say that there was preaching in five villages, namely Smalley, Denby, Heanor, Horsley and Kilbourn.

On May 19th 1839 a Sunday School began under the Superintendency of Edward Abraham Brown. The first Sunday School Anniversary was held on April 5th 1840, preached by Rev William Underwood of Wirksworth.

Smalley reported in 1845 that there was a "pleasing revival of religion at Kilburn." But the growth at Kilburn was slow. By 1867 the Church still owed £100 on the building that was already 35 years old. Not until 1875 was that debt actually cleared.

The village Church was susceptible to all the vicissitudes of every day life. On Denby Wakes Monday, September 1860, a terrible accident happened at Kilburn colliery when four young men were thrown from the pit cage to the bottom of the shaft. One of these men, John Annable, was a member at Kilburn Baptist Church.

The Report to the Association from 'Smalley and Kilbourne'[3] in 1876 referred to the liquidation of the chapel debt at Kilburn, "with the hope of buying ground on which to build a new chapel." The following year it was noted that at Kilburn congregations were much improved. "We have £65 in the bank towards buying land to build a new chapel which is much needed." In 1880 they reported that they had a good Sunday School, "but the cause is very low, nine being reported as lost. To meet the present times we want a new chapel."

No such chapel was to be forthcoming. Land purchase proved a problem, and in 1886 Kilburn Baptists decided to substantially renovate their existing premises and have the chapel re-pewed. Rev E. Hilton had taken pastoral charge of Smalley, Heanor and Kilburn in 1884. By 1886 he decided to concentrate his endeavours on Smalley and Kilburn. He did so to very great effect.

In 1889 Kilburn reported to the Association: "Our congregations on the whole are very good, and we have encouraging signs of having an increase in members. Our pastor is a faithful working servant of the Lord; his pastoral visits are very good, calling upon the poor as well as the rich."

The first year that a membership figure was issued separately for Kilburn was 1890 when it was listed in the Association returns as having 30 members. In 1894 this was 49. In 1900 and 1903, however, Kilburn was recorded as having a membership of only 19. Fred Annable's 'History' refers to a spiritual awakening that occurred at the turn of the twentieth century in Kilburn akin to what was taking place in Wales at the same time. In 1905 Kilburn is listed with 40 members and in 1906 with 51.

This upward momentum once again gave rise to the desire for a new chapel. Fred Annable states that by 1903 "we were overcrowded, both in Sunday School and Church services, some of us having to stand during service." The first site identified for the chapel again fell through, but eventually Frederick Kerry Brown made available the land on which the present chapel stands. Messrs. Harris and Hunt builders obtained the contract, but the men of the Church also gave a hand. They dug the foundations of the building and the sewers as well as a water cistern, fire hole for the heating apparatus, and a hole for the baptistery.

The Stone Laying ceremony was on September 23rd 1908, and the building was officially opened on June 30th 1909. The building cost £1,492 which was completely met "in a short space of time."

Church Membership did grow. At the outbreak of World War One, Kilburn Baptist Church had a membership of 70. Their Sunday School, however, was quite extraordinary. Only 70 children were recorded in the 1903 Association entry. In 1906 there were 282 children identified as part of the Kilburn Baptist Church Sunday School. This figure reached 300 in 1914. Pressure of numbers was eased by using two of the vestries in the new Church to accommodate all the children.

Postscript
Other churches embarked on building schemes throughout this period. In 1879 **Melbourne Baptist Church** completed a £700 renovation of their sanctuary.

Loscoe Baptist Church had a Stone Laying ceremony for its Schoolrooms on Furnace Lane on October 21st 1905. The buildings were opened on Good Friday, April 13th 1905. The building work cost £510 and all debt was paid off by 1908 when the Church submitted its report to the Association: "We are sincerely grateful to the many friends in the Association who so heartily responded to our appeal for help."

In 1880 **Langley Mill Baptist Church** reported to the Association that both the Chapel and Schoolroom had been badly damaged "by the undermining of one of the Butterley Company's Collieries." Thankfully they were also able to report that "The Company agreed to make good repairs which are almost complete." Langley Mill developed plans during the 1910s for a complete new Church building. The intervention of the First World War put paid to these ideas permanently.

1. A brief article by Heather Eaton in the Derbyshire Family History Society News for June 1981 explained that the graveyard at Agard Street had been closed for burials since 1st May 1855. Heather found a number of headstones from the Agard Street graveyard in 1981 under the railway arches in a garage mechanic's yard, but access to this area, she said, was very difficult. A full inventory of the gravestones was carried out by J Brian Radford in 1964. The details of 16 memorial inscriptions are still available at Derbyshire Family History Society Library in Bridge House Chapel.

2. Rev E.W.Cantrell came from Birmingham to Overseal. He served as minister until 1908 and died shortly afterwards.
3. The Baptist Handbook spells the village as 'Kilbourne' until 1906. The Association Reports follow the same spelling until 1905 after which point both sources adopt the spelling 'Kilburn'.

Littleover Baptist Church

Kilburn Baptist Church

Trinity Baptist Church

Belper Baptist Church

Wirksworth Baptist Church

Boyer Street Mission

THE PRESENT CHAPEL BUILDING
— ERECTED IN 1876 —

A glimpse is seen of the School Hall, at the
rear of the Chapel.

Heanor Baptist Church

Crich Baptist Church

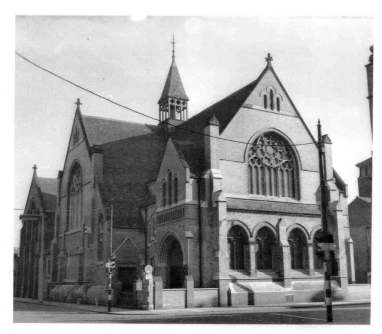

Burton, New Street

Derby Street Tabernacle,

Overseal Baptist Church
Burton

CHAPTER 25

THEOLOGICAL MOVEMENT

The theological and organisational differences between Particular and General Baptists in the early nineteenth century had been sufficient to require J.G.Pike to set up a completely different Missionary Society to that of the BMS. This was not Pike's wish. Rather it was forced upon him by necessity. If the New Connexion General Baptists were to express their international concern it would have to be through their own missionary structures.

By mid century some of those theological differences were becoming harder to find. In 1842 J.G.Pike, a lifelong General Baptist, was elected President of the Baptist Union, from its inception a Particular Baptist organisation. In June 1861 Wirksworth Baptist Church minutes reveal the Church's mind that "the distinction between General Baptists and Particular Baptists should be abolished." By 1870 one sixth of New Connexion pastors came directly from Particular Baptist Colleges or from Particular Baptist Churches.[1] At Rev Joseph Wilshire's Induction at St Mary's Gate General Baptist Church (June 1872) it was noted that both the new minister and his predecessor, Rev Crassweller, were from the Particular Baptist tradition.

Theological realignment was only one factor contributing to the convergence of the two wings of the English Baptist family. One practical incentive to merger was numerical decline. The New Connexion churches in the towns of the East Midlands had seen a drop in membership between 1847 and 1867[2]. While forming a majority of the Baptists in the East Midlands, nationally the New Connexion Generals were in a decided minority[3]. From weakness some General Baptists were beginning to look to merger with the Particulars for their future.

On September 18th 1866 the Midland Conference of the New Connexion met at Friar Lane, Leicester. Item 5 on their agenda was "The union of the Baptist Associations of Nottinghamshire and

Derbyshire [i.e the Particular Baptists] with the Midland Conference. [i.e the General Baptists]" The motion put to the meeting was:

"That this conference, believing in the duty of union and co-operation among Christians wherever practicable, respectfully and affectionately invites the churches forming the Notts and Derbys Association to unite with the General Baptist Churches of this district so as to form one Midland Association or Conference of Baptist churches. It is believed that there are not now any doctrinal differences between us such as need prevent hearty sympathy and common action."

The minutes of the Midland Conference went on to say that two of the ministers of the Particular Baptist Notts and Derbys Association were once in connection with the Generals, while in the Midland Conference there were "no less than six ministerial brethren who were formerly identified with the other section of the Baptist body."

The Midland Conference gave a lengthy discussion to the motion, at the end of which it was resolved that "We heartily approve of the proposed alliance between the Particular and General Baptist Churches in this district." A small working group was set up to meet with the Particulars and take the matter further. The group was comprised of Revs W.R. Stevenson, Samuel Cox, Harris Crasweller and Dr Underwood[4].

When the General Baptists met again in June 1867 the Particulars were meeting at the same time to consider their response. The subsequent reply from the Notts and Derbys Association was disappointing:

"That the most careful deliberation and enquiry have convinced this Association that the practical difficulties in the way of a completer union between this Association and the Conference are insurmountable."

But these were practical not theological difficulties that were keeping them apart.

Throughout the 1870s a resurgence of the New Connexion churches tended to keep talk of amalgamation off the agenda. But self confidence among General Baptists dipped again in the 1880s when it became clear that the number of baptisms was also on the decline. In 1882 there were 1542 baptisms; in 1883 this had dropped to 1344; while in 1884 the annual baptisms in New Connexion churches fell still further to 1291[5].

The Particular Baptists themselves were now more persuaded about reunion than they had been a generation earlier. On Tuesday February 10th 1885 the Derby Daily Telegraph reported on the (General) Baptist Missionary meetings that had just taken place in Derby at which Rev W.F.Harris from Trinity (Particular) Baptist Church was present. Rev Harris addressing his General Baptist colleagues expressed the humble hope:

"That the day was not far distant when they would be able to drop the terms Particular Baptist and General Baptist and become simply Baptists (hear, hear). They were one in spirit and he did not see why they should not be one in faith (hear, hear)."

Charles Williams, in his Presidential address to the Baptist Union Assembly of 1886, argued from John 17 the imperative and irresistible logic for reunion: "Can we justify the division of our denomination into two sections?... We preach the same Gospel.... What hinders?"[6] The General Baptists took the bait, and in meetings at Walsall in 1889 delegates voted 51 to 12 in favour of a 'complete and thorough –going union' with the Particular Baptists.[7]

By this time, however, another theological tussle had taken its grip on the Baptist body politic.

For a number of years developments in Biblical scholarship; the influence of German theologians; and a broadening and liberal mindset had led to a questioning of some of those older theological axioms that Baptists had always taken for granted. This was ultimately to lead to the Down Grade controversy in 1887 and 1888 and the withdrawal of C.H. Spurgeon from the Baptist Union.

In Derby this theological crisis was focused on the ministry of one man, Rev T.R. Stevenson, who became minister at St Mary's Gate in 1881.

Stevenson had been minister at Ilkeston between 1854 and 1859, and had also ministered on a regular basis at Langley Mill. His departure from Ilkeston seemed to precipitate the secession of 50 members from the Church, although the breach was eventually repaired.

From ministry in Colombo, Ceylon, he was called by the St Mary's Gate Church in September 1881 (132 votes to 5). His ministry was appreciated, and in December 1884 the Church threw a party for Mr and Mrs Stevenson on the occasion of their Silver Wedding Anniversary. Generous donations from the congregation resulted in the purchase of a Tea and Coffee Service as well as a bag of silver.

During 1885, however, T.R.Stevenson began to get into significant hot water. He was a keen supporter of Dr Samuel Cox, the minister of Mansfield Road, Nottingham, who had seriously questioned the doctrine of Eternal Punishment. The 'Salvator Mundi' school of thought was very controversial, and T.R. Stevenson was not averse to making his views known.

Whilever he remained minister of St Mary's Gate his theological views were solely the concern of that congregation. But during the course of the year Stevenson was appointed Chairman of the Midland Conference, a position which brought him into wider ministry, and subject, therefore, to the wider scrutiny of the Midland Baptists.

On 20th October 1885 at the Midland Conference in Quorndon, Mr H.W. Earp of Melbourne Baptist Church challenged the appointment of Stevenson because of the unorthodox views he had expressed in an article in the 'Christian World' on May 28th 1885. (See Appendix 4) The article, entitled, 'A true Minister of Christ' refers to a sermon he gave in Derby on Whit Sunday which already indicated his need to defend himself from mounting criticism. W.H.Tetley ruled Mr Earp's motion both out of time and out of place, and the meeting endorsed Tetley's stance.

The St Mary's Gate Church, aware of the motion of no confidence prepared by Mr Earp, had given Rev Stevenson their full support at the close of the Sunday Evening service (18th October):

"The members of his Church and congregation desire it to be known that they do not recognise the right of a conference to sit in judgment upon the theology of any man, and would assure Mr Stevenson of their heartiest sympathy and unabated confidence in him and in his public ministry and work."

Very little is recorded about the controversy. But clearly issues rumbled on. In December 1886, for example, there is a reference to the 'unsettled state of the Church' and in January it was deemed appropriate to read the Church's Trust Deed to the Church AND to the minister.

S.T. Hall, Church Secretary at St Mary's Gate from 1910 – 1930, produced his own survey of the Church's history and includes some of his own reminiscence. He refers to 'the heresy hunt' which followed, and to one press article headed, 'more brimstone wanted.'

On 26th February 1888 Stevenson tendered his resignation. Mr Samuel Hall, on behalf of the Church, expressed deep regret that he had "found it necessary to come to such a decision," and expressed complete confidence in his gospel teaching. Farewell Services were held at the end of July, and there was extensive coverage of the event in the Derby Gazette (August 3rd). Mr Stevenson was magnanimous in his closing words, and the Church was equally generous in their response to him, presenting him with a gift of 100 guineas.

T.R. Stevenson subsequently assumed the pastorate of Union Church, Shanghai, China where he served from 1889 to 1893. He was compelled to return home to Derby following a series of mild strokes. On arrival in Derby he suffered an even more severe bout of paralysis, and died on December 5th 1893. He was 61 years old.

His obituary in the Baptist 'Freeman' (December 15th 1893) said that his statements "were sometimes both strange and startling, and required the usual grain of salt before they could be accepted."The East Midlands Baptist Magazine (January 1894), was more generous: "His great catholicity of spirit, no less than his fearless defence of what he deemed Gospel truth, won for him many admirers abroad as well as at home."

Mr H.W. Earp was nominated for the diaconate of Melbourne Baptist Church in 1886, but failed to get elected. He was elected a deacon three years later, but died in August 1893, four months before Stevenson himself.

T.R. Stevenson was the major casualty of theological intolerance in the county. But he was not the only victim. Rev Kenneth Bond was invited to become the minister at Swadlincote in November 1890. His popularity led to the Church offering him a pay rise in January 1892[8]. In May 1894 Swadlincote's report to the Association was very upbeat referring to a 'vigorous and healthy Church' and stating that the 'labours of our pastor in and out of the pulpit are highly appreciated.'

In October 1895, however, a resolution was brought to the Church Meeting by two members calling on Mr Bond to resign. They declared that the Church had not made sufficient progress in the four and a half years he had been with them (especially considering the growth of the neighbourhood). More to the point they were not happy with the way he had questioned certain Baptist fundamentals from the pulpit, namely the veracity of the Bible and 'the everlasting punishment of the finally impenitent.'

The Burton Evening Gazette provided a detailed coverage of the developing crisis. On Wednesday October 30th they produced a lengthy article covering Mr Bond's sermon the previous Sunday evening on the subject of "The doctrine of Everlasting Punishment." Mr Bond had made known his intention of addressing this subject with the result that half the town seemed to have crammed into Swadlincote Baptist Chapel. Extra seats were placed in any available space including the rostrum itself, "and many stood at the open doors during the whole of the service which lasted close upon three hours."

Mr Bond was extremely thorough, providing in depth analysis of key biblical terms such as Sheol and Gehenna before moving on to the moral arguments against Everlasting Punishment[9]. "In conclusion the Rev gentleman said they could not make people good by frightening them. It was not true religion to believe in the Lord Jesus Christ for the sake of escaping punishment."

A vote on Mr Bond's fate was deferred until 28th November 1895 by which time there had been a flurry of follow up articles and letters in the Burton Evening Gazette. When the Church Members did meet to decide whether to part with their minister there were 62 votes in favour of retaining Mr Bond, and 12 for his removal. It was pointed out, however, that some of those who voted for him were not happy with the way he had said things, but had given him the benefit of the doubt being "impressed with his reverence for the truth – his deep toned piety and his sacrificing labours for the spiritual welfare of the Church."

Mr Bond weathered the storm and remained as minister at Swadlincote until 1905.

The amalgamation of the General and Particular Baptists was completed nationally during 1891 and 1892. The amalgamation included the two missionary societies. Regionally, this was expressed through the formation of a new Association. The Notts and Derbys Particular Baptist Association disappeared along with the New Connexion's Midland Conference. In its place was formed the East Midland Baptist Association with its own county structures and its own county secretaries. The first county secretary for Derbyshire was Rev W.F.Harris of Trinity, Derby.

Individual churches were asked to ratify the amalgamation process. Heanor Baptist Church minute books (May 11 1891) refer to a letter from Dr. S.H.Booth of the Baptist Union and one from Rev Firth, Secretary to the Midland Conference asking for the Church's response to the amalgamation. Heanor had no difficulty in giving their consent. Junction Baptist Church, Derby, had an address from their pastor (of St Mary's Gate) in May 1891 on the advantages of union of Particulars and Generals at home and on the mission field. The Church readily endorsed his recommendation. The Particular Baptist Church at Chesterfield "heartily approved" of the amalgamation at their Church Meeting on June 11th 1891, and equally endorsed the proposed formation of the East Midland Baptist Association.

One or two churches had some qualms about the coming together of the two wings of the Baptist family. Sawley Baptist Church formerly passed a resolution, "That we are in favour of the fusion of the two sections of the Baptist denomination." But the resolution went on to say, "though we continue to hold that 'Christ died for all the sins of all men.'" Swadlincote were even more reticent. Their Church Meeting on April 1st 1891 declared: "While strongly approving of the principle of amalgamation, we are impressed with the importance of preserving as far as possible the advantages of our present organisation."

In time, amalgamation became an accepted and natural part of the life of Baptist Churches in the county. In 1908 Birches Lane Baptist Church, South Wingfield, agreed to replace the words 'Particular Baptist Church' on the stone at the front of its building, with the words 'Baptist Church.' It was a physical and symbolic illustration of the transition the denomination had made.

The ease with which ministers crossed from Particular to General Baptist churches in Derbyshire (and vice versa) can be seen from a short survey of the ministry of Rev J.T.Owers.

Mr Owers began his ministry in 1869 at Loscoe Baptist Church, one of the few Particular Baptist Churches in the county. By 1872 he had moved to Station Street, Burton, another Particular Baptist Church in the Notts and Derbys Association. In the 1880s he moved to Grimsby, but in 1900 he returned to Derbyshire where he became the pastor of the General Baptist Church in Heanor. He exercised very fruitful ministries in each of his churches, and remained as minister of Heanor Baptist Church until his death in 1917. The transitioning of this one minister illustrates something of the experience of the whole denomination.

It should perhaps be pointed out that even with the merger of the two wings of the Baptist family, there were still Baptist churches that remained outside these structures. There had been Baptists in Charlesworth, near Glossop since 1816 through the work of William Gadsby, George Mellor and Squire Booth. A building was erected in 1838 and a succession of ministers (John Beard, George Drake, and J Hand) saw the work develop. Charlesworth had an entry in the 1851 Religious Census. For a number of years during the 1860s – 1880s Charlesworth Baptist Church appeared in the Baptist Handbook although it was never identified as belonging to a specific Association. Membership in 1864 was 27. From 1871 – 1882 membership remained stable at 22. The 1884 entry records only 12 members. But by the beginning of the twentieth century the Church was clearly identified with the Northern Counties Strict and Particular Baptist Committee. Membership had been boosted by an influx of people from Manchester. By 1911 it was recorded that Charlesworth Baptists had an average of 100 people attending their services of worship.[10] Another Strict and Particular Baptist Church appears to have met at Barmoor Clough, three miles from Buxton, where a Church was formed by John Kershaw in 1852. They make no appearance in statistics submitted to General or Particular Baptist Associations regionally or nationally.

1. J.H.Y.Briggs English Baptists of the Nineteenth Century p.124
2. J.H.Y.Briggs English Baptists.... P.128
3. Ernest Payne The Baptist Union p.78
4. Dr William Underwood (see appendix 5) was a passionate advocate of union between the two sections of the Baptist family. As President of the Chilwell College he carried considerable influence. In 1870, at the centenary celebrations of the New Connexion he made a strong plea for the union of all Baptists.

"No doubt we have our distinctive opinions still, but they are so seldom made prominent that the bulk of the people do not understand them. For all practical ends what might be called the Calvinism of one party is exactly the same as the supposed Arminianism of the other...... And when pulpits have been exchanged, or services shared by ministers of both sections, what

impartial hearer could detect any theological difference in the sermons and speeches?"
Quoted A.C.Underwood, 'History of the English Baptists' p.214

5. J.H.Y.Briggs English Baptists ….. p.138
6. J.H.Y.Briggs English Baptists ….. p.139
7. J.H.Y.Briggs English Baptists ….. p.141
8. Mr Bond was offered a pay rise that would have given him a salary of £120 a year. The salary of the minister at St Mary's Gate, Derby at this time was £300 per annum. This illustrates something of the huge differences in salary that Baptist ministers could receive. In actual fact Mr Bond refused to accept the pay rise until the debt on the new chapel was cleared.
9. "The doctrine of everlasting punishment was antagonistic to their idea of God as the infinitely loving, and he could not believe that even for the accumulated sins of a life lasting even 70 years any man could be condemned to endless death. He contended also that the doctrine did not square with their conception of a God of justice." (Crimes committed in time did not warrant a punishment meted out in eternity.) 'Burton Evening Gazette' October 30th 1895. Mr Bond was interrupted a couple of times during his lengthy discourse.
10. This information is found in 'The Christian's Pathway' for October 1911. The data was supplied by the then Secretary to the Northern Counties Strict and Particular Committee, W.G.Hawkins. I am grateful to David Woodruff of the Strict Baptist Historical Society for making this information available.

Rev T.R.Stevenson   Rev J.T.Owers
Source: Matlock Record Office

Rev W.F.Harris   Charlesworth Particular Baptist Chapel

325

CHAPTER 26

THE TURN OF THE CENTURY

The Baptists of 1900 looked very different to those of 1800. In 1800 there were no more than 11 or 12 Baptist Churches in the county. While several churches had day schools connected to them, the idea of the Sunday School was very new. William Pickering, when he was minister at Ilkeston and Smalley, appears to have been one of the first to introduce the idea into the county in 1804. It took quite a while for the idea to become generally accepted. According to W.A. Richards' Report to the EMBA in 1907 there were 43 Baptist churches in the county plus 5 preaching stations, and there were 46 Sunday Schools. The number of registered Sunday School scholars in Derbyshire Baptist Churches peaked in 1902 with a total of 9,450.[1] Many of these Sunday Schools were of colossal size; involved small armies of volunteers; and developed elaborate organisational structures to manage the flow of children. Churches with small adult memberships could sustain a proportionately large Sunday School. Belper Baptists in 1903 had a Church membership of 55 but a Sunday School of 232. South Street, Ilkeston had a Church membership of 51 in 1903, but 270 Sunday School scholars. In fact the two Baptist Churches in Ilkeston had a combined Sunday School population of 570 in 1903. But this was small in comparison to some of the larger Schools. In 1903 Loscoe; Queen Street, Ilkeston; Melbourne; New Street, Burton; Watson Street, St Mary's Gate, and Trinity, Derby all had Sunday Schools with 300-340 children. Hill Street, Swadlincote had 400 children; Pear Tree, Derby had 450, but this was still small in comparison to Osmaston Road which had 688 Sunday School scholars, and Junction Baptist Church which had an incredible 989 children on their books. In 1906 Junction actually had 1012 Sunday School scholars, and while numbers slipped in the following years, they still remained the king of the Derbyshire Sunday Schools. In 1914 there were 774 children still on their books. Their nearest challenger was Pear Tree Road with 470 children.

Baptist Church life in 1900 revolved around its programme of activities for children in a way that could never have been imagined a century earlier. Churches in 1900 saw the future of the Church in the nurture and training it provided to the young. The work of the Sunday School was considered a sound investment, and a guarantee of the Church's survival. But this was a focus that would have been quite novel to the Baptists of 1800 for whom preaching to adults was the main missionary endeavour.

Not only did the Sunday School represent a major new innovation in the Baptist Churches of the nineteenth century, so too did the emergence of the Temperance movement.

There would scarcely have been a Baptist Church in Derbyshire that did not have a Band of Hope or some other Temperance organisation attached to it by 1900. Temperance Sunday would have been a major event in most Church's annual calendar. The social ills associated with abuse of alcohol were all too apparent; whole families could be rendered penniless through the wanton drunkenness of one or more of its adult members. The 'demon drink' was the enemy to be confronted, and churches in 1900 were at the vanguard of crusading movements for changes to licensing laws[2], and the education of the young.

All this was a far cry from the attitude of Baptists in the eighteenth and early nineteenth centuries. It is hard to imagine a Baptist Church in 1900 providing its baptismal candidates with a tot of gin or rum to keep out the cold as Smalley Baptist Church did. Evidence from the Smalley accounts from 1799 – 1809 list both gin and rum as items of expenditure in connection with baptisms. Warming the outside of the person was not an option in an open air baptistery, river or pond. In October 1799 Mr Felkin laid down his terms for remaining as minister at Smalley and Ilkeston. His requirements included:

"To have a little red wine kept in the vestry at Smalley that I may have one glass before and after preaching when I please."

None of this was in the slightest unusual. The Barton Preachers, it will be recalled, fell foul of the excise laws in 1759 at one of their monthly gatherings for the Lord's Supper by trading alcohol in unlicensed premises. The Particular Baptists equally had no qualms about supporting local hostelries. The Northamptonshire Baptist Association, to which the Derbyshire and Staffordshire Particular Baptist Churches belonged in the early nineteenth century, held annual meetings throughout its geographical area. But invariably they were accommodated in a Public House. In 1799 delegates were put up at The White Swan at Olney, Buckinghamshire; in 1805 at The Bell, Humberstone Gate, Dunstable; in 1806, at The George in Leicester; in 1807, at The Bull in Spalding. They returned to Olney in 1808, but this time settled on The White Lion for hospitality. In 1817 when they returned to Olney they met at The Cross Keys. In 1818 the Annual Meetings were held in Loughborough, and delegates were accommodated at The Crown.

In the extensive writings of Rev J.G. Pike very little is said about the dangers of alcohol. His 'Persuasives to early piety' (1818) and 'Guide for young disciples' (1823) are concerned more with the sins of 'falsehood,' 'pride,' and 'waste of precious time.' In the 'Sacramental Accounts' of Ripley Baptist Church there were numerous purchases of British Port Wine recorded throughout 1840-1842.[3]

The Baptist newspaper, the 'Freeman' carried regular advertisements for Kilnahan's Irish Whisky right up to 1870. For a number of years after this it persisted in the adverts but argued for the product's medicinal properties. By 1880 the adverts had been dropped altogether[4].

One of the main indicators of this shift towards tee-totalism amongst Baptists was the transition to non–alcoholic (unfermented) communion wine.[5] In 1800 every Baptist Church would have used fermented wine. By 1900 unfermented wine at Communion would have been much more common. In 1875 Swadlincote deacons felt it would be prudent to introduce unfermented wine at Communion, sensing that some of the congregation were absenting themselves from the Lord's Supper because of their objection to alcohol. In May 1881 Sawley Baptist Church decided to try the unfermented wine for a six months trial, while the Castle Donington deacons felt the need to discuss the transition to unfermented communion wine in October 1892.[6]

The transition to tee-totalism would have been faster in some congregations than in others. In July 1882 at Swadlincote, Rev E. Carrington complained about the disparaging remarks made about his Christian character and conduct by members of the Gospel Temperance and Blue Ribbon movement who had been using the school room. A grudging and half hearted apology of sorts was received but not to his satisfaction. In 1883 Mr Carrington decided to leave the Church. Presumably his unwillingness to embrace the tee-total movement had given rise to a whispering campaign. In Ilkeston (a hot bed of Baptist tee-totalism) the local Anglican vicar complained bitterly at the way he had been lampooned by the Baptists for speaking at the Annual Banquet of the Ilkeston and District Licensed Victuallers and Beersellers' Association in November 1887. The vicar (Rev Buchanan), writing in the 'Ilkeston Pioneer' considered intemperance in language as lamentable as intemperance in drink.

A third feature of Baptists at the turn of the twentieth century was their increasingly politicised nature. It would be quite wrong to see the Baptists of 1800 as somehow disinterested in politics. They had always been concerned about issues that affected their civil liberties. (Opposition to Church Rates was a perennial hobby horse). Many Baptist Churches campaigned on the evils of the slave trade (see appendix 3) and forwarded petitions to Parliament. But by the end of the nineteenth century there was a growing movement among all the Free Churches to defend education from narrowly sectarian religious instruction, and it was this campaign more than any other that produced a very close and almost inseparable union with the Liberal Party of the day. The Liberal Party's concern for educational and religious liberty; for changes to the Licensing laws; and the conditions of housing and working conditions, were all issues that chimed well with the Non-conformists agenda. W.A.Richards' County report to the EMBA for the year 1904 made mention of the construction and opening of his own Church's new building on Pear Tree Road, Derby. But this was not considered the highlight of the year. That honour was given to the town of Derby playing host to the Baptist Union meetings in October 1903. These were large and inspiring meetings Mr Richards recorded, "culminating in the huge Drill Hall demonstration addressed by Dr Clifford and D.Lloyd George esq. MP. For this gathering with the leading Liberal politician of the country, and future Prime Minister, there was "Uncontrollable enthusiasm."

The shape, style and content of Baptist services of worship would have changed markedly over the hundred years since 1800. The earliest Baptist gatherings had debated whether singing should be allowed at all. There had been a gradual recognition of its legitimate place in a service of worship, and accompaniment in 1800 would usually have been by a handful of makeshift musicians with stringed instruments and horns. Victorian sensibilities gradually became intolerant of some of these amateur performances. Disputes over the standards of the bass viol playing could frequently be encountered in Church Meeting minutes. The harmonium became the instrument of choice for early Victorian worshippers. This in turn gave way from the mid century onwards to the full blown pipe organ which churches had installed in their new, grandiose chapels. Baptist Church music became increasingly professionalised and centralised. The organist became a figure of enormous importance in the life of the Church, alongside the choirmaster. Growing and extensive Baptist Church choirs emerged often developing quite sophisticated repertoires and party pieces. The choir and the organ came to dominate the worship of the Baptist Church.

The celebration of the Lord's Supper began to undergo a revolution towards the end of the nineteenth and into the twentieth century. The main item to be changed was the replacement of the common cup with the individual glasses. Willington Baptist Church made this transition earlier than most in 1880. The Osmaston Road Church Magazine for November 1901 contained an article by Rev Joseph Gay, reproduced from the Baptist Times and Freeman, entitled, "The Individual Communion Cup". The writer argued for the possible transmission of contagious diseases through the common goblet. A tray of individual glasses would not only remove these health risks, but would also serve to enhance the unity of the Church by allowing everyone to drink together. Osmaston Road were persuaded to adopt this scheme shortly afterwards. Station Street, Long Eaton went over to the individual glasses in 1911. Pear Tree Road adopted the practice in 1912, and were probably persuaded to do so less by the theological explanations of the pastor and more by the fact that someone was willing to donate the Church a new Communion set and glasses! This was the same situation in Birches Lane, South Wingfield when they were presented with a set of glasses in 1915.

The other major sea change in worship in the life of Baptist Churches between 1800 and 1900 was in connection with the financing of the local Church. In 1800, and for many years afterwards, pew rents were the principal source of Church income. A family agreed to pay a certain amount of money to sit in a particular seat or pew in Church. More prestigious seats, in better positions, could exact a higher price. The 1851 Census revealed just how extensive this system of Church financing had become. But from the 1860s onwards a new, novel and quite radical idea emerged. It was known as "The Weekly Offering Scheme." Churches debated the scheme in Church Meetings for many years. It involved asking people to contribute to the work of the Church each week rather than on a quarterly basis as was invariably the case with pew rent income. The system was more inclusive than its predecessor, and opened up the whole of the congregation to contribute to the maintenance of the Church. Some churches went over to the system quite early: (Crich in 1860; Ripley in 1861; Wirksworth in 1862). Others were much later. St Mary's Gate renovated and re-pewed its chapel in 1897 and repriced its pews. Station Street, Long Eaton didn't give up pew rents until 1910, and Clay Cross was still operating with pew rents as late as 1913.

On the surface Baptist strength at the turn of the century was impressive. In his County Report to the Association in 1906 W.A.Richards was able to list 44 churches that were part of the Derbyshire Baptist scene. Total membership from those churches (year ending 1905) amounted to 4,823[7]. This represented an increase of 252 on the previous year, and Richards attributed this rise to the influence of the Welsh Revival. Overall membership rose again the following year so that by the end of 1906 there were 4915 members in

Baptist Churches in Derbyshire. This compares with figures of approximately 2298 members from 16[8] churches in 1851.

These figures, however, masked an underlying weakness in the overall situation. The membership totals were heavily skewed by the large memberships of five urban churches in particular:

Pear Tree, Derby	-	180 members
Junction Street, Derby	-	299 members
New Street, Burton	-	319 members
St Mary's Gate, Derby	-	355 members
Osmaston Road, Derby	-	486 members

Collectively these five churches represented approximately 34% of the total Baptist membership within the county.

In addition to the Pear Tree and Junction churches the growth and energy in the county was clearly coming from other newly formed churches.

Membership totals

	1880		1906
Chesterfield	100		129
Clay Cross	67		103
Watson Street	78		87
Heanor	67		106
Long Eaton	120	(2 churches)	237
Swadlincote	87		130

By contrast, many of the older churches were showing a marked and remorseless decline in membership.

Membership totals

	1851	1906
Belper	71	63
Crich	42	34
Duffield	88	53

Melbourne	282	146
Milford	73 (1855)	16
Riddings	109	58
St Mary's Gate	544	355
Smalley	102	74
Swanwick	76 (1848)	35
Wirksworth	176	130

These figures become even more disturbing when account is made of the rapid growth in population that occurred over that fifty year period, and the inability of the churches to keep pace with that population growth.

Perhaps the most salutary lesson comes from an analysis of Church peaks: when churches attained their highest membership total.

Church membership peaks

	Highest total	year
Belper	110	1842
Crich	53	1853
Duffield	103	1850
Melbourne	325	1861
Milford	107	1858
Ripley	187	1872
Smalley	173	1845
St Mary's Gate	676	1861
Wirksworth	210	1844

Even a brief assessment indicates that all these churches peaked about the mid century, and experienced decline throughout the rest of the nineteenth century. By 1906 the majority of Baptist churches in Derbyshire had long since passed their best.

County Membership reached its peak in the 1909 report when the total at the end of 1908 was 4,950. Thereafter totals showed a year on year decline.

County Membership

1909[9]	4,950
1910	4,923
1911	4,888
1912	4,836
1913	4,808
1914	4,729

Factors and forces were already at work contributing to the decline of Baptist Churches long before the onset of World War One and the ensuing carnage.

None of this was missed by the Baptists at the time. As early as 1875/6 John Clifford was writing in the General Baptist Magazine about the duplication of Free Church work in some of the smaller towns. He observed that there were 10 Methodist places of worship in Belper and no less than 16 in Alfreton! By contrast there were some newer communities with little or no Free Church provision. Clifford pleaded for some form of co-operation or Concordat between the denominations to ensure that Free Church work wasn't fragmented, and to facilitate a systematic approach to Church extension. His pleas fell on deaf ears.

The EMBA Report for 1894 gave a summary of a Conference held at Belper in November 1903 at which Mr J.H. Starkey read a paper on "Church extension in the county." The outcome of the Conference was the formation of a sub committee to look into the advisability of commencing work in such towns as Buxton, Matlock and Glossop with a view to founding Baptist Churches there. The Baptists were well aware that one third of the county (in the North West) had no Baptist presence at all.

(Interestingly, the 1894 Report also mentioned that Dr Clifford had offered a site of land for a Baptist Chapel at Draycott.)

New causes did begin during this period. The 1899 County Report mentioned the formation of Wilmot Road, Swadlincote with a membership of 35. The 1903 Report mentioned that in July 1902 the Derbyshire Baptist Union had commenced a work at Alvaston, a rapidly growing suburb of Derby. Services had been held in the old Wesleyan Chapel and there was already a membership of 20. The same Report also mentioned that the Baptist cause at Chellaston[10] was enjoying the most prosperous times after years of discouragement.

The 1903 County Report also details the beginning of a Baptist cause in Matlock:

"In the month of June (1902) a few Baptists residing in Matlock who were anxious that a Baptist cause should be started in that town, appealed for the help and guidance of the Association. As a result of this appeal services were commenced on July 20th in the Town Hall."

The 1904 County Report mentioned that services had carried on throughout the year in the Town Hall, but that the work was being seriously hampered by the lack of a more suitable place to meet.

The 1905 Report, however, brought glad tidings on that front. The Twentieth Century Fund had awarded £750 for the erection of a Baptist Church at Matlock, to be paid in three instalments. Astonishingly, the County Union Executive declined the grant, unless it could be followed up with a Home Mission Grant for a resident minister in the town. No further mention is made either of a Home Mission Grant or of a Baptist cause in Matlock.

In truth, with the exception of the barren North West, Baptists had reached saturation point in the county by the early twentieth century. There were far fewer new causes started because there were far fewer places that did not have some Baptist or other Non-conformist presence. With notable exceptions like Pear Tree, Junction, and New Street, Burton in the industrial heartlands, most Baptist Churches in

Derbyshire by the turn of the century were already in decline, and some of them had been so already for over half a century.

<u>Footnote: Barton in the Beans, Castle Donington & Kegworth</u>
The General Baptist cause in Derbyshire traces its main root to the Baptist Chapel in the hamlet of Barton in the Beans. How had this cause faired over the nineteenth century?

In 1906 Barton still recorded a membership of 263. This included its branch churches at Bagworth, Barlestone, Bosworth, Congerstone and Newbold. (Desford had separated in 1905). This still represented a substantial fall from 1851 when the Church and its group recorded 327 members, and was well below its peak year of 1840 when it had a membership of 420.

Castle Donington had peaked in 1847 when it had a membership of 335 (which would have included the Sawley members). In 1851 membership stood at 285, but by 1906 this had fallen right back to112.

The Kegworth and Diseworth Church by contrast had a quite different tale to tell. With an average membership of 90 in the 1840s and 120 in the 1850s, it stabilised at an average of 160 throughout the 1870s to 1890s. In 1906 the Church could boast a membership of 171 which had grown to 177 by the eve of the First World War.

1. This is the EMBA figure which <u>includes </u>the Burton churches. The Baptist Handbook has a separate section for the Staffordshire churches so that their Derbyshire statistics <u>exclude </u>the Burton churches.
2. Rev T.R.Stevenson of St Mary's Gate, Derby spoke at a packed meeting held in the Temperance Hall, in favour of the closure of Public Houses on a Sunday. (Derby Daily Telegraph Wed. October 29th 1884)
3. Frank Rinaldi gives a contemporary account of how the Sunday School at Stoney Street, Nottingham celebrated Queen Victoria's Coronation by providing the children with a dinner at which a "quantity of Ale was supplied to the children." The result was "they became very demonstrative and we could not keep them in order as part of them were intoxicated."

4. Michael Walker Baptists at the Table p.149
5. Michael Walker (p.147) says that the majority of London Baptist Churches were using unfermented Communion wine by the end of the century.
6. Frank Rinaldi records that Friar Lane, Leicester decided to provide unfermented (non-alcoholic) wine as an option for its communicants in 1869. By 1881 the only Communion wine used was non – alcoholic.
7. The published membership figure was 4,783, but 40 members were subsequently added for the Cotmanhay Church transferring over from The Tab. Nottingham
8. There were 12 GB churches and 4 PB churches for which figures are available. There were no figures for Swanwick for several years.
9. The Report was compiled in 1909 for figures at year ending 1908
10. Melbourne records having a branch Church at Chellaston by 1831. St Mary's Gate considered Chellaston becoming a branch of its Church in 1843. The cause at the turn of the century dated its origin back to 1868 and was serviced by the Derbyshire Baptist Preachers Association. It secured a building in 1877. Membership was never high. In 1877 there were 22 members. In 1906 there were 16.

The outbuildings/stables of Peartree Cottage c.1960. For a number of years the building was used by the Baptists as their chapel. In earlier days it housed the plaster works of Samuel Rose. Demolition of the outbuildings took place in 1978.

Chellaston Baptists Meeting Place
From 'Chellaston then and now' pbd by Chellaston History Group
Source: Derby Local Studies Library

Rev Dr. John Clifford

Birthplace of John Clifford, a few doors down from Sawley Baptist Church, opposite the Railway Inn

CONCLUSION

I have the utmost admiration for the eighteenth and nineteenth century Baptists covered in this book. Their dedication and commitment were exemplary. Their evangelistic and Church planting work was impressive. Their achievements were highly significant. To move from a modest cluster of Baptist churches in 1800 to well over forty churches by 1900 was no mean feat. It took hard work; struggle and, above all, faith to accomplish. While some individuals and some churches failed to live up to their high calling in conduct and in attitude, many more showed evidence of the New Life in Christ, and the power of the Spirit. The Baptists of Derbyshire during the nineteenth century became a force for goodness, and made a positive impact on the development of society. Their contribution to the moral and social improvement in the county should not be underestimated.

Frank Rinaldi, in his excellent PhD thesis 'The Tribe of Dan', noted the shift in the New Connexion General Baptists from a Revival Movement in 1770 to an established denomination by the time they disappeared in the merger of 1891-1892. The same process could be observed for the Particular Baptists as well. While some may lament such a transition, and regard it as a falling away from its original purpose, the fact remains that the shift was quite natural and understandable. The multiplication of the churches required a more robust organisational structure than the loose and informal connexionalism that marked the earlier years. The Baptists, in that sense, became a victim of their own success.

Others too may lament the theological shifts that took place throughout the nineteenth century. There is often nostalgia for the theological surety of Sam Deacon, Francis Smith, William Fletcher or J.G.Pike compared to the theological subtleties and range of T.R.Stevenson, Samuel Cox, John Clifford or W.A.Richards. In truth the awareness of the social dimension of the Gospel represents not a dilution of the Gospel or a distraction, but rather the recognition that the world at the end of the nineteenth century was infinitely more complex than it had been a century earlier. The industrial revolution

339

had produced a range of social issues, and on such unprecedented scale, that addressing those concerns was an inevitable response from people of conscience striving to relate the Christian message to a new generation. The world had moved on. The mission strategy of the eighteenth century Baptist pioneers at Barton, walking 20 miles to preach in a cottage or market place, no longer fitted a society where churches (especially Non-Conformist churches) abounded, and where men and women were more concerned with the harsh day to day realities of this life than those of the life to come. Old solutions no longer satisfied the general public. But then neither did they satisfy the people within the churches themselves. New answers were needed for new questions.

Sociological factors inevitably impinged upon the fortunes of the Baptists. Springing up as a rural (though not agricultural) movement, the New Connexion Baptists found themselves by the mid nineteenth century to be adversely affected by migration to the larger towns. The mechanisation of the framework knitting industry had a detrimental impact on Baptists who had eeked out an existence through the old cottage industry practices. When the population moved to the towns the Baptists found it hard to follow, leaving urban centres to newly emerging churches or to those who had had the good fortune (or foresight) to be there already.

It is possible to point to areas where nineteenth century Baptists perhaps 'went wrong.' Frank Rinaldi has pointed with some clarity to the fixation with Sunday School as the antidote to the churches' problems. The ablest men and women in the churches were channelled into using their skills to coach and nurture the young, and yet the results from this massive investment were sometimes derisory. Sunday School as such could be seen as a diversion from the real evangelistic work that needed to be done. In fairness, however, during the nineteenth century in Derbyshire there was undoubtedly considerable dividend gained from the Sunday Schools. A number of churches regularly reported baptismal services where the majority if not all the candidates were from the School. Adult Church Members were produced from the ranks of the Sunday School scholars. The problem was that the conversion rate was certainly not on the scale anticipated, and certainly not in sufficient quantity to maintain numbers. A failure to advance at a time of rapid population growth was symptomatic of the churches' inability to engage with the world beyond the Church. Children were easier targets; a captive audience. But the failure to connect with the parents of this vast army of children was to seriously undermine the investment in the young and to render so much of that investment as null and void.

John Clifford chastened his contemporaries for their indolence. Perhaps he had a point. Churches easily became places of respectability and status; bastions of middle class Victorian values. Evangelistic zeal and mission mindedness appeared to be absent. There was a failure to mobilise congregations into every member ministry. The Primitive Methodists are often looked to as a more avowedly itinerant and evangelistic grouping. The Methodists consistently outstripped the Baptists in the county in terms of Church growth and Church extension. Had the Baptists adopted their methodology and practice our fortunes may have improved. In truth, the Primitive Methodists succumbed to the same pressures and tendencies as the Baptists. Inertia set in with the 'Prims' by the time they had moved to the second or third generation just as it had with the Baptists. Churches became the aspirational focus of the upwardly socially mobile. With one or two rare exceptions they became ineffective at reaching and attracting the poorer elements in society. And in industrialised England it was the poor that were in plentiful supply.

It is easy to 'blame' the Baptists of the nineteenth century for these faults and weaknesses. But all this is easier to see with hindsight. Curiously, inspite of all our cute analysis and perception, and our ability to identify the failings of a past generation, we still seem incapable of doing and being more than our Victorian predecessors. Their mistakes are our mistakes as well. We continue to replicate the practices we concede were flawed. The only difference is that we stand in judgement over those who were never blessed with our understanding of the problem.

There is one observation that has emerged from extensive reading of the minutes of Derbyshire Baptist Churches. It was certainly not one that I had considered before embarking on this study. This is the critical role that money played in the success or otherwise of a Baptist Church. Over and over again it becomes clear that a cause developed or took off as a result of some wealthy benefactor. This might be the Ward-Swinburne family at Agard Street; John Taylor at Duffield; Mr Stanhope at Langley Mill; Richard Thomson at Salem, Burton; Mr Bradley at Kegworth; John Dunnicliffe at Ashbourne; the Pegg, Swingler, and Wilkins families within Derby churches; the Parkinson and Bennett families at Sawley; the Spencer family at Wirksworth or the Nortons at Cauldwell. Land was donated; legacies made; building costs met; ministry subsidised. It is easy to despise such influence, but in reality it was only through such generosity that some of our churches came into being or survived at all.

Though an unpalatable and unpopular thing to say, the reality is that money made things happen. It did then. It does now. And many churches struggled because they were never able to develop a sufficiently robust financial base. There is an assumption that all our present churches were once large. We assume that once upon a time there was a golden age. A brief analysis of the membership statistics would reveal that churches like Windley, Milford, Littleover, and Willington have always been small, and that membership figures in recent times are as healthy as they have ever been.

Modest Church Membership figures, however, affected the financial viability of many congregations, and led in part to an ecclesiastical poverty trap. A small financial base invariably meant that a Church could not afford paid ministry. This hadn't been a problem in the days of Francis Smith or Sam Deacon. They exercised bi-vocational ministries, earning their living from their trade and exercising ministry for little or no recompense. Congregations would be satisfied with itinerant and occasional preachers. But as churches experienced growth, and as congregations became increasingly educated, they demanded more of their preachers than a rehearsal of the basics of the gospel each week. A learned, trained and better equipped ministry was required. This wasn't a bad thing, as some have tried to imply, but a legitimate development in the desire to cultivate a Christian mind. But this tendency towards professionalised ministry did have financial ramifications, and did leave some churches behind. Undeniably, those churches with full time ministers progressed further than those who did not. The inability to afford a minister invariably hindered a Church's development and often left it languishing in the doldrums. Some churches have never escaped this poverty trap, and maybe ministry patterns in the twenty first century need to consider the bi-vocational model more seriously in order to address this very specific problem.

Here we might point to the weakness of the Baptist polity for perpetuating this predicament. Time and again the North Derbyshire Conference and the Midland Conference appealed to Baptist Churches to work in collaboration with neighbouring churches. Yet fierce rivalry, old grudges, petty jealousies, and sheer human cussedness prevented such arrangements. For decades the churches at Milford, Belper and Crich were unable to afford ministry on their own. Yet there was a singular unwillingness to explore any form of joint ministry. A similar problem bedevilled Smalley, Heanor, Langley Mill, Kilburn and Loscoe. Churches would rather 'make do' with what 'lay' ministry they could find than co-operate in such a way as to be able to afford full time and trained ministry despite the evidence that growth was more likely to come through that route. Other systems of Church government could arrange for clustering. The Methodist circuit pattern ensured the availability of trained ministry for the smallest congregations. But the Baptists clung tenaciously to their independence and only paid lip service to the notion of interdependence. Only through the auspices of Home Mission did any form of shared support and sharing begin to break down the walls of isolationism.

It would, however, be fair to say that some churches brought this predicament upon themselves. The mid to late nineteenth century saw a period of intense chapel building. A Church like New Street, Burton had three chapels in 60 years. This worked well for them, and the buildings helped both to develop and complement the ministry of the Church. Part of me stands in admiration of the bravery and risk taking

343

of these churches with their chapel building programmes. They weren't wedded to particular edifices. They were willing to build and to tear down to meet their perceived needs. They were willing to invest in Church plant; to adapt, moderrnise and keep up to date in ways that the twentieth century churches have just failed to do. After the First World War little imaginative new building work took place unless it was forced on a Church through fire, subsidence, structural damage or an offer too good to miss. Maybe there are significant lessons for us all in this.

But while a Church like New Street, Burton managed investment well, other churches over-reached themselves. The buildings were too large and too expensive, and the debt that was incurred proved to financially cripple the Church and massively curtail the possibility of ministry. The Baptists in Ilkeston took out huge loans on their Queen Street building and spent over 20 years paying them back during which time they lost at least two ministers because they didn't have enough money. At one stage the Treasurer, Mr Sisson, had to pay the minister out of his own pocket! Crich Baptist Church built its first chapel in 1839 and were still carrying debts from that in 1871. No sooner had they cleared the debt than they purchased their new chapel and entered into a further £1,500 of debt. Throughout this period they were unable to afford any settled ministry. St Mary's Gate in Derby celebrated the extinction of their chapel debt in 1878, some 36 years after they moved into the prestigious site. By my calculation Kilburn Baptist Church took 43 years to pay off the loans on their first chapel. Heanor Baptist Church was not untypical in taking out a loan of £700 in 1875 on a chapel building project estimated to cost £800. There were cries of 'poverty,' 'help!' and pleas for assistance for years to come. Chapel debt was probably the main cause of the failure of the Parker Street Church in Burton, and would have finished off Sacheverel Street had St Mary's Gate not bailed them out. Little wonder that the Melbourne Church in its Report to the Association in 1879 following a £700 renovation to its sanctuary could boast that they had done this "without entailing an enormous debt to fetter future action." This was a lesson that many churches never learned. Chapel building and chapel debt were frequently placed ahead of financing ministry. This was often a disastrous, even fatal choice. Both Clay Cross and Swadlincote lost ministers because of their financial commitments to debt repayment.

Money made things happen, and money still makes things happen within the life of our Baptist churches.

There is, I believe, one major lesson to be learned from a study of the Baptists of Derbyshire; a lesson that should still speak into the life of all our churches: the creative role of sacrifice. People like Sam Deacon, J.G.Pike, William Pickering, Francis Smith, and William Fletcher were men who put their lives on the line. They put themselves out for the sake of the Gospel. For some it was the 24/7 lifestyle that made the difference, being willing to walk thirty miles for a preaching opportunity; it was the willingness to spend and be spent; to be considered 'fools for Christ'. The sacrificial actions of Messrs Jeffrey and Dossey at Gamston in supplying the materials for the chapel and manse at Ashford in the Water, or of Mrs Pegg selling her wedding ring to help build the Melbourne Chapel, all ultimately made a real difference. If that early generation can teach modern Christians something it is the value of sacrifice, and the need to regard our faith less as a recreational pursuit and more as a way of life. To make ourselves wholly available for the cause we believe in is a view most Baptists would endorse but few of us ever seem to practice.

If the Church of Jesus Christ in Derbyshire and in Britian is ever again to make a vital impression on society it will require men and women to literally become 'living sacrifices.' We will need to step outside our comfortable lifestyles; readjust our priorities; pay more than lip service to the faith we espouse; and learn all over again to take up our cross and follow Christ.

There is nothing inevitable about decline, provided that we modern-day disciples live out of conviction, mean what we say, and practice what we preach.

BIBLIOGRAPHY

In addition to primary sources consulted and an array of chapel histories, the following secondary sources were used in the compilation of this study:

History of the Derby and District Free Churches –	B.A.M. Alger
Evangelicalism in Modern Britain -	D.W.Bebbington
The English Baptists of the Nineteenth Century –	J.H.Y.Briggs
The English Baptists of the Eighteenth Century –	Raymond Brown
Melbourne Baptists: story of 200 years –	T.J.Budge
Historic Memorials of Barton, Melbourne... –	J.R.Godfrey
Life and thought of Baptists of Nottinghamshire: unpublished M.Phil thesis –	F.M.W Harrison
Bonsall at Prayer –	John March, Dudley Fowkes & Pam McInally
The Baptist Union –	Ernest A Payne
Brook Street Chapel, Derby: a charge to keep –	J.Brian Radford
The English Baptists of the Twentieth Century –	Ian M Randall
The Tribe of Dan: unpublished PhD thesis –	Frank Rinaldi
The making of a northern Baptist college –	Peter Shepherd
Derbyshire in the Civil War –	Brian Stone
History of the General Baptists vol.2 –	Adam Taylor
Baptists at the Table –	Michael Walker
Spiritual Pilgrim: the Countess of Huntingdon –	Edwin Welch
Congregational Connexionalism: unpublished M.Phil. thesis –	Margaret Wombwell
History of the General Baptists of the New Connexion –	J.H.Wood

APPENDICES

APPENDIX 1

An account of Nathaniel Pickering's preaching expedition to Sawley

"On May 8th 1766 Mr N. Pickering was preaching in a dwelling house in that village (Sawley) when the curate of the parish, much intoxicated, came at the head of a numerous mob, many of whom were in the same state as their leader; and, entering the room, ordered the preacher to cease or they would put him in the stocks. Mr Pickering, hoping to stop the violence, read his licence; but this had no effect. The curate seized him; and he, without resistance suffered himself to be led out of the house to the stocks. But here the clergyman and his associates were too much overpowered by liquor to be able to complete their design; and Mr Pickering quietly went home. The congregation had dispersed, amidst the insults of the drunken rabble; and the whole village was in an uproar. The bells of the Church were rung, hand bells were jingled in the ears of the Baptists, dirt was thrown in their faces, and a bucket of blood was brought from a butcher's shop to throw over them. Mr Pickering, however, took an opportunity of acquainting the bishop of the diocese with the disgraceful conduct of the curate; and was assured, that he should receive a severe reprimand.*

*One of the rabble, who rung the handbell and used every means to provoke some of the Baptists to fight him, having continued in a drunken rage for several days, on crossing the ferry, while abusing his fellow passengers, fell out of the ferry boat and was drowned."

Extract from Adam Taylor, 'History of The English Baptists' vol.2 pages 50-51. His information was gleaned from the General Baptist magazine vol.2

(Adam Taylor went on to mention, that thwarted in their endeavour to present the gospel in Sawley, the Baptists went instead to Dale Moor on the road to Ilkeston, subsequently constructing a Meeting House at Little Hallam)

Appendix 2 – The Barton branches (an indicative not exhaustive list)

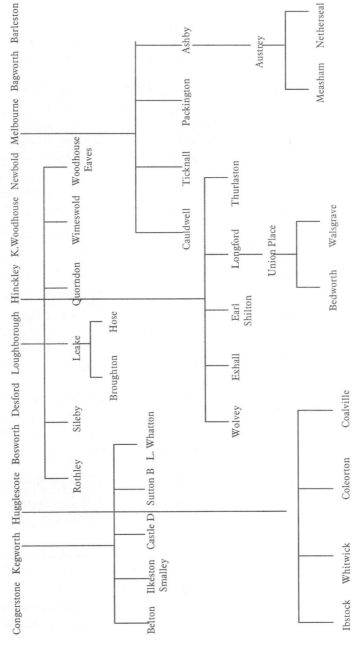

Source: Christine Meller   Compiled by Rachael Greasley

349

APPENDIX 3
Baptist Involvement in Anti Slavery Movement

DERBY, FEB. 8th, 1833.

WE the undersigned Inhabitants of the Town of Derby, respectfully request your Worship to call a MEETING of the Town on the earliest convenient day, to consider the propriety of petitioning the Houses of Parliament for the ABOLITION of COLONIAL SLAVERY.

Charles M. Lowe	John Steer
G. H. Woodhouse	John Hall
William Fisher	Charles Dewe
J. G. Pike	Robert Bennett
William Hawkins	William L. Newton
J. Gawthorn	Joseph Lewis
Philip Gell	Samuel Holmes
Thomas Cox	Henry Flower
Thomas Boden	John Jones
Archibald Fox	Daniel Hobson
Anthony Thomas Carr	George Wilkins and Son
R. W. Birch	A. Pick
Samuel Fox, jun.	Thomas Wooler
William Pike	John Hill
Walter Pike	John Edwards
Robert Forman	Samuel Hope
William Turner	John Henley
William Shaw	J. Latham
William Williamson	Samuel Ayrton
Thomas Storer	

BOROUGH OF DERBY.

In compliance with the above most respectable Requisition, I DO hereby appoint a General Meeting of the Inhabitants of this Borough to be holden at the Town Hall, in the said Borough, on SATURDAY the 16th day of February instant, at 12 o'clock.

JOHN CHATTERTON,

Derby, 12th Feb. 1833.   MAYOR.

Source: Dr Alasdair Kean
Note the names of J. G. Pike, George Wilkins and son (from Brooke Street Chapel), and Samuel Ayrton (from Sacheverel Street).

APPENDIX 4
Rev. T.R. Stevenson: The Christian World 25th May 1885

A TRUE MINISTER OF CHRIST.

IN a sermon preached by Rev. T. R. Stevenson, at Derby, on Whit-Sunday evening, he strongly urged his Christian brethren to "allure rather than alarm men" if they wished to do spiritual good. He added: "On account of supposed heresy, I have been sharply reproved and denounced. Some religious people seem to think a denial of eternal punishment will lead to its infliction! To all such four considerations are commended. First, will God send men to perdition for error? Surely not. Mistakes and sins are totally different things. The one calls for pity, the other for penalty. Wickedness, not heterodoxy, is the way to ruin. Secondly, even supposing the benevolent ?) opinion of my adversaries is correct, let it be remembered that heaven and hell are not things of the future only. A servant of God has heaven *here*, whatever his coming fate may be. The faithful friendship of man, the sweet love of woman, the affection of dear little children, the ability to cry 'I believe in God the Father Almighty, Maker of heaven and earth,' help given habitually to the miserable, the unfortunate, the neglected, the friendless—these, and the like, constitute sources of happiness and satisfaction which the New Jerusalem itself can hardly exceed. Thirdly, if one is to be lost because of heresy, it will be because such is God's will, and one can only say, 'Thy will be done.' If the Supreme One will derive pleasure from consigning to torment those who sought truth, but missed it, be it so. *In that case, however, the victim is less to be pitied than the Judge.* But no! it cannot be true that God will act thus. If He did, would the 'Judge of all the earth do right'? Fourthly, I, for one, if doomed to hell, would carry on my present work, namely, seeking and saving the lost. How could I do any other, if I had a spark of humanity? And in so doing, I should be accurately following the example of Christ, who 'went and preached to the spirits in prison.'"

Source: Bodleian Library

351

APPENDIX 5

The career of Rev Dr William Underwood

One of the figures who pops in and out of this study is William Underwood. Born in Wymeswold, Loughborough on 27th March 1812 he was baptised by the Minister at Loughborough Baptist Church, Rev Thomas Stevenson, and began to preach in 1833. He became a student at the Loughborough College and in July 1836 assumed his first pastoral charge as Minister of Wirksworth Baptist Church. During this ministry he preached three times each Sunday and three or four times during the week. By 1840 he was already being approached by a Sheffield Church eager to obtain his services. Eventually in 1841 he accepted the call to Praed Street, Paddington. Within a short space of time the Church needed to construct galleries to cope with increased numbers. In 1852 he returned to Derbyshire as Minister of Sacheverel Street, Derby from whence he moved to Chesham in 1855. Two years later he was elected President of the General Baptist College then in Nottingham, and was instrumental in shifting the College to new premises in Chilwell. Underwood remained as President of the College until 1873. Along with his colleague Rev W.R.Stevenson (one time assistant minister to J.G.Pike) he trained between 40 – 50 men for the Baptist ministry which he regarded as the chief work of his life. Underwood had a reputation of being stern and unbending.

In 1873 he accepted a call to become minister of Castle Donington and Sawley. The arrangement did not work well. His refusal to take more than one service a fortnight at Sawley precipitated the split between Castle Donington and Sawley. In 1875 his son Alfred accepted a call to Zion, Burton, and by the following year William Underwood's name appears in connection with that Church. When Alfred Underwood left to form the Parker Street Church, Burton in 1879 William Underwood went with him and provided ministerial assistance (unpaid) until 1884. He was still active in that Church at the time of its closure in 1888. Dr Underwood also features prominently in the life of Watson Street, Derby where his presence was regularly acknowledged in reports to the Association between 1880 – 1889.

On the national stage Dr Underwood was a warm advocate of the Union of General and Particular Baptists in 1891, and he features extensively in the debates that were raging at that period.

He died in Burton on 1st November 1898. In June of that same year he had provided the obituary in the Baptist Handbook for his son, Alfred, who had died aged 46. In 1899 Alfred's widow presented a clock to the Osmaston Road, Derby, Church to be placed in the front of the Church tower. The clock was in memory of her late husband who had served as a deacon of the Church and her father in law who had been minister in the 1850s. The minute book for the New Street Church, Burton recorded the death of Dr Underwood, who was in membership with them at the time of his death. It listed his many achievements and included this heartfelt tribute:

"The members of this Church desire to put on record their high appreciation of the sterling Christian character and rare mental gifts of the late Dr Underwood."

APPENDIX 6 - Derbyshire Baptist Churches 1906

Churches	Date	Seats	Members	Teachers	Scholars	Preachers	Pastors
Belper	1818	600	63	16	132	3	W. C. Davies
Birches Lane (Alfreton)	1863	250	20	15	116	1	.. .. ..
Bonsall	1823	150	16	9	63	2	.. .. ..
Cauldwell (see Staffordshire)							
Chellaston	1868	116	16	8	27	1	.. .. ..
Chesterfield (27,185)	1861	350	129	17	168	3	.. .. ..
Clay Cross	1863	225	103	21	212	6	W.R. Ponton
Crich	1839	240	34	21	105	2	
Derby (105,912):-							
Green Hill, Trinity	1795	400	140	29	251	9	E.M. Yeomans
Junction Street	1897	400	299	52	1012	6	P.A. Hudgell
Osmaston Road	1831	1000	486	55	639	10	(G.H. James)
Pear Tree Road	1873	700	180	29	393	..	(W.A. Richards)
St Mary's Gate	1791	1000	355	32	308	13	J.H. Rushbrooke,M.A.
Boyer-street	..	250	11	13	198		
Littleover	..	200	41	12	86		
Willington	..	120	31	10	57		
Watson-street	1867	200	87	20	306	4	
Dronfield	1846	450	127	21	160	3	
Duffield	1810	200	53	8	91	2	A.Wilson
Heanor, Derby Road	1861	450	106	29	332		J.T Owers
Ilkeston (25,384):-							
Queen Street	1784	550	113	18	315	2	A. Copley (Lay pastor)
South Street	1882	225	66	25	230	1	

354

Churches	Date	Seats	Members	Teachers	Scholars	Preachers	Pastors
Kilburn	1832	120	51	21	282	1	
Langley Mill	1845	300	85	18	160		B. Smith (Lay pastor)
Long Eaton:-							
St John's	1889	420	94	32	233	2	J.T. Heselton
Station-street	1877	450	143	30	312	1	J. Cottam
Loscoe	1783	400	93	32	290	3	
Melbourne and Ticknall	1750	600	146	31	218	7	J.F. Archer
Melbourne, Derby Road	1902		65	16	105		A.H. Coombs
Milford	1849	150	16	4	20		
New Whittington	1862	300	31	11	120	1	
Riddings	1806	400	58	19	120	1	O. Henderson
Ripley	1833	450	112	37	303	2	
Sawley	1783	250	90	31	128	1	
Shirebrook	1901	150					
Smalley	1785	300	74	23	95	1	E. Hilton
Stonebroom (Alfreton)	1877	250	91	13	121		
Swadlincote, Hill Street	1867	500	130	23	405	5	
Hartshorne	..	..	12	13	31		
Wilmot Road	1898	300	64	19	163	2	
Swanwick	1796	500	35	23	225	2	F. Todd
Wirksworth and Shottle	1818	300	130	26	128	9	

Staffordshire (Burton on Trent) Baptist Churches 1906

Churches	Date	Seats	Members	Teachers	Scholars	Preachers	Pastors
Derby Street	1871	600	149	23	240		J. Askew
New Street	1824	840	329	42	335		J. Porteous
Castle Gresley	1877	200		8	74		J.Porteous
Cauldwell	1785	100		2	33		J.Porteous
Overseal	1854	350	74	9	129		E.W.Cantrell
Willington St.				13	62		
Station Street	1792	630	181	35	241	10	D.L.Donald
Walton on Trent	1877	200					

Source: Baptist Handbook 1906
Compiled by Rachael Greasley

APPENDIX 7

DERBYSHIRE BAPTIST CHURCHES IN EMBA 2006

CHURCH	MEMBERSHIP	CHURCH	MEMBERSHIP
Belper	50	Ilkeston	37
Burton, New	85	Langley Mill*	--
Chesterfield	70	Long Eaton	34
Clay Cross	5	Melbourne	26
Cotmanhay	16	Milford	11
Derby, Alvaston	20	Overseal	10
Derby, Boulton Ln	19	Sawley	22
Derby, Broadway	125	Smalley	17
Derby, The Haven	14	Swadlincote	41
Derby, Junction	24	Swanwick	22
Derby, littleover	57	Willington**	57
Derby, Ozzy Road	83	Windley	3
Derby, Pear Tree	91	Wirksworth	19
Heanor	22		

** Willington is officially an Associate congregation of the EMBA

Total Membership from 27 churches = 980

* Langley Mill submitted no entries for year ending 2006. The previous year their membership figure was 76. If that figure is used for the current year then the Derbyshire Baptists membership = 1056

During the last 100 years only 3 new Baptist churches have been established in the county, all of them within Derby: Alvaston, Boulton Lane, The Haven (Ecumenical Partnership).

During the last 40 years the following 12 Baptist Chapels have closed: Bonsall; Derby, Boyer Street; Derby, Watson Street; Diseworth; Hartshorne; Riddings; Ripley; Shottle; Stonebroom; Swadlincote, Wilmot Road; Ticknall; and Weston on Trent. There have also been mergers in Burton and Long Eaton resulting in the closure of chapels in those towns. Ilkeston's two Baptist Churches merged before the Second World War.

The following 6 churches have also withdrawn from the EMBA and the Baptist Union: Birches Lane, South Wingfield; Crich; Derby, Trinity; Duffield; Kilburn; and Loscoe. Burton, Salem has withdrawn from the EMBA but remains in the Baptist Union.

For the year ending 2006 Castle Donington and Kegworth (both officially in Leicestershire) had memberships of 14 and 25 respectively. Barton in the Beans withdrew from the Association in 1999. Its entry in the Baptist Union Handbook for 1999/2000 recorded a membership figure of 6.